Class, Race, Gender, and Crime

Social Realities of Justice in America

Gregg Barak
Eastern Michigan University

Jeanne Flavin
Fordham University

Paul Leighton
Eastern Michigan University

D0061211

Roxbury Publishing Company
Los Angeles, California

Library of Congress Cataloging-in-Publication Data
Barak, Gregg
Class, Race, Gender, and Crime: Social Realities of Justice in America
Gregg Barak, Jeanne Flavin, and Paul Leighton
p. cm.
Includes bibliographical references
ISBN 1-891487-34-5
1. Criminal Justice, Administration of—United States 2. United States—
    Social conditions I. Flavin, Jeanne, 1965– II. Leighton, Paul, 1964–
    III. Title
    Criminology
    HV9950.B34 2001
    364.973—dc21   00-028097
                                                            CIP

Publisher: Claude Teweles
Managing Editor: Dawn VanDercreek
Production Editor: Renée M. Burkhammer
Assistant Editor: Monica Gomez
Typography: Synergistic Data Systems
Cover Design: Marnie Kenney
Cover Photo: Paul Leighton

Printed on acid-free paper in the United States of America. This paper meets
the standards for recycling of the Environmental Protection Agency.

ISBN 1-891487-34-5

ROXBURY PUBLISHING COMPANY
P.O. Box 491044
Los Angeles, California 90049-9044
Tel.: (310) 473-3312 • Fax: (310) 473-4490
E-mail: roxbury@roxbury.net
Website: www.roxbury.net

Ed,

In a place where even moments of decency and generosity are as rare as original thinking, your kindness (and Marianne's) during my first six weeks here will be the most memorable and cherished moments of my stay.

To Our Families

May retirement bring both of you the mix of serenity, adventure, and excitement you both desire and deserve.

Love,
Ernesto

Contents

List of Boxes

Preface

Is it race or gender that interferes with the full realization of the "justice" part of criminal justice? A few people would indicate that social class is also important, then join the chorus of responses: "Well, it depends." The challenge remains, however, to specify what we mean by "it depends"—that is, to understand how class, race, and gender operate independently and in combination with each other to influence people's experience in and of the criminal justice system and larger society. This challenge is being taken up by an increasing number of scholars who are developing more sophisticated, inclusive theories. The resultant literature frequently assumes a baseline level of knowledge of class, race, *and* gender that many readers do not have. This lack of knowledge prevents many people from appreciating the full range of barriers to justice, the overlapping nature of these constructs, and how they form an interlocking system of oppression that is reflected and re-created in criminology and criminal justice.

To address this gap, our text provides a solid foundation for more advanced studies of intersectionality, while introducing readers to more recent or lesser known developments. Our intention is not to generate cutting edge (or "undercutting edge") theory but rather to provide a map of the terrain and an incitement for readers to consider class *and* race *and* gender more deeply. Our goal is to move the discussion beyond the mantra of class, race, and gender.

To that end, this book devotes a full chapter each to exploring class, race, gender, and the intersections thereof. Each chapter is similarly organized, with the aim of guiding the reader through common issues that are important regardless of the larger construct being examined. Thus, in addition to defining key terms and describing social, political, and economic distributions, we also examine the constructs as they pertain to criminology, the law, victimization, law enforcement, judicial processing, sentencing, criminal justice workers, and media representations. However, class, race, and gender are ultimately different phenomena, so a "cookie cutter" approach that produced identical chapters would not be appropriate or desirable. Readers should expect and appreciate some variation in how these topics are discussed in different chapters.

Although we have tried to write a comprehensive introduction to intersectionality, our discussion is not—and indeed cannot be—exhaustive. Barriers exist, both practical and intellectual. Practically speaking, even restricting the discussion to a three-class, two-gender, two-race (white, nonwhite) model results in 18 possible race, gender, and class combinations. This simple model would immediately and correctly be attacked for reducing race to white and black while omitting a discussion of Hispanic ethnicity, Asians, and Native Americans (for starters). By having separate chapters for class, race, and gender, we can provide a more extensive overview, say, of racial and ethnic categories. We believe the organization of this book will leave the reader in a better position to make sense of the permutations of class, race, and gender than if we tried to cover 36 or 72 possibilities through several stages of the criminal justice system.

Another barrier to comprehensiveness is lack of data. Few data exist on class and criminal justice; other data are frequently broken down only by race or gender. With limited resources, the government cannot produce data covering the extensive permutations discussed above. These data limitations must necessarily influence the coverage in our book, but we have made every effort not to re-create silences and exclusions. The greater barrier, however, is that the disciplines of criminology and criminal justice are still in the process of constructing adequate conceptual frameworks to help grasp the multiple meanings and implications of intersectionality. The disciplines are still developing a vocabulary that permits meaningful communication about multiple crosscutting social relations in a clear, comprehensible way.

Acknowledgments

In writing this book, we have sifted through the feedback of no fewer than ten reviewers and have had to make difficult decisions about incorporating their numerous suggestions. Tackling class, race, gender, and intersection in one volume increases exponentially the possibility for legitimate disagreements about content and organization. Nevertheless, we believe that we have created a reasonable balance here.

We owe thanks to a number of reviewers who read the "first" draft in total, to a few others who read the introductory framework of subsequent drafts, and to publisher Claude Teweles for his efforts in soliciting much of this feedback. One person in particular, Raymond Michalowski, who read both the manuscript as a whole and the reworked introduction, believed strongly in the inherent value of this project and helped most in bringing the book to fruition. Toward the end of the rewriting process, Ray e-mailed us: "Like you, I still believe we are all involved in a collective project to challenge the hegemonic story about crime and justice." In this regard, Ray provided yeoman's service to the cause. Ray also noted that he had been impressed by a preface to one of Albert Szymanski's books on social class wherein he had indicated—quite contrary to most acknowledgment pages—that if his book contained errors or inadequacies, the blame was not only his but was to be shared by all colleagues who had read and commented on it and by the wider discipline for failing to develop better ideas.

In this context, we would like to thank a number of people. First, the seven Roxbury reviewers did a splendid job in communicating what needed to be done to make the transition from a "promising" and "interesting" project to the book it is now. In alphabetical order, they are Ronald L. Akers (University of Florida), Werner J. Einstadter (emeritus professor, Eastern Michigan University), Raymond

Michalowski (Northern Arizona University), Al Patenaude (University of Arkansas, Little Rock), Claire Renzetti (St. Joseph's University), Norman White (University of Missouri, St. Louis), and Richard A. Wright (Arkansas State University). Next, we would like to thank Jean Ait Belkhir (Southern University at New Orleans), founder and editor-in-chief of the journal *Race, Gender, and Class,* for his enthusiastic support of this book project and for his feedback on the working draft. We would also like to thank Robert Bohm (University of Central Florida) for his critical and editorial read of the introductory framework as it went through fine-tuning. Finally, we would like to thank Mandy Barclay from the Department of Sociology, Anthropology, and Criminology at Eastern Michigan University for the unenviable task of producing one formatted set of references from numerous files.

In addition, Gregg Barak would like to thank Eastern Michigan University for a faculty fellowship for the Fall 1999 semester that allowed him to work on this book without any teaching distractions. Jeanne Flavin would like to thank Fordham University for awarding her the 1999 Ames Fellowship funds to support her research on this book. Paul Leighton would like to thank Eastern Michigan University for the Provost's New Faculty Award for Fall 1999 that provided for a reduced teaching load and some much-needed time for writing and research.

About the Authors

Gregg Barak is professor of criminology and criminal justice at Eastern Michigan University. He is the editor of six books, including *Crime and Crime Control: A Global View* (2000). He has also written three books, including *In Defense of Whom? A Critique of Criminal Justice Reform* (1980), the award-winning *Gimme Shelter: A Social History of Homelessness in Contemporary America* (1991), and *Integrating Criminologies* (1998). Barak has served as chair of the Critical Division on Criminology of the American Society of Criminology and received the Critical Criminologist of the Year Award in 1999.

Jeanne Flavin is assistant professor in the Department of Sociology and Anthropology at Fordham University. She is committed to doing research that has important applications to society at large. Her scholarship has examined how society responds to offenders with HIV/AIDS and victims of domestic violence, how child-care responsibilities influence the sentencing of men and women drug offenders, and, more generally, how people's experiences in and of the U.S. justice system are shaped by class, race, and gender. In 2000, Flavin received the Fordham University undergraduate teaching award.

Paul Leighton is assistant professor of criminology and criminal justice at Eastern Michigan University, where he is coordinator of graduate studies in criminology. He is co-editor, with Jeffrey Reiman, of *Criminal Justice Ethics* (Prentice Hall, 2001). His current research, "Televising Executions, Primetime 'Live'" has appeared in *The Justice Professional* (Vol. 12, no.2, 1999). Leighton is a technology fellow at Eastern Michigan University and webmaster for http://www.paulsjusticepage.com and http://www.stopviolence.com.

Chapter 1

Crime, Inequality, and Justice

Most studies of crime and justice take a narrow approach and treat crime as simply a violation of a legalized social norm that carries a penal sanction. Justice is equated with the fulfillment of legally guaranteed "due process" rights or "equal protection." Without abandoning these meanings of crime and justice, we adopt a broader cultural approach. Our approach explores crime control and the administration of criminal justice from a position of "social constructionism" (Barak 1994, 1996). We view the criminal justice system as a culturally powerful, label-conferring institution that has developed in relation to the changing meanings of criminal law. We also view the definitions of "crime" and "criminals" as a product of moral agents, social movements, political interests, media dissemination, and policymakers (Best 1990; Jenkins 1994; Potter and Kappeler 1998). Among the main factors involved in producing "crime" and "criminals" are class, race, and gender.

We expand on the narrower legalistic meanings of crime control by examining the historical and contemporary practices of criminal justice as they have been shaped and experienced by the rich and poor, by racial and ethnic majorities and minorities, by men and women. We also provide richer contexts for understanding the numerous social realities of justice in America. Analytically, for example, we look at social groupings in America in isolation and in combination. This analysis reveals many "social realities" of crime, crime control, and criminal justice, encouraging the reader to see crime and justice from multiple perspectives rather than from the one-dimensional perspective of legal order. Thus, as used in this text, "justice" can refer not only to criminal justice but to political, economic, social, racial, ethnic, sexual, and religious justice.

One of the underlying assumptions that drives our study has to do with the fundamental distinction that anthropologists, sociologists, and others make between insider and outsider groups. Whether we are talking about matters within nations or between nations, the ages-old interactions and conflicts among social groups have always possessed an element of we/they or us/them. Accordingly, "insiders," or members of one social group, tend to see themselves as possessing virtues not possessed by "outsiders," or members of other social groups. For example, members of one's own group of origin are typically seen as less violent, aggressive, or criminal and more trustworthy, peace-loving, and law-abiding than members of the "other" group.

For many millennia and throughout the world, these ethnocentric beliefs have shaped social relations across lines of what we now think of as class, race/ethnicity, gender, nationality, sexuality, religion, and more. In our own contemporary period, when it is politically incorrect to hold bigoted views about "others" (i.e., racial and ethnic minorities, gays, Jews), it is still politically acceptable to hold such views about "criminals." So when public discourse has dwelled on "welfare cheats" or "violent criminals," what typically comes to mind are racially charged subtexts with images of the "other." In the 1980s, this phenomenon was classically demonstrated when the media and ethnographers alike talked about drug-addicted mothers, perpetuating racial stereotypes of African American women trading sex for crack, rather than middle-class white women snorting the more expensive powder cocaine. While pregnant poor and black women became targets of the criminal justice system, middle- and upper-class women escaped scrutiny of criminal justice agents into the confines of private detoxification facilities (Humphries 1999).

In other words, we see crime as more than the violation of a legalized social norm and justice as more than the equal application of laws. Similarly, we see the study of crime and crime control as more than analyzing the behavior of criminals and the institutional agents of the criminal justice system. Visano emphasized the following:

> *The study of crime is an analysis of being, becoming and experiencing 'otherness.' Crime is a challenge to a particular socially constructed and historically rooted social order. The study of crime, therefore, is an inquiry into expressions of power, cultural controls and contexts of contests. Accordingly, the designated criminal is set apart and relegated to the margins according to a disciplining discourse about differences. (1998, p. 1)*

This book is an attempt to locate the study of crime control in the context of being and becoming a person of "class, race, and gender" and in experiencing "otherness" in the social realities of crime and justice. We are interested in how class, race, and gender biases become reflected in the criminal justice system—and how criminology, law, and criminal justice practices help (re)create the "other." This book is an attempt to show that "crime" and "criminals" are socially and materially constructed phenomena, reproduced daily through various discussions in the streets, the media, the home, the government, the courts, and other cultural bodies.

What does not become subject to crime and crime control because of cultural silences is important too. In other words, we will discuss those otherwise harmful and injurious behaviors that have not been marginalized or made deviant and criminal. Criminality and crime range from relatively minor infractions, such as petty theft, to trafficking in illegal contraband, to extremely violent acts of commission and omission. Similarly, criminals may equally vary from "single, simple, so-called situated and clearly pathologized individual offenders to more elusive, complex, global, sovereign and corporate organizations" (Visano 1998, p. 1). Some harmful acts and offenders are not defined as crime or criminals, but among those that are, only some actors and offenses are regarded as "real" threats to the social order and, therefore, worthy of managing and controlling. For these reasons, crime control becomes the regulation of a relatively small number of acts that have been designated as threatening to the social order. The administration of criminal justice becomes the institutionalized or patterned responses for processing those threats. This way of functioning becomes accepted and normalized; ideology convinces people that the patterns are inevitable and "just."

However, justice is more than the patterned reactions to criminal offenders. It is also more than the operations and functions of the criminal justice system that consist of legislative codes, judicial decisions, law enforcement practices, sentencing policies, and penal sanctions.

Although such practices are important, the meanings of justice entail larger political, economic, and social relations. The late Judge Bazelon commented that "it is simply unjust to place people in dehumanizing social conditions, to do nothing about those conditions, and then command those who suffer, 'Behave—or else!' " (in Leighton and Reiman 2001, p. 39). Although the police might not coerce a suspect into confessing and the defendant might have a lawyer for representation in court, Bazelon points to important additional considerations about the justice involved with "tough on crime" policies in the inner cities. Likewise, crime control policies that do not take into account larger contexts are not likely to be effective. As Bazelon comments,

"We cannot produce a class of desperate and angry citizens by closing off, for many years, all means of economic advancement and fulfillment for a sizable part of the population, and thereafter expect a crime-free society" (Leighton and Reiman 2001, p. 39).

The point is that the narrow conceptions of crime and justice are valid and pragmatic but are not sufficient by themselves. Instead, we believe that our analysis of criminal justice is strengthened when the broader social and cultural conceptions of crime and justice, in conjunction with the more narrow and legalistic ones, are investigated and evaluated together. We also believe that this kind of comparative inquiry sheds more light on important (but frequently neglected) questions of "equal justice for all." Finally, in the spirit of critical pedagogy, we believe that this type of integrative analysis and its implications can help move the administration of justice closer to the ideals of peace and human liberation.

Class, Race, Gender, and Justice: A Historical Overview

It has been recently argued that the criminal justice policies of postindustrial America are the preferred methods for managing the rising inequality and surplus populations of the United States (Michalowski and Carlson 1999; Parenti 1999). *Surplus populations,* or what Marx called the *lumpenproletariat,* refer primarily to occupationally marginal persons and those who are unemployed or unemployable; they are people with little attachment to the conventional labor market and little "stake in conformity" (Anderson 1974). In this book, we will use interchangeably such terms as "marginal classes" or "dangerous classes" to refer to surplus populations.

A historical overview of the relations of class, race, gender, and crime control reveals that on the frontier as well as in industrial America, the administration of justice was about regulating and controlling the "dangerous classes," as they were first referred to in the mid- and late-nineteenth century. Of course, the "war on crime" has rarely, if ever, been publicly discussed as a war on the "down and out" or contextualized as involving inequality and privilege. Usually, it has been described as a war on the "bad" and "mad" in the context of law and order.

Although the regulation and control of the dangerous or marginal classes has remained an essential function of the American criminal justice system, it has rarely been addressed within the changing and competitive relations of order, law, and crime (Michalowski 1985). Instead, the social relations of difference and conflict based on class, race, or gender are typically reduced to narrowly shaped questions about equal treatment under law. Similarly, the tensions or contradictions between political, economic, and social inequalities on the one hand and legal, ideological, and philosophical equalities on the other hand have always been an essential part of both the processes of criminalization and the larger struggles for social justice. Even though these social relations are fundamental to the cultural production of crime and justice, they are usually suppressed in most analyses of the criminal justice system.

In the context of combating dangerous criminals and securing justice for all, the patterned behaviors and trends in policing, adjudicating, and punishing have always been the subject of political evaluation, legal review, and public scrutiny. Over time, the criminalizing of behavior has been subject to periods of legal and constitutional reform that have gradually expanded the meanings of "due process" and "equal protection" for a wider and more diverse group of people. Despite the "democratization" of criminal justice during the late nineteenth and twentieth centuries, the effects of crime control have always been to the disadvantage of the nation's most disentitled and marginalized members (Auerbach 1976; Barak 1980; Harring 1983; Walker 1980). When it was a young nation, the political and legal apparatuses of the United States were dominated by the organized power of wealthy, white, and male interests, to the detriment of slaves, freedmen, workers, nonworkers, women, people of color, and (ex)convicts. Since our nation's beginnings, then, the various struggles for justice, inside and outside the administration of criminal law, have included the goal of empowering people and granting all access to the same political and legal bodies of rule making and rule enforcing.

In the seventeenth, eighteenth, and nineteenth centuries, the rate of profits was constantly rising, initially due to the low costs of agricultural slavery, and then to the developing mechanization of labor and the increased productivity of industrial capitalism (Anderson 1974). At the beginning of this period, punishment and social structure reflected a situation in which the systems of production (e.g., agricultural, industrial) had discovered rewards and punishments that corresponded to the social relations of producing men (e.g., slaves, freedmen, convicts). During the early nineteenth century or preindustrial America, for example, there was the continuation of slave labor in the South and the introduction of imprisonment at hard labor in the North (Rusche and Kirchheimer 1939/1968).

By the end of the nineteenth century, however, the institutions of slavery and penal labor had been formally put to rest. With the increased application of machinery to the production process and the increased rates of profit, the need for inexpensive labor was declining (Platt and Takagi 1980). Nevertheless, during this period, workers' wages were lowered as a series of economic depressions, beginning in the 1880s, contributed to rising unemployment. At the same time, most forms of prison labor were outlawed and new ideologies of correctional reform and rehabilitation emerged (Sellin 1976).

During the Progressive Era (1900–1920), there were other changes in the criminal justice system as well, such as the birth of juvenile justice (Platt 1969) and the emergence of the public defender (Barak 1980). With respect to the differential treatment of people of color and women, and in connection with their lack of full legal and political rights, "equal protection" made some headway during this period. For example, in the early twentieth century the Black Codes and Jim Crow laws were abolished, eliminating some forms of legal discrimination against African Americans. In 1920, the Nineteenth Amendment passed and women received the right to vote in political elections. Each of these legal changes was expanding and conforming to the intent of the Fourteenth Amendment, enacted in 1868, guaranteeing to all people "equal protection under the law." Keeping with this tradition and indicative of the enduring struggles for justice were the social movements of the 1950s, 1960s, and 1970s.

Before turning to our portrayals of the history of class justice, racial justice, and gendered justice in America, we need to stress that we are not trying to suggest that some kind of linear progression of ever-greater equality exists. Equality is always a struggle, and is always resisted by those who are "more equal." Moreover, new forms of inequality often arise to take the place of old forms that have become illegal. Finally, it should be understood that simply granting a right in law does not make it so in practice.

Class Justice

Throughout most of the nineteenth and well into the twentieth century, a blatant kind of class justice prevailed in the selective enforcement and differential application of the criminal and civil laws to the "haves" and the "have nots" (Auerbach 1976; Barak 1980). The laws themselves were heavily influenced by a reverence for private property and laissez-faire social relations. In terms of commercial transactions, the philosophy of the day was "buyer beware." In the area of business, farmers and merchants alike were subject to few regulatory laws of any kind. In other words, both groups were allowed the freedom to expand their particular domains and to compete and acquire both property and capital with little legal interference. By contrast, labor was highly regulated. Unions were an illegal interference with "freedom of contract" and an unlawful conspiracy that interfered with the employer's property rights.

Railroads were crucial to the expansion of the economy at the turn of the century, and companies were amassing large fortunes from this industry. However, they fought attempts at minimum wages for employees and often required employees to live in a company town, rent dwellings from the company, and shop at company stores. The prices charged by the company were usually more than the wage, so families became bound to the company as indentured servants. For industry as a whole, the average work week was 60 hours. Fatigue, combined with the employers' indifference to workplace safety, created "an appalling record of industrial accidents. An incomplete survey showed that at least half a million workers were killed, crippled, or seriously injured on the job in 1907" (Gilbert 1998, p. 57).

In other areas, exposés on the meat packing industry shocked the public and motivated legislators to enact the first Food and Drug Acts. The journalists, called muckrakers, believed that "big business was 'bad business' insofar as it was more concerned with profit than human life" (Frank and Lynch 1992, p. 13). Their concerns were shared by lawyers such as Louis Brandeis, who would soon become a Supreme Court justice. He was writing about the "curse of bigness" and the problems of companies becoming large in the interests of being a monopoly—one that violated the public trust rather than worked in its interest. "No country," he wrote, "can afford to have its prosperity originated by a small controlling class" (in Douglas 1954, p.

187). Justice Douglas (1954) explained that "Brandeis did not want America to become a nation of clerks, all working for some overlord."

The administration of criminal (and civil) justice was chaotic, often corrupt, and subject to the buying of law enforcement and juries (Barak 1980). An independent and decentralized criminal justice system designed for a more homogenized, pioneer, and primarily agricultural society was ill-adapted for the needs of an increasingly complex, urban, and industrialized society. A social and cultural environment that was experiencing increasing numbers of immigrants from southern and eastern Europe, a changing means of rapid communication and transportation, and an expanding presence of wage-earning working classes called for a coordinated system of criminal justice.

By the turn of the century, the buying of justice that had prevailed earlier (available to those who could afford representation in the legislatures, in the courts, and in the streets) was threatening the very legitimacy of criminal justice in America (Cantor 1932). The initial laissez-faire emphasis on the right to acquire private property had blossomed into a full-fledged national preoccupation with wealth and power. Political corruption became widespread, and political machines dominated urban areas: "The machines controlled city governments, including the police and the courts. Payrolls were padded and payoffs were collected from contractors" (Edelstein and Wicks 1977, p. 7). Graft and other forms of bribery contributed not only to the buying of justice by those who could afford it, but to a changing national morality. "Rackets," "pull," and "protection" were common antidotes for stubborn legal nuisances. Prevailing values of wealth and success predominated as guiding principles of right and wrong. "The ability to 'make good' and 'get away with it' offsets the questionable means employed in the business as well as professional world. Disrespect for the law and order is the accompanying product of this scheme of success" (Cantor 1932, p. 145).

Those who were marginalized, especially the poor, unemployed, women, and people of color, were rarely, if ever, in a position to buy justice. As the marginalized groups of immigrants and others grew in urban cities across America, and as the miscarriages of justice flourished, the need to reform the institutions of criminal justice grew, because the country was beginning to experience bitter class wars. The working classes aggressively resisted exploitation through on-the-job actions and wider social movements. To combat challenges to the emerging monopoly or corporate order of industrial capitalism, the wealthy and ruling classes initially employed illegal violence, such as the hiring of thugs and private armies. Later, they retained the services of private security companies, such as Pinkerton's, to infiltrate and break up worker organizations. However, as the number of violent incidents increased, and as the contradictions of American democracy became more apparent, other methods for regulating and controlling the masses were needed, ones reflective of a modern system of crime control and a criminal justice system based on a more equal-appearing application of the rule of law (Barak 1980).

During the Progressive Era, the plight of the poor gained the attention of some industrialists and political leaders. The discontent of those who were not benefiting from the expanding economy threatened the growing prosperity of those who were. As a response to the growing resentment of the lower and working classes, and from the middle-class Progressives who believed in the "perfectible society," the ruling strata sought to stabilize the social order in general and to reform the administration of criminal justice in particular. With respect to the former relations of class justice, there emerged mass education, working-class citizenship, assimilation of ethnic groups, voting privileges, political parties, and economic mobility for a growing middle class. With respect to the latter relations of class justice, there emerged within the administration of crime control a number of reforms, some "hard" and some "soft" (Center for Research Criminal Justice 1975).

Examples of the harder or technical reforms included the formation of systems of state policing, the initiation of truancy laws, and the forced sterilization of some "mentally defective" persons, poor people, and sex offenders. Examples of the softer or humane reforms included the development of the juvenile justice system, the public defender system, and a bit later, systems of treatment and rehabilitation. Each of these soft reforms aimed at a fairer, more objective, scientific, and humane administration of criminal justice. In combination, these reforms helped secure and legitimate the needs of an emerging corporate capitalism as they contributed to more rational, bureaucratic, and efficient systems of criminal justice. At the same time, these legalistic reforms not only improved the practices and the images of due process and equal protection under the law, they also legitimated greater state intervention into the lives of those marginally defined and segregated on the basis of their class, race, and gender. The practice of forced sterilization, for example, continued until as recently as the 1970s and provided the foundation for chemical castration as well as policies aimed at getting women on welfare to agree to be implanted with the contraceptive Norplant.

Racial Justice

The consistencies in the practice of racial justice in the Americas date as far back as Christopher Columbus and his ill treatment of the indigenous peoples, and subsequently the early colonists' treatment of Native-American Indians, and the institutionalized enslavement of Africans by the slave codes. This intense and sustained history of mistreatment has raised questions about genocide in the United States with respect to both Native Americans (Churchill 1997; Weyler 1992) and African Americans (Johnson and Leighton 1999; Patterson 1970, 1971).

Russell has shown that one constant remained as the slave codes became the black codes and the black codes became Jim Crow segregation statutes:

> Blackness itself was a crime. The codes permitted Blacks to be punished for a wide range of social actions. They could be punished for walking down the street if they did not move out of the way quickly enough to accommodate White passersby, for talking to friends on a street corner, for speaking to someone White, or for making eye contact with someone White. (1998, p. 22)

Each of these "systems of racial justice" operated in racially oppressive and discriminatory ways. Some were blatantly "double standards" and some were subtly so, as in the "separate and equal" ruling of *Plessy v. Ferguson* in 1896.

Slave codes, from 1619 to 1865, constituted the criminal law and procedure applied against enslaved Africans (Gorman 1997; Oshinsky 1996). The codes regulated slave life from cradle to grave and were virtually uniform across the states in upholding the institutions of chattel slavery. "Under the codes, the hardest criminal penalties were reserved for those acts that threatened the institution of slavery (e.g., the murder of someone White or a slave insurrection). The slave codes also penalized Whites who actively opposed slavery" (Russell 1998, p. 15). But their primary purposes were to enumerate applicable laws and to prescribe the social boundaries for slaves: where they could go, what types of activity they could engage in, and what type of contracts that they could enter into. Slaves were not only subject to the administration of separate, special tribunals, but to procedural practices that did not accord them the same rights as free white men, such as the rights to a jury trial, to be convicted by a unanimous verdict, to be presumed innocent, and to appeal a conviction. Nor were slaves permitted to serve as jurors or to act as witnesses against whites. In short,

> the codes created a caste system under which Whites, Blacks, and mulattoes were accorded separate legal statuses and sanctions. This meant that in addition to the blatant double standards of the slave codes, Blacks were further marginalized by laws that assessed punishment by 'degree of Blackness.' (Russell 1998, p. 15)

Under such a caste system, the slave codes of most states allowed whites to beat, slap, and whip slaves with impunity. When it came to sex crimes, especially ones involving interracial relations, racial double standards of enforcement and punishment prevailed. For example: "A Black man who had sex with a White woman faced the most severe penalty, while a White man who had sex with a Black slave woman faced the least severe penalty" (Russell 1998, p. 16). In fact, more black men were executed for rape than for killing a white person, and under Virginia law, the only law carrying the punishment of castration was the rape of a white woman by a black man. Under most slave codes, however, the rape of a black woman by a white man or by a black slave was not a crime. Under the slave codes, the prevailing modes of enforcing slavery were not only through separate but unequal laws and tribunals, but by the notorious slave patrols, or the precursors to the first American form of policing. Slave patrollers, working in conjunction with the militia, were allowed to stop, search, and beat slaves who did not have proper permission to be away from their plantations. Slave laws also sanctioned extrajudicial forms of justice, such as "plantation justice," which permitted slave owners to impose sanctions, including lashes, castration, and hanging, and to hire bounty hunters to catch runaway slaves (Russell 1998).

After the Civil War and emancipation, newly freed black men and women were given the right to enter into contracts and to marry. At the same time, the first Black Codes adopted in 1865 created a new system of involuntary servitude, expressly prohibited by the recently adopted Thirteenth Amendment. For example, the adoption of vagrancy laws allowed blacks to be arrested for the "crime" of being unemployed, and licensing requirements were imposed to bar blacks from all but the most menial of jobs in the South. Finally, the newly granted rights for blacks served to mobilize white vigilantes, including the likes of the Ku Klux Klan. The harsh nature of racial justice also can be seen by the institutionalization of the "lynching ritual," an extreme form of vigilante racial justice that between 1882 and 1964 in America claimed the lives of 3,000 to 10,000 blacks (Tolnay and Beck 1995).

Jim Crow laws began to take hold in the early 1900s following the *Plessy v. Ferguson* decision. These laws mandated separate public facilities for blacks and whites and applied to just about any type of social interaction, including cemeteries, hospital wards, water fountains, public restrooms, church bibles, swimming pools, hotels, movie theaters, trains, phone booths, lunch counters, prisons, courthouses, buses, orphanages, school textbooks, parks, and prostitution (Myrdal 1944). In effect, the segregation statutes and covenants in the South as well as in the North in terms of where "Whites, Coloreds, and Negroes" could rent or buy property, for example, spoke to the way in which these laws sought to effectively regulate both the private and public lives of blacks. Both before and after *Brown v. the Topeka Kansas Board of Education* in 1954, outlawing "separate but equal," the world of social etiquette made no pretense regarding social equality. Russell offers this explanation:

> Rules of racial etiquette were an integral part of Jim Crow. These unwritten rules required that Black men refer to White men as "Mister" or "Sir." At the same time, however, Whites would commonly refer to a Black man as "boy." The rules governing racial manners also required Blacks to step aide and bow their heads in the presence of Whites. This system of verbal and physical deference reflected the White belief that no matter how much racial equality the Constitution promised, Whites would never view Blacks as their social equals. (1998, p. 22)

African Americans are not the only nonwhite groups who have experienced racial injustice, imposed separation, and cultural imperialism. The thefts of land from Native Americans and the government's subsequent breaking of treaties have left many of them on small, isolated reservations (Churchill 1997; Lazarus 1991). Many Latinos live in rural and inner-city barrios, not unlike the proliferation of Chinatowns and black and brown ghettos that grew up all across America. Patterns of residential segregation have remained the rule, even though "separate but unequal" was struck down (Massey and

Denton 1993). The social isolation experienced by these racial others has created "many deleterious effects, both structural (e.g., systematic differences in opportunities to acquire disposable income and to generate wealth) and psychological (e.g., being unable to understand what life is like for members of other groups)" (Mann and Zatz 1998, p. 5).

Gendered Justice

Historically, the differential treatment of men and women—and later of boys and girls—has reflected gendered notions of public and private space. The expression or legacy of a gendered double standard dates back to the chauvinistic sexual customs and conceptions of private property as first articulated in ancient Greek and Roman laws (Posner 1992). Until recently these customs had prevailed in law. Throughout most of modern Western history, and in the United States, women were considered chattel or possessions of their fathers and husbands, forbidden from holding property in their own names or from entering into business deals or contracts. Women were treated as different or as "second class" citizens, and they were subject to the patriarchal rules of family, usually under the guise of protecting them and controlling them "for their own good." Whether in the public or private spheres, gendered justice denied women equal protection under the law. In fact, it was not until the 1980s that husbands could be charged with the crime of raping their wives. Moreover, the burdens of legal proof involved in extramarital rape cases before then were always hard to meet, making rape the single most difficult crime to successfully prosecute on behalf of women victims seeking justice from the criminal law.

Early European feminists worked to raise awareness of women's oppression, a tradition that continued in spite of social revolutions in Europe and passionate discourses about equality and brotherhood. Indeed, in the late 1700s, Mary Wollstonecraft "observed the inconsistency of radical males who fought for the freedom of individuals to determine their own happiness and yet continued to subjugate women, leaving them to 'procreate and rot' " (Kandal 1988, p. 12).

In the United States, few advocates of abolishing slavery saw any connection with women's suffrage. For example, the Grimke sisters used their status as part of a prominent Southern family to argue that female slaves "are our sisters" and have a "right to look for sympathy with their sorrows and effort and prayer for their rescue." But the New England abolition society chastised them for forgetting "the great and dreadful wrongs of the slave in a selfish crusade against some paltry grievance . . . some trifling oppression" of their own (Kandal 1988, p. 214). After the Civil War, a gendered reaction began similar in effect to the earlier purity crusades in Victorian England (Posner 1992).

With the arrival of the Progressive Era, social reformers sought to address the widespread prostitution and venereal diseases that resulted from the temporary shortage of women that accompanied the great waves of immigration in the late nineteenth and early twentieth centuries. Laws were passed that tried to suppress abortion, pornography, contraception, and prostitution. Federal laws such as the Mann Act of 1910 outlawed the importation of contraceptives, the mailing of obscene books and other materials, and the interstate traffic in prostitutes. The selective enforcement of those laws against the female sellers and the male purchasers of sex remains to this day a *de facto* component of the social relations of gendered justice and social control.

To be sure, persons handled formally by the criminal justice system and who ended up in prisons throughout the nineteenth and twentieth centuries were 95 percent male and 5 percent female (Rafter 1990). However, at least since the nineteenth century, the social control of girls and women has also included the patriarchal institutions of marriage and family, the associated treatment of females for their recalcitrance and waywardness, and the medicalization and hospitalization of their problems (Foucault 1980; Platt 1969).

Women also experienced gendered justice in other ways besides the chivalry that has been shown primarily to white women but denied to other women. For instance, when the first wave of organized imprisonment of women occurred between 1870 and 1900, many reformatories were opened as alternatives for white women. These women were regarded as in need of moral reform and protection. Women's case files in the American West in the late 1880s "rarely expressed an official opinion that an incarcerated female offender represented a threat to society. Instead, parole boards denied a woman freedom because she 'had not been sufficiently punished,' or she 'traveled with bad companions in the past,' or she 'broke the hearts of her respected parents'" (Butler 1997, p. 226).

At the same time, as the reformatory movement "resulted in the incarceration of large numbers of white working-class girls and women for largely noncriminal or deportment offenses," such offenses did not extend to women of color (Chesney-Lind 1996, p. 132). Rather, African-American women, for example, continued to be warehoused in prisons where they were treated much like male inmates (Butler 1997). In the South, black women often ended up on chain gangs and were expected to keep up with the men in order to avoid beatings (Rafter 1990).

Gendered justice has also socially constructed the "normal" criminal as male and the "abnormal" criminal as female. In other words, men were seen as rational creatures of culture and women as governed by their nature. Thus, criminology constructed the crimes by men as being bad choices that reflected a normal weighing of gain and loss, but crimes by women were seen as "unnatural" because they went against the allegedly docile and submissive "nature" of women (Hart 1994; Rafter 1990). Links have also been made between the "unnaturalness" of female criminality and lesbianism (Faith 1993; Hart 1994).

The Social Relations of Class, Race, Gender, and Crime Control: Inequalities of Crime, Culture, and Production

Examining class, race, and gender in relationship to law, order, and crime control provides an appreciation for the unique histories of the individual social groupings and interrelated axes of privilege and inequality. At any given moment, class, race, and gender may "feel more salient or meaningful in a given person's life, but they are overlapping and cumulative in their effect on people's experience" (Andersen and Hill Collins 1998, p. 3). As we have already shown, in terms of the history of the social realities of justice in America, the experiences of diverse groups of people in society have contributed to the shaping of conceptions of criminals and victims. These experiences have helped to shape not only the way racial and ethnic majorities have come to regard specific legitimate and illegitimate behaviors but the patterned ways in which they have (or lack) access to institutional power and privileges.

For example, Roberts (1993), in her examination of the intersections of crime, race, and reproduction, discusses the convergence between the racial construction of crime and the use of reproduction as an instrument of punishment. She links crime, race, and reproduction to show how racism and patriarchy function as mutually reinforcing systems of domination that help determine "who the criminals are, what constitutes a crime, and which crimes society treats most seriously" (Roberts 1993, p. 1945). More specifically, in terms of abortion, birth control, and social control, Roberts discusses how this domination is meted out through the control of black women's bodies that discourages procreation, subordinates groups, and regulates fertility. As part of our integrative analysis of class, race, and gender, we similarly attempt to explore how each of these hierarchies helps sustain the others and how they reinforce the types of crimes and justice in our society.

Our study of class, race, gender, and crime reveals several broad themes about how bias undergirds the construction of what will and will not be criminal, as well as affects the implementation and administration of those biased rules. This bias also shapes the construction of individual experience and identity, which varies according to one's socioeconomic position in society. More specifically, we bring at least four related assumptions to this study of the social relations of class, race, gender, and crime control:

- First, these categories of social difference all share similarities of justice, especially as they relate to power resources and to the allocation and distribution of rewards and punishments in society.

- Second, the systems of privilege and inequality derived from the social statuses of class, race, and gender are overlapping and have accumulating effects on the type of crime control that various groups of people receive.

- Third, there are connections between these systems of difference, inequality, and privilege, as each helps to reproduce the social divisions of hierarchy and stratification that dynamically affect people's life experiences, inside and outside the criminal justice system.

- Fourth, according to relationships of power, status, and authority, systems of crime control socially construct selectively enforced and differentially applied norms to social groups.

Historically, we know that the legal differences favoring corporations over individuals, workers, and consumers, or the wealthy over the middle and poor classes, have remained fairly constant over time despite efforts to regulate and control monopolies of wealth or to assist society's destitute. We also recognize that, on the one hand, during the twentieth century the more blatant forms of discrimination based on alleged differences of race and gender were significantly reduced in the United States. On the other hand, we recognize that although many legalized and institutionalized forms of bias have been reformed or abolished by law, in practice, differential treatment based on race and gender still persists. Hence, in terms of the operations of crime control, poor persons still have fewer resources or less power working for them in negotiating outcomes within and without the criminal justice system than the affluent or middle classes. And, when poor persons are of color or are women too, they hold even less power, and if they are all three—poor, of color, and women—they possess less power still. To put it most simply, the social relations of class, race, and gender help construct the kinds of crime and justice that we have in American society.

Our study is not an ethnographic study of victims or victimizers. It is an analytical investigation into the institutionalized practices and outcomes of crime control. Nevertheless, we share the desire to unravel the complexities of class, race, and gender as they interact with the cultural production of crime, justice, and inequality. We also share an appreciation that crime, justice, and crime control cannot be separated from the totality of the ordered, structural, and cultural contexts of their productivity. Each of our cultural approaches shares the belief that the inequalities in control and justice are part and parcel of the social constructions of class, race, and gender differences as they are experienced in relationship to place, order, conflict, and perception.

Public perceptions of what constitutes unacceptable social injuries and acceptable social controls are shaped by the underlying elements of social organization, including the production and distribution of economic, political, and cultural services (Michalowski 1985). We are not talking about conspiracies of elites and decision makers here, but rather about crime and crime control institutions that reflect and recreate capitalist economic relations. So "serious crime," defined from above or below, from the suite or the street, or from official reports of the Federal Bureau of Investigation or the cultural media, becomes statistically mediated and socially constructed. In culturally structured numbers, narratives, and pictures alike, a distorted view and limited perception of harmful behavior emerges. Crime and criminals are restricted primarily to the tabulations and representations of the conventional criminal code violations: murder, rape, burglary, robbery, assault, and larceny-theft. Traditionally omitted from these images and narratives of street crime are the underreported and hidden crimes, such as trafficking in and possession of stolen merchandise, illicit sex, gambling, loan sharking, internal pilferage, and weapons smuggling. Almost all crimes in suites are ignored and invisible, such as the frauds and embezzlements of white-collar and professional criminals as well as corporate offenses against the environment, workplace, and consumer.

Culturally produced images of crime and criminals reinforce one-dimensional notions that criminality and harmful behavior are exclusively the responsibility of the poor and marginal members of society. The images of crime control and the administration of justice leave impressions that reproduce limiting social realities of social control and crime prevention. As mass consumers, we all share mediated facsimiles of lawbreakers and crime fighters. Common stories of crime and criminal justice appear and reappear over and over in the news, in films, on television, and in literature. Consequently, most Americans imagine similar renderings of crime, criminals, law enforcement, adjudication, and punishment.

It is no wonder that when most people try to picture the typical American crime, the common image that emerges is one of young male victimizers and victims of color. In repetitive news stories, African-American and Hispanic male youths in particular are encountered lying dead in pools of blood, victims of so-called senseless violence or gang-related drive-by shootings. There are also the numerous police action reenactments that can be viewed regularly on such television programs as *Top Cops* or *America's Most Wanted* that similarly recycle images of these young men as dangerous drug dealers whose dwellings must be invaded during the early hours of dawn by "storm troopers" and other law enforcement personnel in order to secure the "war on crime." In like fashion, the images of crime control that are constructed throughout the criminal justice system as we move from law enforcement to adjudication and from sentencing to incarceration again serve to reinforce limited and fairly distorted realities of criminal justice.

When we think of a criminal courtroom, for example, images come to mind from relatively long and involved trials exposed in feature-length films, or from *Court TV's* gavel-to-gavel coverage of such celebrated cases as that of Sandy Murphy and Rick Tabish for killing multimillionaire and former Las Vegas casino owner Ted Binion in September 1998. The actual trial of these two "sympathetic" murderers did not convene until February of 2000 and ended in May with their receiving the minimum sentence possible under Nevada law. The public is also led to believe, based on succinct and curt shots of highly charged courtroom scenes from various television series such as *The Practice* and *Law and Order,* that attorneys for each side, engaged in vigorous battle, always do their legal best to secure justice for all. However, in these dramatizations, whether fictional or "reality television," the images that do not come to mind are the ones in which the rights of defendants have been watered down. We refer to the overwhelming majority of criminal cases (90 percent) that are plea-bargained everyday in courthouses throughout America. These negotiated deals in lieu of trials usually take less than a few minutes for judges and courts to process and uphold. In the process, they virtually eliminate the possibility of appeal (see Kipnis in Leighton and Reiman 2001).

Turning from adjudication to punishment, popular images of dangerously violent offenders who need to be locked up indefinitely are prevalent in the media. For the last 30 years, politicians have appeared before the media talking about a "get tough(er)" platform that criticizes the current "leniency" of the previous election cycles. Such pictures influence penal policies and make unimaginable the possibility of ever reuniting the offender, the victim, and the community. As part of the politics of American punishment and the political economy of incarceration, the languages and images of retribution serve to negate rehabilitation efforts and contribute to the United States' $100 billion-a-year criminal justice-industrial complex (Dyer 2000; Shelden 1999). Representations of offenders convey the images of feuding convicts divided into racial and religious cliques doing "scared time"; not of inmates engaged in school or the learning of a vocation, or of former offenders "fitting back" into society.

The award-winning HBO dramatic series of life in a maximum security prison, *OZ*, portrays a based-on-facts fictional account of the complexity of one of those "hell on earth" archipelagos. On the one hand, this representation ignores the social realities of some 1,500 other state and federal prisons of lesser pain. On the other hand, *OZ* does not actually do justice to the growing apartheid-like conditions of crime and punishment that disproportionately affect black and brown Americans. Meanwhile, commercially successful prison films, such as *Lock Up* (1989), *The Shawshank Redemption* (1994), and *The Green Mile* (1999) tend to present images of ethnic and cultural diversity in prison as they tell stories of mostly white inmate protagonists in conflict with mostly white correctional antagonists, against a background of "out of control" systems of criminal justice (Horton 1996). Box 1.1 provides more information on mass culture and the relations of class, race, and gender in the context of O. J. Simpson's trial.

Box 1.1

Murder, Criminal Justice, and Mass Culture: A Case Study in Class, Race, Gender, and Crime

One of the most celebrated courtroom dramas of all time was the televised trial of O. J. Simpson for the cold-blooded murder of his ex-wife and her male friend. For more than 18 solid months, the Simpson case was both a media circus and a public obsession, not to mention a small cottage industry of consumer goods, legal pundits, and television specials—the latter still going on at the time of this writing. One can certainly surmise that the interest, appeal, attraction, disgust, or whatever with this case had much to do with its converging issues of class, race, and gender.

One can also safely say that the Simpson trial, both inside and outside the courtroom, represented the civics lesson of the 1990s, as it socially constructed and reconstructed, over and over again, the general workings of the American systems of law enforcement and criminal justice. More particularly, the trial became a "crash course" for the masses in constitutional and criminal law and in articulating the rights of the individual versus the rights of the state. Beyond the social realities and legal realisms of whether the criminal justice system was "fixed" or "broken" were the historical experiences and perceptions that whole groups of people, based on the complexities of their class, race, and gender backgrounds, brought to their evaluations of the systems of law and justice in the United States. These real (and imagined) differences in experience of the legal system undoubtedly shape and influence people's views of the administration of justice. The evidence is clear that people's social experiences based on class, race, and gender were more important than the actual facts of the case.

In other words, for the most part, people's views of the criminal justice system and of Simpson's guilt or innocence remained the same from beginning to end. In short, beliefs and attitudes were consistent before, during, and after the criminal trial. Some commentators have claimed that the case was an exercise in the reification of whatever people believed in the first place. Other commentators claimed that the Simpson case represented a Rorschach test of sorts. Thus, people could make anything they liked out of it. We believe that the first of these two claims is much closer to the truth. After all, in reality there were many more "spinners of" than there were "spins on" the O. J. phenomenon (see Barak 1996). For us, however, the interesting question has less to do with the fact that people's views of criminal justice and Simpson remained fairly constant throughout the debacle and more to do with the ways in which class, race, and gender shaped those views.

Take the question of guilt or innocence. Generally, persons from higher socioeconomic groups thought that O. J. committed the murders, and it appears that race and gender made no significant difference. Among blacks, 70 percent thought O. J. was innocent; more African-American males than females thought he was guilty. Among whites, 70 percent thought that Simpson was guilty, with slightly more affirmative women than men. How did the jury compare to the public at large? The jury officially voted 12–0 not guilty on the second round of "polling" themselves. On the first round it was different, as one Hispanic and eight black women and one black man had voted not guilty, while the two white women had voted guilty. So the breakdowns of the first jury reactions appear similar to those of the general public.

As meaningful as some of these differences appear, such black and white distinctions were incomplete and misleading to the extent that they failed to poll the reactions of Asians, Hispanics, and other societal groupings. More important, these polls in black and white, unlike the more complex and sophisticated polling of the body politic or electorate, failed to break down the interpretations by age, occupation, class, gender, sexual orientation, religion, and other demographics. Such data would have helped shed light on the background similarities and differences, for instance, between the 30 percent of whites who agreed with 70 percent of blacks that he was not guilty. In future public discussions of crime and punishment, for example, expanded data of other ethnic and racial groups in relation to their socioeconomic and gender positions would help the body politic move beyond simple black and white distinctions and closer to the more complex relations of class, race, and gender.

What was particularly interesting to observe during the O. J. saga were the mass-mediated reconstructions to "normalize" this case within the context of everyday practices of criminal justice in America. In other words, the Simpson case was an aberration in the administration of criminal justice as it departed from the more traditional images and stereotypes of criminal defendants, trial attorneys, expert witnesses, and juries of one's peers. For example, criminal prosecutors and criminal defense attorneys are much more often than not white and male, the bailiffs are usually men and more often than not of color, court reporters are invariably women, and juries, as infrequent as they are, are rarely constituted of one's peers. Typically, juries are from higher socioeconomic classes than criminal defendants. Ordinarily, both the behavior of the police and the credibility of expert witnesses are beyond reproach. That is, they are generally treated with a decorum of deference and respect.

In the circumstances of defendant O. J., the status quo was ripped apart. After all, Simpson was a wealthy African American male accused of murdering his formerly dependent—psychologically and economically—white wife and her white working-class male friend in a "sexual triangle" of sorts. Of course, Simpson was also a media celebrity from television and films, and a former all-Pro running back for the Buffalo Bills, who was able to retain a million-dollar "dream team" of well-known criminal attorneys, eventually led by the indefatigable Johnnie Cochran. In fact, unlike 99.9 percent and higher of criminal defendants, O. J. had "deeper pockets" than the prosecution did. As for the prosecuting team, they were led by the unusual combination of a white woman and an African-American man. As for the jury, they were composed of eleven women and one man: nine African Americans, one Hispanic, and two whites, all members of the working classes. Finally, presiding over this trial was an Asian rather than an Anglo- or Euro-American judge.

These and other differences from the normal relations of class, race, and gender that usually surround a murder trial accounted for the differential applications of the law, or for the special privileges, that O. J. received during his incarceration period, prior to and pending the outcome of his trial. For example, even before the trial began, Simpson reached an unheard of deal in the annals of American criminal justice history. He was able, through his attorneys, to successfully negotiate a deal with the prosecution that should he be convicted of the double murder, the state would not execute him. Generally, if such deals are reached, the accused has to, in exchange, plead guilty to some crime or another, saving the state the expense of a costly trial and eliminating any chances of a nonconviction. O. J. traded nothing except for his incredible popularity.

Similarly, because of the high-powered nature of the defense team, Simpson's attorneys were able to effectively put the motives and competencies of the Los Angeles Police Department and District Attorney's Office on trial. In the process, they raised what appears to have been the "reasonable doubt" in this jury's mind—the key to his acquittal in the criminal trial. In sum, the differences in the management of justice between the Simpson case and the normal case were informed by a novel combination of class, race, and gender relations of crime control.

At the same time, the public reactions to this criminal event were also shaped and influenced by class, racial, and gendered experiences with law enforcement and crime control. More specifically, differences in social group experiences with the criminal justice system determine one's trust or lack of trust in justice, or whether one views, for example, the police as professional and competent or as biased and discriminatory. In terms of analyzing the relations of class, race, gender, and justice, then, it is important to account for the diversity of views and experiences.

Barak, Gregg (ed.). 1996. *Representing O.J.: Murder, Criminal Justice, and Mass Culture*. Albany, NY: Harrow and Heston.

Overview of the Book

The disciplines of criminology and the fields of criminal justice have always been about the real and imagined differences between "criminals" and "noncriminals." Theoretically, explanations of crime and crime control, regardless of perspective or school of thought, have sought to make sense out of these differences. In the process of trying to sort out these differences, virtually every theoretical framework has made both explicit and implicit assumptions about class, race, and gender. Up until recently, the problem with this line of inquiry was not only a lack of agreement on the effects of these three critical constructs but, worse yet, the fact that folks were still debating whether or not these variables matter.

By the turn of the twenty-first century, however, a growing number of criminologists from several orientations, including critical, feminist, Marxist, positivist, and integrative, had come to appreciate, in different yet related ways, that class, race, and gender matter. Today, many inquiries are interested in finding out just exactly how class, race, and gender matter in the production of crime and criminal justice. Of course, key questions on the complexities of these relations and on the means of exploring them still remain. Our goal is to contribute to the analysis and exploration of the complexities of class, race, gender, and crime and crime control.

In the rest of this book, we strive to portray the social realities of justice in America, vis-à-vis an examination of class, race, and gender and the administration of criminal justice. Although class, race, and gender are viewed here as interconnecting systems of difference and as belonging to a larger system of privilege and inequality, we still appreciate the uniqueness of these categories and the importance of viewing them both alone and in combination. Hence, Chapters 2, 3, and 4 tend to treat class, race, and gender, respectively, as separate phenomena, delineating the meaning and conceptualizing the experiences of each in relation to the practices of criminal justice.

The formats of these three chapters are quite similar. Each chapter begins with a narrative example that reflects on actual situations of class, race, and gender and that attempts to locate connections between criminal justice policies and culturally structured realities. Following these examples are overviews of what is meant by the terms "class," "race," and "gender." Many key related terms are defined in our effort to provide a broad understanding of class, race, and gender. This initial introduction also includes a discussion of the social, economic, and political aspects of class, race, or gender.

The next sections of each chapter start to explore more specific relationships with crime. Specifically, class, race, or gender is first related to the discipline of criminology, then law and law making. Each chapter then surveys the various critical points in the current criminal justice process, with particular attention to the distribution of victimization, policing and the identification of criminals, adjudication, and punishment. Unlike many other books, we examine how class, race, and gender relate to workers within the criminal justice system rather than look only at the offenders and clients of the system. Each of these chapters finishes with a survey of media representations. Finally, we draw some general conclusions concerning the relationships between the administration of crime control and class, race, and gender.

In Chapter 5, the connections between class, race, and gender are drawn more explicitly. The opening narrative in this chapter focuses on the treatment of Rosa Lopez, a witness in the Simpson trial, and on the need generally to account not only for class or race or gender in the social construction of crime and crime control but also for all three acting in relation to each other. After the Lopez illustration, the chapter follows an outline similar in topics to Chapters 2 through 4 (but with the focus on intersections rather than just class, race, or gender). The chapter ends with an examination and evaluation of the changing race and gender relations of criminal justice workers.

In the final chapter, we conclude by providing an overview of crime control and the administration of justice in America. In the context of class, race, and gender, we try to characterize and summarize the thrust of our findings about these relations on crime and justice. We also discuss the differences between individual and social justice and how both are related to the kinds of justice practices inside and outside the administration of criminal law. In this context, we examine three systems of justice—equal, restorative, and social—and the policy implications of each for reducing crime and maximizing justice. Finally, we consider how these systems or scenarios of justice affect the social and criminal relations of class, race, and gender. ✦

Chapter 2

Class

Habitually Unequal Offenders

In 1964, William Rummel received three years in prison after being convicted of a felony for fraudulently using a credit card to obtain $80 worth of goods. Five years later, he passed a forged check in the amount of $28.36 and received four years. In 1973, Rummel was convicted of a third felony— obtaining $120.75 by false pretenses for accepting payment to fix an air conditioner that he never returned to repair. Rummel received a mandatory life sentence under Texas' recidivist statute. He challenged this sentence on the grounds that it violated the Eighth Amendment's prohibition of cruel and unusual punishment by being grossly disproportionate to the crime.

In Rummel v. Estelle (1980) the Supreme Court affirmed Rummel's life sentence for the theft of less than $230 that never involved force or the threat of force. Justice Louis Powell's dissent noted that "it is difficult to imagine felonies that pose less danger to the peace and good order of a civilized society than the three crimes committed by the petitioner" (445 U.S. 263, 295). However, Justice William Rehnquist's majority opinion stated there was an "interest, expressed in all recidivist statutes, in dealing in a harsher manner with those who by repeated criminal acts have shown that they are simply incapable of conforming to the norms of society as established by its criminal law" (445 U.S. 263). After "having twice imprisoned him for felonies, Texas was entitled to place upon Rummel the onus of one who is simply unable to bring his conduct within the social norms prescribed by the criminal law" (445 U.S. 284).

Now consider the case of General Electric, which is not considered a habitual criminal offender despite committing diverse crimes over many decades. In the 1950s, GE and several companies agreed in advance on the *sealed bids they submitted for heavy electrical equipment. This price-fixing defeated the purpose of competitive bidding, costing taxpayers and consumers as much as a billion dollars. GE was fined $437,000—a tax-deductible business expense—the equivalent of a person earning $175,000 a year getting a $3 ticket. Two executives spent only 30 days in jail, even though one defendant had commented that price-fixing "had become so common and gone on for so many years that we lost sight of the fact that it was illegal" (in Hills 1987, p. 191).*

In the 1970s, GE made illegal campaign contributions to Richard Nixon's presidential campaign. Widespread illegal discrimination against minorities and women at GE resulted in a $32 million settlement. Also during this time, three former GE nuclear engineers—including one who had worked for the company for 23 years and managed the nuclear complaint department—resigned to draw attention to serious design defects in the plans for the Mark III nuclear reactor because the standard practice was "sell first, test later" (Hills 1987, p. 170; see also Glazer and Glazer 1989).

In 1981, GE was convicted of paying a $1.25 million bribe to a Puerto Rican official to obtain a power plant contract. GE has pled guilty to felonies involving the illegal procurement of highly classified defense documents, and in 1985 it pled guilty to 108 counts of felony fraud involving defense contracts related to the Minuteman missile. In spite of a new code of ethics, GE was convicted in three more criminal cases over the next years, plus paying $3.5 million to settle cases involving retaliation against four whistleblowers who helped reveal the defense fraud. (GE subsequently lobbied Congress to weaken the False Claims Act.) In 1988, the government returned another 317 indictments against GE for fraud in a $21 million computer contract.

In 1989, GE's stock brokerage firm paid a $275,000 civil fine for discriminating against low-income consumers, the largest fine ever under the Equal Credit Opportunity Act. A 1990 jury convicted GE of fraud for cheating on a $254 million contract for battlefield computers, and journalist William Greider reports that the $27.2 million fine included money to "settle government complaints that it had padded bids on two hundred other military and space contracts" (1996, p.350; see also Clinard 1990; Greider 1994; Pasztor 1995; Simon 1999).

Because of tax changes GE had lobbied for and the Reagan tax cuts generally, GE paid no taxes between 1981 and 1983 when net profits were $6.5 billion. In fact, in a classic example of corporate welfare, GE received a tax rebate of $283 million during a time of high national deficits even though the company eliminated 50,000 jobs in the United States by closing 73 plants and offices. Further, "Citizen GE" is one of the prime environmen-

tal polluters and is identified as responsible for contributing to the damage of 47 sites in need of environmental cleanup.

Currently, GE advertises that it "brings good things to life," and it owns NBC television. Even though felons usually lose political rights, GE's political action committee contributes hundreds of thousands to Congress each year. In spite of having been convicted of defrauding every branch of the military multiple times, GE is frequently invited to testify before Congress. If the corporation's revenue were compared to the Gross Domestic Product of countries, it would be the 53rd largest economy in the world. In 1997, GE's CEO, Jack Welch, Jr., made $8,800,797 in salary, bonuses, and other compensations. He had an additional $18,783,000 in stock options, for a total yearly pay package of $27,583,797. Jack Welch, Jr., also has $182,243,818 in unexercised stock options from previous years (Executive Paywatch, http://www.paywatch.org). "Three strikes and you're out" does not apply to GE, which is still at bat after hundreds of felony convictions.

Introduction

The Constitution of the United States claims that everyone is entitled to equal protection under the law. The statues of Lady Justice that adorn many courts show her blindfolded so she can impartially weigh the claims on the scales she carries. But most Americans know that being rich has its advantages, including in the areas of crime and law. Death-row inmates joke that people who have capital do not get capital punishment, and the statistics support their observation. Being wealthy makes it more likely that someone can literally or figuratively get away with murder. Several observers see this pattern as so pervasive that they argue the criminal justice system is about controlling the poor and keeping them in their place (Chambliss and Seidman 1982; Quinney 1977). Further, "crime" refers to "crime in the streets" rather than "crime in the suites," or corporate crime (like that of GE), which is more prevalent and more costly to society. These observations raise important questions about the connections between class and criminal justice which is the subject of this chapter.

For most Americans, discussions of class are often suppressed, denied, or ignored. Fundamentally, class revolves around questions of the distribution of income and wealth. At the same time, these questions are related to racial and gender identity, as women and minority men tend to occupy the lower levels of the income distribution. At the same time, America also has a strong myth of being a classless society, so issues of class usually take a back seat to issues of race and gender. In fact, more than one-third of people questioned in a survey about class identification said they had never thought about it before. In keeping with the notion of class as taboo, when asked a simple question of whether she thought there were social classes, one woman responded, "It's the dirtiest thing I've ever heard of" (Fussell 1983, p. 16).

Most people have heard (or said) something dirtier. And, even though most people would agree that class relates to what type of car people drive, the home they own, and the quality and quantity of consumer goods they possess, few people wish to engage in a substantive dialogue about the concept. Resistance to the topic is so real that one author has commented that the reaction from people when he told them he was working on a book about social class was as if he had said, "I am working on a book urging the beating to death of baby whales using the dead bodies of baby seals" (Fussell 1983, p. 15). Discussions of class are also problematic because the distributions of income and wealth directly contradict many of the ideas associated with a classless society.

For example, discussions of rich and poor draw attention to the disparity between how few Americans are middle class and how many believe themselves to be. Such discussions also highlight the "hourglass" shape of wealth distribution that reflects a growing inequality between the rich and the poor as well as a shrinking middle class. Indeed, since the mid-1970s, the distribution of wealth has become more unequal. Many people who have experienced downward mobility and reduced expectations react bitterly to the notion that anyone can make it if they work hard enough, given the double-shift lives of many of these persons. Jim Hightower, a Texas populist, does talk about economic inequality and how the economy is not working for many Americans—including downsized employees who have been kicked through "the goal posts of global greed" (1998a, p. 71). He says bluntly that "the rich are getting richer and the rest of us are getting taken," and as a result, he is accused by his critics of trying to start "class warfare" (1998a, p. 105). In short, the discussion of class is fraught with many emotionally charged and repressed feelings. Yet, a complete understanding of crime and crime control requires that we venture into this taboo area.[1]

We begin this exploration by defining some of the key terms related to social class and reviewing how some of the major theorists have approached this topic. We then provide an overview of income and wealth distributions, as well as offer some preliminary observations on how these inequalities affect political power (and thus law making) in the United States. We then discuss the relationship between class and criminology, with a focus on theories relating inequality to crime and raising questions about the relative lack of theory about white-collar, corporate, and state crime. A section on class, crime, and law reviews the various theoretical understandings of how the elites use their position to influence law making. The chapter also addresses important issues related to current criminal justice processing by examining the relationship between class and victimization, the identification and adjudication of criminals, and the punishment and imprisonment of offenders. We conclude the chapter by discussing how class applies to workers in the criminal justice system and how it plays out in media representations of crime.

Social Class and Stratification in Society

Definitions of Key Terms

In a most generic sense, *class* may be defined as "any division of society according to status" or social ranking (*New Webster's Dictionary of the English Language,* 1984, p. 186). For example, Horton and Hunt (1976, p. 234) defined social class as a "stratum of people of similar position in the social status continuum." Consequently, the janitor and the college president are not of the same class and are not treated the same way by students. The study of classes, however, is not only a way to identify social units (such as bourgeoisie, proletariat, middle class, underclass, and ruling class), but also a means for examining the history of capitalist society. Since the time of the French "utopian" socialists at the turn of the eighteenth century, the use of such terms as "class," "stratum," "rank," and "position" have not been interchangeable names for identical groupings.

For Marx, the principal social classes were the wage workers (the proletariat), the capitalists (the bourgeoisie), and a middle group (the petty bourgeoisie) that was supposedly on its way out. Before the rise of industrialism in the seventeenth century, Adam Smith had divided society into those who lived by wage labor, by renting out land, or by profiting from trade. Writing at the turn of the twentieth century, Thorstein Veblen (1919/1969) divided society into the leisure class and the working class: the former had become so wealthy that their main preoccupation was "conspicuous consumption," the latter so poor that they were forever struggling for their subsistence. Each of these descriptions of social class signifies that money separates people into different groupings.

The study of class is part of a larger question about what sociologists call *stratification*, which is concerned with the distribution of social goods such as income, wealth, and prestige. Because most of these goods have an (extremely) unequal distribution, part of studying stratification (or privilege and inequality) is an attempt to explain how small minorities maintain control over a disproportionate share of the social resources. Although *class* can cover many attributes that relate to social position, we will use it here mostly to indicate income and wealth. Elements of status—such as prestige and respectability—are also important for understanding the functioning of the criminal justice system, especially in terms of such "master statuses" as race and gender that transcend one's socioeconomic status. For the time being, however, we confine our discussion of class to its purely economic rather than its social manifestations. The aspects of class that refer to "good" or "high" taste or to a sophisticated sense of style or judgment are further removed from criminal justice concerns, though they may be related to both the social reality and the social construction of one's positions in society.

Many social thinkers have tried to devise meaningful ways to divide up the spectrum of income and wealth. As already noted, Marx identified the capitalist class, or the *bourgeoisie*, who owned the means of production (factories, banks, and businesses); the *petty bourgeoisie*, who do not have ownership but occupy management or professional positions; and the *proletariat*, or workers, who need to sell their labor to make a wage. Marx also identified the surplus population or *lumpenproletariat*, who have no formal ties to the system of economic relations because they are unemployed or unemployable (see Lynch and Groves 1989). In developing his theory of class and class conflict, Marx also contributed a useful critique of capitalism. Marx's description of economic classes is tied to his ideas about class struggle and his belief that history could be described in terms of an ongoing war of the rich against the poor for control of wealth.

Although Marx himself did not write much about crime, his suggestion that law and criminal justice are tools used in this class warfare have been utilized by criminologists to provide important insights and questions that are further explored in this chapter.

Many other attempts to describe the class system have been less useful because they are not tied to a theory of power relations or offer no useful insights for understanding criminal justice. For example, the distribution can be described in terms of upper, middle, and lower classes. There are many variations on this scheme, in part because people feel uncomfortable describing others as "low class" (but see Reiling in Henry and Hinkle 2001). To avoid possible value judgments, the lower segment of the income distribution has been described by such terms as "working class," "working poor," and "underclass." However, there is a growing literature in the field of "white trash studies," which examines the poorest whites who have none of the power and prestige of most whites. These people tend to have resources equal to or even fewer than minorities but have white skin, so studying them can potentially shed theoretical light on issues of race and class (Wray and Newitz 1996).

One interesting attempt to describe the distribution is Fussell's typology of nine classes: top out-of-sight (rich), upper, upper middle, middle, high proletarian, mid-proletarian, low proletarian, destitute, and bottom out-of-sight (1983). People in the first category include media mogul Ted Turner, who recently gave one *billion* dollars of his own money to the United Nations. One of Turner's seven properties is a New Mexico ranch that covers 578,000 acres, or enough room for 22 lakes, 30 miles of fishing streams, and more than 8,000 elk (Gilbert 1998, p. 90). People in the last category include homeless people, such as mentally ill people and Vietnam veterans who live in the subway tunnels of major cities (Barak 1991b; Toth 1995).

Many schemes for understanding class have difficulty placing women who work in the home and are not wage earners. Indeed, radical feminists often argue that women represent a social class. More generally, feminists argue that women's relationship to the class structure is mediated by "the configuration of the family, dependence on men, and domestic labour" (in Gamble 1999, p. 206). Chapter 5 examines these issues in more detail, so for now the important point is that underlying all these ideas about how to create meaningful divisions are some basic concepts related to income, wealth, and financial assets. *Income* is the most straightforward indicator of class. It represents sources of individual revenue such as salary, interest, and other items that must be reported on income tax forms. By contrast, *wealth* includes income *and* possessions such as cars, savings accounts, houses, stocks, and mutual funds, but it also takes into account debts and loans. *Financial assets* is a measure of usable wealth or ownership of the economic system. It excludes houses, cars, and items people could turn into cash at a garage sale. Instead, it focuses on stocks, bonds, and trusts—"the kind of ownership that gives a person distinct advantages in a capitalist society" (Brouwer 1998, p. 13).

Economic Distributions

Income, wealth, and financial assets are all distributed unequally in the United States. To illustrate income distribution, Gilbert (1998) uses the example of a parade, where all the households in the United States pass by in one hour (see Figure 2.1). The height of the marchers in the parade is used to represent their income, with the smallest being the poorest and the tallest being the richest. An average 1994 household income of $43,000 corresponds to a height of 5 feet, 10 inches. The first 50 minutes of the parade, in which people range from the size of matches to 12 feet tall, covers almost 85 percent of all households. The last 10 minutes show a greater range—from 12 feet to thousands of feet tall—illustrating the large income a relatively few households command (think of Ted Turner and the CEO of General Electric).

Gilbert suggests that the parade opens on an odd note because "it seems that the first people are marching in a deep ditch" (1998, p. 86). These people have suffered income losses and perhaps had to borrow from the bank. At five minutes into the parade people are all about a foot tall and earn about $7,500 a year, at least part of which probably comes from public assistance, social security, or veteran's benefits. Women and minorities are overrepresented in the first 15 minutes of the parade. Overall, only 8.4 percent of white families were living below the poverty level while 23.6 percent of African-American families and 24.7 percent of Hispanic families were (Bureau of the Census 1999c, p. Table 768). Fifteen percent of white children live below the poverty level, compared with 36.8 percent of African-American children (Bureau of the Census 1999c, p. Table 761). Most of the children living in poverty are part of households headed by single women.

Figure 2.1
The Income Parade

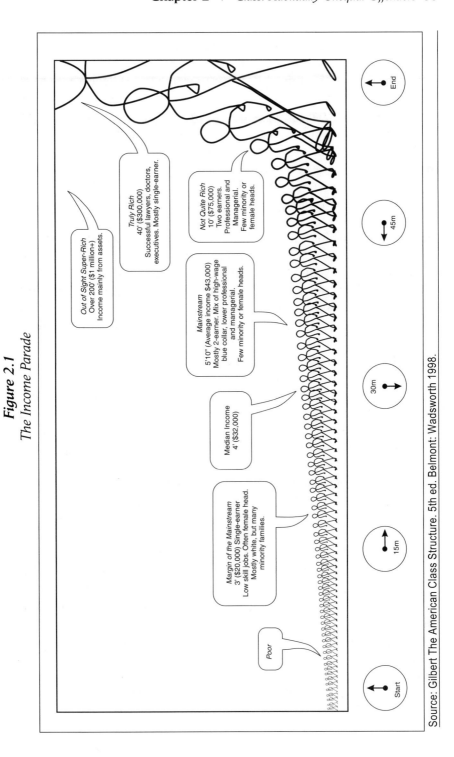

Source: Gilbert The American Class Structure. 5th ed. Belmont: Wadsworth 1998.

After 20 minutes, one-third of all households will have passed, but the average height would be about three feet—people who are just above the 1997 official poverty rate of $15,500 for a family of four. After 30 minutes, households that receive the median income ($32,000) would parade by, and seven minutes later would come people who receive the average income and are thus of "normal" height. Some of these households have a single wage earner in a good job, but many make an average income because of several wage earners.

As the parade advances to 50 minutes, people are in the 10- to 12-foot range and more frequently have two wage earners to pull in $75,000 to $85,000. Female-headed households and minorities are infrequent. Fifty-nine minutes into the parade, "we would be looking at 50-foot Goliaths, seconds after that, 200-foot King Kongs, and then towering leviathans, thousands of feet tall" (Gilbert 1998, p. 89–90). Marchers from the first part of the last minute are likely to be professionals such as doctors and lawyers, then corporate executives, who in 1995 had an average compensation of $3,746,392 (Brouwer 1998). Marchers in the last seconds would typically be single-wage-earner households whose income is from jobs but also includes interest or gains from stocks, bonds, and real estate.

Table 2.1 further illustrates this point by comparing the compensation of various people in the United States, from minimum wage earners to the President to the CEOs of some Fortune 500 companies. (Note: The average worker in Table 2.1 does not correspond to the average in the parade because Gilbert's parade uses *households* that may have more than one worker or wage earner.)

Income is only one way of examining the finances of households, and other ways indicate even more inequality. Table 2.2 summarizes several of the most common ways of examining the distribution of financial resources. The table indicates that the wealthiest 1 percent of the population receive almost 16 percent of all income that is distributed in the United States; the top 10 percent receive 40 percent of all income. As noted above, wealth reflects not only income, but possessions such as cars, savings accounts, houses, stocks, and mutual funds. It also takes into account a wide variety of debt (such as from credit cards), which helps reveal what economist Juliet Schor calls *The Overspent American* (1998). Even though measures of wealth include such items as Individual Retirement Accounts, the poorest 10 percent of American families have an average *negative* net wealth of $14,494 (Hurst, Luoh, and Stafford 1998, p. 276).

Table 2.1
Yearly and Hourly Compensation of Selected Workers, 1997

Worker	Yearly Wage	Hourly Wage
Minimum wage	$10,721	$5.15
Poverty level (for family of four)	15,500	7.21
Average worker	25,501	12.26
Supreme Court justice	167,900	80.72
President of the United States	200,000	96
August Busch III (CEO, Anheuser-Busch)	10,065,211	4,839
Michael Eisner (CEO, Walt Disney)	10,653,820	5,122
Alex Trotman (CEO, Ford Motors)	13,359,020	6,422
Geoffrey Bible (CEO, Philip Morris)	20,553,755	9,881
Lee Raymond (CEO, Exxon)	26,731,648	12,851
Jack Welch, Jr. (CEO, General Electric)	27,583,797	13,261
John Reed (CEO, Citicorp Bank)	40,277,500	19,364

CEO compensation figures from Executive Paywatch, http://www.paywatch.org
CEO figures include stock option grants from 1997 but exclude value of unexercised stock options. Unexercised stock options include: August Busch III, $16,683,495; Michael Eisner, $59,579,999; Alex Trotman, $27,113,625; Geoffrey Bible, $73,566,322; Jack Welch, Jr., $182,243,818; John Reed, $81,144,375.
Hourly pay figures based on a 40-hour work week for 52 weeks a year.

If these people sold their house and car, emptied their bank accounts, and held a large garage sale, they could not pay off all their bills. If Gilbert's income parade became a wealth parade, about six minutes would pass before a spectator could see anyone. Even then, many figures in the parade would be minuscule because the poorest 40 percent of the United States owns only about 1 percent of the wealth (Hurst et al 1998, p. 277). Table 2.2 shows that the top 10 percent own more than 70 percent of the country's wealth, so marchers would remain quite small until the last six minutes. The size of the last marcher in the wealth parade—Bill Gates of Microsoft—is examined in Box 2.1. More generally, this concentration of wealth is much greater in the U.S. than in other industrialized democracies. The ratio of wealth held by the top 20 percent compared to the bottom 20 percent is 11:1 in the U.S., 7:1 in Great Britain, and 4:1 in Japan (Mantios 1996: 97).

Table 2.2
Distributions of Financial Resources

	Income	Wealth	Financial assets
Very rich (top 1%)	15.7%	37%	46%
Affluent (next 9%)	25.2	35	36
Rest of us (bottom 90%)	59.1	28	18

Source: Brouwer (1998).

Box 2.1

Bill Gates and the Fortunes of Microsoft

The last person in a wealth or financial assets parade would be Bill Gates, founder and head of Microsoft, whose Windows operating system is on upward of 80 percent of the personal computers in the world. In 1998, he led *Forbes* magazine's list of the world's richest people and has now been the wealthiest person in the United States for five years. His net worth is estimated to be between $48 and $66 *billion*. Most of his assets are in Microsoft stock, so his worth can change several hundred million in reaction to regular daily stock fluctuations.

When we wrote an early draft of this chapter, Microsoft stock traded for $106, and an increase of $1.25 per share translated into a nearly $650 million increase in his wealth. His total worth from Microsoft stock alone would be $55 billion based on that stock price. Before we finalized this chapter, the Department of Justice and the attorney generals of many states filed an antitrust case against Microsoft, charging that it had unfairly used its monopoly position with the Windows operating system to promote its Internet Explorer browser and harm competitors like Netscape. Partly because of this lawsuit and the possibility of Microsoft being broken up into several smaller companies, its stock price fell to about $70 in August of 2000. However, because he now owns more shares of Microsoft, Bill Gates' net worth is still more than $53 billion.

That amount of money is difficult to conceptualize. For example, someone who makes $50,000 a year for 20 years earns a total of $1 million; one thousand people earning $50,000 a year for 20 years would collectively make $1 billion. The Bill Gates' Net Worth Page has some additional illustrations to put that figure into perspective. The $53 billion

- Could fund NASA and America's space program for 4 years.
- Is $13.3 billion more than all the gold in Fort Knox.
- Is enough to give $8.77 to every person on the entire planet (and still have $12,102,392 left over). Or, it is enough to give every person in the USA $194.
- Could be depleted by spending $369,000 per *hour*, 24 hours a day, seven days a week, 365 days a year for 17 years.

Alternatively:

- At a minimum wage of $5.15 per hour, if you worked continuously, 24 hours a day, 7 days a week, and saved every bit of your earnings (disregarding taxes), you would need to work for 1,182,989.65 years to earn Bill's money. If you took the wimpy approach, and only worked 40 hours a week, it would take 4,968,556.54 years. Note that man's oldest known hominid ancestor, *Australopithecus,* lived between 3.5 and 4 million years ago.

- On December 3, 1998, Bill announced that he was donating $100 million to vaccinate third-world children. Although this is certainly a generous donation, $100 million represents 0.187 percent of his total net worth. Proportionally, this is the same as someone with a net worth of $100,000 making a donation of $187.24.

- According to the people at Save the Children, it costs $240 to sponsor one child for a year. This means that Bill could save 222,524,790 (222.52 million) children. Of course, there are only 58.5 million people (adults included) in all of Ethiopia.

Source: Bill Gates' Net Worth Page, *http://www.quuxuum.org/~evan/bgnw.html.* For more information on the Microsoft antitrust case, explore the resources in the elite deviance section of *http://www.paulsjusticepage.com.*

Financial assets is a measure of ownership of the economic system that focuses on stocks, bonds and trusts. Table 2.2 indicates that the wealthiest 1 percent of the population own almost half of all financial assets in the country, so the power that goes with this ownership is highly concentrated. Further, in U.S. society blacks own one-fifth (20 percent) of the wealth that whites do, and this wealth tends not to be financial assets (Blau and Graham 1990; Swinton 1993). About 14 percent of African-American families own stock, compared with almost 45 percent of Caucasian families (Hurst et al 1998). Thus, ownership of the economy is in white hands, but more than half of all white families are also excluded from the benefits of economic ownership.

The uneven distribution of income and wealth is not a recent phenomenon and has a stable quality. Even in times when economic indicators point to a growing economy, the unequal distribution remains or may even become more unequal. Further, economic indicators have only a marginal relationship to how the average person experiences the economy. (There's a story of a man in a café reading to the waitress a headline proclaiming the good news that a healthy economy created 100,000 jobs. "Yeah," she says, "I have three of them.") Also, the benefits of economic expansion are not evenly distributed and tend to accrue to those who already have substantial assets. From 1995 to 1996, the average compensation of CEOs jumped 54 percent and "the average boss collected an options-fueled package worth $7.8 million for 1997, pulling down a 35 percent raise over 1996's $5.8 million" (Light 1998, p. 65). More generally, Wolff writes in his aptly named book *Top Heavy* that the 1980s "were a party for those at the very top of the wealth distribution" but "the wealth of the rest of the population did not simply grow more slowly; it actually fell" (1995, p. 2).

Political Sphere

For at least some purposes, American law treats corporations as "persons." The legal fiction of corporate "persons" means their size should also be considered to have a full understanding of how wealth affects the treatment of persons under the law. The intense concentration of wealth in corporations generates considerable political power, makes accountability increasingly difficult, and increases inequality in a way that is invisible to criminological theory.

Corporations grow to unlimited size so that their money power now dwarfs that of (most) individuals. For example, if General Motors marched in the income parade, it would be more than 17 *million* feet tall! Such an income makes it gargantuan not only in relation to individuals but also cities, states, and even the federal government. Indeed, corporations make up slightly more than half of the largest economies in the world, as demonstrated in Table 2.3. They continue to merge and form alliances, increasingly becoming global in their reach. Problems of jurisdiction compound problems of resources as we approach a time, in the words of Korton, "When Corporations Rule the World" (1995).

Filmmaker Michael Moore demonstrated this principle in his movie *Roger and Me,* where he tries to get an appointment with the CEO of General Motors to persuade him to come to Flint, Michigan, to see the devastation that resulted from the massive downsizing of auto workers. Moore is the average Joe—he presents a Chuck E Cheese card as a credential—and is constantly rebuffed by Roger Smith, who claims that the town's collapse had nothing to do with him.

Table 2.3
Ranking of the World's Largest Economies (Countries & Corporations), 1995

1. United States	36. EXXON	69. Ukraine
2. Japan	37. NISSHO IWAI	70. Portugal
3. Germany	38. Saudi Arabia	71. SIEMENS
4. France	39. ROYAL DUTCH/SHELL	72. BRITISH PETROLEUM
5. Italy	40. Finland	73. Colombia
6. United Kingdom	41. South Africa	74. Ireland
7. China	42. TOYOTA MOTOR	75. TOKYO ELECTRIC POWER
8. Canada	43. WAL-MART STORES	76. Pakistan
9. India	44. HITACHI	77. U.S. POSTAL SERVICE
10. Spain	45. NIPPON LIFE INS	78. VOLKSWAGEN
11. Brazil	46. AT&T	79. SUMITOMO LIFE INSURANCE
12. Netherlands	47. NIPPON T & T	80. TOSHIBA
13. Australia	48. MATSUSHITA ELEC & INDUSTRIAL	81. UNILEVER
14. Korea, South	49. TOMEN	82. IRI
15. Russia	50. Algeria	83. Egypt
16. Iran	51. Hong Kong	84. Philippines
17. Switzerland	52. Poland	85. NESTLE
18. MITSUBISHI	53. GENERAL ELECTRIC	86. New Zealand
19. Taiwan	54. Vietnam	87. DEUTSCHE TELEKOM
20. MITSUI	55. DAIMLER-BENZ	88. FIAT
21. Sweden	56. INTL. BUSINESS MACHINES	89. ALLIANZ HOLDING
22. ITOCHU	57. Malaysia	90. SONY
23. Belgium	58. MOBIL	91. VEBA GROUP
24. SUMITOMO	59. Israel	92. HONDA MOTOR
25. Mexico	60. NISSAN MOTOR	93. Singapore
26. GENERAL MOTORS	61. Venezuela	94. ELF AQUITAINE
27. MARUBENI	62. NICHIMEN	95. Nigeria
28. Austria	63. KANEMATSU	96. STATE FARM GROUP
29. Indonesia	64. DAI-ICHI LIFE INSURANCE	97. NEC
30. Argentina	65. SEARS ROEBUCK	98. PRUDENTIAL INS.
31. FORD MOTOR	66. PHILIP MORRIS	99. ESTERREICHISCHE POST
32. Denmark	67. Greece	100. MEIJI LIFE INSURANCE
33. Turkey	68. CHRYSLER	
34. Thailand		
35. Norway		

Source: Combustion in the Rain Forest, *http://www.geocities.com/~combusem/ WORLDEC.HTM. For a 1990 comparison, see Ending Corporate Governance, http:// www.ratical.com/corporations/.*

This large concentration of wealth translates into political power that is also exercised through corporate lobbyists and Political Action Committees (PACs). PACs that donate thousands—or even millions—of dollars can achieve considerable clout at a time when only 0.06 percent of the U.S. population contributes more than $1,000 to political parties or candidates (Hightower 1998b, p. 6). Many corporate interests donate heavily to both political parties to ensure access to legislators and favorable action on their legislation, regardless of which party wins the election. Further influence and consideration comes from the corporate use of "the slush fund, the kickback, the stock award, the high-paying job offer from industry, the lavish parties and prostitutes, the meals, transportation, housing, and vacation accommodations, and the many other hustling enticements of money" (Simon 1999, p. 24).

The result of this influence can be tax breaks, less regulation, or limits on the extent of punishment, such as the size of damages juries are allowed to award against businesses in product liability cases. An excellent example is the process to establish sentencing guidelines for corporate misconduct. In 1984, Congress established the U.S. Sentencing Commission to help create guidelines that would make federal sentencing more certain and uniform in criminal cases. The guidelines are a grid that judges use to plot both the severity of the offense and an individual's record to find an appropriate range for the sentence. The first set of guidelines in 1987 did not address corporate crime, although the 1990 ones did.

> Instead of $5,000 or less—the amount levied in four-fifths of all corporate convictions from 1975 to 1976—fines were set as high as $364 million. In addition, the commission had devised innovative new punishments—including probation and community service for convicted organizations. (Etzioni 1990, p. C3)

After a "steamroller of business lobbyists" took notice, the Commission released a revised set of guidelines in which the potential fines were "slashed," mitigating factors were given more weight, and aggravating factors (such as a prior record) were removed from consideration (Etzioni 1990, p. C3). Under the original plan, a level 10 offense carried a penalty of $64,000, while the post-lobbying guidelines suggested $17,500; level 25 was revised down from $136 million to $580,000; and the maximum fine went from $364 million to $12.6 million. Later, then-Attorney General Thornburgh, who had called fighting crime in the suites one of his top priorities, withdrew the Justice Department's long-standing support for tough mandatory sentences for corporate criminals following an intense lobbying campaign by defense contractors, oil companies and other Fortune 500 firms. (Isikoff 1990, p. A1)

Also, although real people convicted of felonies lose their voting rights, corporations convicted of multiple felonies lose none of their political rights—and in some cases, like with GE, try to lobby Congress to weaken the law under which they were convicted. Further, corporate charters themselves act as a shield from the public and give the corporation permission to act in the best interests of shareholders rather than the larger public good. Thus,

the corporation is now a superhuman creature of the law, superior to you and me, since it has civil rights but no civil responsibilities; it is legally obligated to be selfish; it cannot be thrown in jail; it can deduct from its tax bill any fines it gets for wrongdoings; and it can live forever. (Hightower 1998a, p. 34)

Class and Criminology

Criminological theory is frequently based on an unquestioning acceptance of how the criminal law defines crime. Because class is related to political power and law making, class is also deeply implicated in theoretical understandings and constructions of crime. This section of the chapter provides an overview of the issues, then focuses on two specific issues: the link between inequality and crime, and the underdeveloped state of theory about white-collar, corporate, and state crime. The next section provides more comprehensive analysis on the relationship between class and law.

Frequently, the formation of the criminal law is not part of any theorizing about class, so the definition of crime is seen as more of an absolute than the contingent outcome of a political process that includes class conflict and class biases. At other times, crime theory assumes that criminal law is a direct reflection of consensus, or of folkways hardening into custom and finally law. In other words, criminologists' and others' focus on the crimes of the poor as a "natural state of affairs," rather than as an expression of inequality and privilege, provides theories of criminal law that exclude inequality as part of their explanation. In turn, the criminal law's controlling of the offenses of the poor rather than the offenses of the rich appears to reflect the legitimacy of an agreed-upon definition of crime.

When crime theory unreflectively takes the criminal law as a given and works within it, the fiction of crime as neutral law sets in (Platt 1974). Working within the confines of "crime" as defined by the law cedes control of the disciplinary boundaries of the field to law makers and the political process that produces law. It also means that many social harms—from tobacco smoke to environmental pollution, from neo-colonialism to crimes against humanity—are excluded from study even though they present more of a threat to people's well-being and security than much of what is officially designated as a crime (Barak 1991; Robinson 1998). If criminology makes

> no moral judgment independent of criminal statutes, it becomes sterile and inhuman—the work of moral eunuchs or legal technicians. If moral judgments above and beyond criminal law were not made, the laws of Nazi Germany would be indistinguishable from the laws of other nations. (quoted in Simon 1999, p. 37)

Among the main theorists in exposing the myth of the neutral criminal law were Karl Marx and Friedrich Engels, who noted that the law and the order it upholds is one based on very unequal distribution of property and resources. Marx and Engels thus "insisted that the institutions of the state and law, and the doctrines that emerge from them, serve the interests of the dominant economic class" (Beirne and Messerschmidt 2000, p. 110). For them, crime was not about the defects of morality or biology, but rather about the defects of society and the product of the demoralization and alienation caused by the horrible conditions of industrial capitalism. Crimes were defined as violations by the state of natural or human rights and as forms of primitive rebellion.

Subsequent Marxian analyses of crime and crime control in the United States can be subdivided into "instrumental" and "structural" models of crime and criminal control. The work of Richard Quinney (1977), for example, is representative of the instrumental model. He argued that within the overall conditions of the capitalist political economy, two kinds of crimes emerge: "crimes of domination" and "crimes of accommodation." Crimes of domination include *crimes of control* (i.e., acts by the police and FBI in violation of civil liberties), *crimes of government* (i.e., political acts such as Watergate or Iran-Contragate), *crimes of economic domination* (i.e., corporate acts involving price-fixing, pollution, planned obsolescence), and *social injuries* (i.e., acts that may or may not be illegal but deny basic human rights, such as racism, sexism, and economic exploitation). These crimes of domination, according to the instrumentalist view, are necessary for the reproduction of the capitalist system itself.

In contrast, crimes of accommodation are committed by relatively powerless people of the lower and working classes. Quinney identified three crimes of accommodation, or of adaptation to the oppressive conditions of capitalism and to the domination of the capitalist class: *predatory crimes* (i.e., burglary, robbery, drug dealing), *personal crimes* (i.e., murder, assault, rape), and *crimes of resistance* (i.e., protests, sabotage). For Quinney, the real danger to society comes from the crimes of domination rather than the crimes of accommodation. However, the former acts are not criminalized as they serve the interests of the ruling classes; the latter acts are criminalized and punished as they threaten the political and economic status quo. Hence, crime control is really class control.

As an example, consider the following quote taken from one of the founding fathers of the classical school, Cesare Beccaria, in his book, *Essay on Crimes and Punishments,* first published some two hundred years ago and still in print today. In trying to reason through the appropriate punishment for an offender, he takes the imagined voice of the criminal:

> What are these laws that I am supposed to respect, that place such a great distance between me and the rich man? He refuses me the penny I ask of him and, as an excuse, tells me to sweat at work he knows nothing about. Who made these laws? Rich and powerful men who have never deigned to visit the squalid huts of the poor, who have never had to share a crust of moldy bread amid the innocent cries of hungry children and the tears of a wife. Let us break these bonds, fatal to the majority and only useful to a few indolent tyrants; let us attack justice at its source. I will return to my natural state of independence; I shall at least for a little time live free and happy with the fruits of my courage and industry. The day will perhaps come for my sorrow and repentance, but it will be brief, and for a single day of suffering I shall have many years of liberty and of pleasures. (quoted in Vold and Bernard 1986, p. 29)

The speaker points out the social injuries that are part of the crimes of domination that help secure the unequal distribution of resources. At the same time, the speaker advocates unspecified crimes of accommodation in response to the oppression. Vold and Bernard (1986) note that the revolutionary implication behind the passage is obvious and that crimes of need could be better prevented by a more equal distribution of money than by the severity of the penal law. Instead, Beccaria argued that the death penalty is an ineffective deterrent that should be replaced by the more protracted suffering of life imprisonment. Indeed, he believed that overuse of the maximum penalty is an incentive for escalating rather than curbing class conflict.

William Chambliss (1988) articulated a structural-contradictions theory of crime and crime control, in which recognition is given to the resistance and pressures from other classes besides the ruling classes. In his model, Chambliss identifies certain contradictions inherent within capitalism, such as the contradictions between profits, wages, and consumption—or between wages and the supply of labor. These contradictions ultimately culminate in crime as underclasses are formed that cannot consume the goods that they were socialized to want as necessary for meeting the conditions of happiness. One solution for these underclasses is to resort to criminal or illegitimate behavior. The state then responds to these acts with crime control. We explore this idea further in the next chapter with respect to scholars who argue that the high rates of incarceration for African Americans are the result of crime control policies put in place to control the minority population denied a place in an increasingly technological society with less need for their labor.

Together, the instrumental and structural views of law, crime, and control in relationship to the political economy help explain "why certain behaviors are criminalized by the state whereas others are not," and "how a capitalist economic system itself generates certain class patterns of crime" (Beirne and Messerschmidt 2000, p. 202). Fuller theories of human behavior, crime, and crime control should strive to integrate individual-level factors with social structure factors (Barak 1998). However, most crime theory continues to emphasize how the crime problem can be located primarily in defective individuals found among the poorer classes rather than to suggest or integrate the possibility of a defective economic system.

For a brief period in the 1960s, the roles of inequality and discrimination were identified as contributing to the "breakdown" in law and order by the President's Commission on Crime and Law Enforcement. Some 30 years later at a retrospective sponsored by the U.S. Department of Justice, criminologist Todd Clear was one of the few who mentioned the issue of inequality and discussed the backlash to President Johnson's Great Society ideas that had been the backdrop for the Commission. The Commission advocated government taking a lead in crime prevention through social programs and opportunities for disadvantaged citizens. The subsequent rise of the law-and-order mentality led to a different and more limited "get tough" pro-incarceration role for the government, because crime was seen more as the result of individual failings and malice (Department of Justice 1998).

Although research on the link between social disadvantage and crime is not a priority for government funding, criminologists have continued to explore it. An important finding is that poverty itself is not the key, because "if that was the case, then graduate students would be very dangerous people indeed" (Currie 1998, p. 134). The important theoretical concepts relate to inequality, relative deprivation, and blocked opportunities. Indeed, Currie notes that the important contribution to violence is "the experience of life year in, year out at the bottom of a harsh, depriving, and excluding social system [that] wears away at the psychological and communal conditions that sustain healthy human development" (Currie 1998, p. 34).

Further, high levels of inequality mean that there are more poor and destitute than would exist under a more equal distribution. Thus, "there are criminals motivated by the need for a decent standard of living, where 'decent' can mean what they perceive most people in their community enjoy, what whites but not blacks enjoy, what they used to enjoy before they lost their jobs, or what they were led to expect to enjoy by advertising and dramatization of bourgeois lifestyles on television" (Braithwaite 1992, p. 82). Braithwaite argues that "inequality worsens both crimes of poverty motivated by *need* for goods for *use* and crimes of wealth motivated by *greed*" (1992, p. 81, emphasis in original). Inequality also produces more structural degradation, which he argues is important because of the links between humiliation, rage and violence. Ultimately, the "propensity to feel powerless and exploited among the poor and the propensity of the rich to see exploiting as legitimate both . . . enable crime" (1992, p. 94).

Because most of criminology tends to be guided by the criminal law, the focus of crime theory is almost exclusively on the behavior of the poor. Notably, one of the first important mentions for criminology of "crime" in relation to the behaviors of the upper classes was in 1908 when E. A. Ross promoted the notion of a "criminaloid." Friedrichs notes that Ross used this term to discuss "the businessman who committed exploitative (if not necessarily illegal) acts out of an uninhibited desire to maximize profit" (1996, p.2). Ross' discussion, however, did not immediately inspire sociologists to explore the topic, partly because criminology was attempting to establish itself as a "science," which meant distancing itself from the passionate outrage that characterized many of the journalists who were busy condemning robber-baron industrialists and pointing to the excesses of the capitalist system.

But this work did get the attention of Edwin Sutherland, who was interested in the criminality of the rich because of his attempt to develop a general theory of crime. He believed that a major deficiency of criminological theory was that it could only explain crime by the poor, which made for not only class-biased criminological theory, but for a practice and policy of criminal and juvenile justice steeped in class biases as well (Platt 1969). In 1939, Sutherland introduced the term *white-collar crime* in his presidential address to what is now the American Sociological Association. The key elements included that the perpetrator be an upper-class or white-collar person, the crime be committed in the course of one's occupation, the crime be a violation of trust, and the crime be processed through civil or administrative proceedings rather than a criminal court.

Once again, criminology was slow to follow up on Sutherland's research, and its primary focus still remains with street crime, although crimes by the upper class exact a far heavier toll in terms of dollars and lives (Clinard 1990; Reiman 1998a; Simon 1999;). Much of the theory that does exist is devoted to explaining shoplifting or employee theft rather than wrongdoing and violence by corporations. Also neglected within the sphere of white-collar crime is state crime, including the denial of human rights, surveillance, and other state crimes of domination. Further, although serial killers are a trendy topic of study for criminologists, criminology devotes little attention to mass murder such as genocide. Indeed, criminologist Margaret Vandiver noted that "if we had as much research and theory on genocide as we do on shoplifting, we would be far ahead of where we are now" in reducing human suffering (1999, personal communication).

Criminologists who have followed up on Sutherland's work have identified a wide variety of activities that fall under the general term "white-collar crime." But books and discussions of the topic do not always note the full range of victim-offender relationships, thus recreating a blindness to some power dynamics. The most frequently discussed white-collar crimes are employee theft and credit card fraud, in which businesses, corporations, and financial institutions are the victims. The least frequently discussed are corporate and government crime, in which the powerful are the perpetrators who are victimizing employees, consumers, taxpayers or the environment. Terms like *economic crime, financial crime, business crime,* and even categories like *technocrime* and *computer crime* should cover the range of possible victimizations, but they are frequently limited to acts against financial institutions. Headlines occasionally proclaim the U.S. is getting tough on white-collar crime, but the stories usually describe a harsh sentence for employees who steal or embezzle from their employers. The criminal justice system rarely applies its tough-on-crime rhetoric to the executive who harms employees by cutting corners on workplace safety, who knowingly markets unsafe products, or who causes environmental damage in order to help boost corporate profits.

More specifically, *occupational crime* is done to benefit the perpetrator personally rather than the business. At times, the victim will be the business, although at others it may be consumers. In each case, the crime is linked to the perpetrator's occupational position. Examples include auto mechanics charging for unnecessary work, bank managers embezzling the institution's funds, or doctors fraudulently billing insurance companies. *Corporate crime* is perpetrated by individuals in a corporation and acting in its interest (and benefiting themselves individually through bonuses and promotions). The victims include workers, consumers, taxpayers, communities, the government, and the environment (Winslow 1999). Acts include fraud (against the government, taxpayers, or consumers) and anticompetitive practices (which cause higher prices). *Corporate violence* refers to acts that inflict physical suffering rather than simply monetary losses, as in the case of dangerous or defective products, unsafe working conditions, and medical conditions caused by pollution or toxic waste. *State crime* is perpetrated by public officials who are trying to perpetuate a specific administration, exercise general government power, or exercise undue influence on behalf of large campaign contributors. The victims can be as widespread as all taxpayers who are forced to pay for corruption and fraud; victims can also be a specific political group—or even its leaders—who are denied basic political rights through surveillance and harassment (Barak 1991a).

Class, Crime, and the Law

Both income and wealth have the potential to translate into political power that can affect legislation. Thus, any investigation of crime must start with the process of law making, which includes a theory of the state. While some law reflects widespread consensus about conduct that should be prohibited, the criminal law also helps shape public perception about what constitutes harmful behavior. Thus, definitions of crime appear to be the result of consensus rather than problems of differential application and selective enforcement based on unequal access to the law-making process. The dynamics suggested in Black's *Behavior of Law* (1976) together with the work of Mills (1956) and those who share that tradition (Domhoff 1998) indicate how the power elite use the law to further their own advantage.

It is not simply that the rich and powerful use their influence to keep acts from becoming crimes, even though these acts may be more socially injurious than those labeled criminal; they are also able to use mass-mediated communication to shape the public discourse and moral outrage about "crime" (Barak 1994). In short, the elite's relative monopoly over the "free" airways allows them to act as "transmission belts" for creating consensus over what is and is not a crime. The outcome of this sort of commonly mediated inequality permits the kind of Orwellian "doublespeak" captured by Michael Moore in "Why Can't G.M. Sell Crack?" Moore asks, if profit is supreme—a company should be able to do whatever it wants to make a profit—why can't they sell drugs? His answer is that crack is illegal because we believe crack destroys people's lives and ruins communities. But then, he asks, why do we let companies downsize during a time of record profits and close factories, because that too destroys communities: "Crime goes up, suicide goes up, drug abuse, alcoholism, spousal abuse, divorce—everything bad spirals dangerously upward" (1996, p. 256). Meanwhile, the behavior of these corporations and their CEOs is not scorned or subject to arrest for "public assault," but, on the contrary, they are treated as cultural icons and heroes by Wall Street; they become "Masters of the Universe simply because they make huge profits regardless of the consequences to our society" (1996, p. 255).

While not everyone agrees with Moore's comparison, many have an intuitive understanding of the concept *analogous social injury*, "which includes harm caused by acts or conditions that are legal but produce consequences similar to those produced by illegal acts"

(Lanier and Henry 1998, p. 19). The mass media rarely present crime stories to engage this question, but the American public frequently regard white-collar crime as at least as serious as street crime and feel that corporate criminals are treated too leniently (Grabosky, Braithwaite, and Wilson 1987). Respondents in polls have supported stiffer sentences than had been handed down under the Food, Drug and Cosmetic Act. People in other surveys favor incarceration for false advertising, unsafe workplaces, antitrust offenses, and the failure by landlords to make repairs, resulting in the death of a tenant. The offense of "knowingly manufacturing and selling contaminated food that results in death" was ranked in seriousness behind assassination of a public official and killing a police officer during the terrorist hijacking of a plane; the selling of contaminated food was considered more serious than "killing someone during a serious argument" and the "forcible rape of a stranger in a park" (Grabosky et al. 1987, p. 34-35). Even though people do see some corporate crimes as being as serious as street crime and as deserving of punishment and incarceration, these sentiments are not reflected in the criminal law, because of intervention in the law-making process by the wealthy and the power elite.

Most of the harmful and illegitimate behavior of the rich and powerful has not traditionally been defined as criminal, but nearly all the harmful and deviant behavior perpetrated by the poor and the powerless is defined as violating the criminal law. Thus, crime control theory and practice evidence a legal and structural class bias by concentrating the coercive power of the state on the behaviors of the poor. These omitted relations of class justice reveal the importance of two systemic operations in the administration of criminal justice: "selective enforcement" and "differential application" of the law. Selective enforcement of the law refers to the fact that most harms perpetrated by the affluent are "beyond incrimination" (Kennedy 1970). Harms committed by the politically and economically powerful that do come within the purview of criminal law are typically downplayed, ignored, or marginalized through differential application.

Criminologist Stephen Box suggests that one of the most important advantages of corporate criminals "lies in their ability to prevent their actions from becoming subject to criminal sanctions in the first place" (in Braithwaite 1992, p. 89). Although certain behaviors may cause widespread social harm, the criminal law does not forbid abuses

of power in the realm of economic domination, governmental control, and denial of human rights (Simon 1999, p. 38). For example,
being a habitual offender is against the law in most areas, where
"three strikes and you're out" applies to street criminals. But habitual
offender laws do not apply to corporate persons (like GE) that can
repeatedly commit serious crimes without being subjected to habitual
offender statutes.

In some cases, harmful actions will be civil offenses rather than
criminal ones, but the difference is significant because civil actions are
not punishable by prison and do not carry the same harsh stigma.
Other destructive behavior may not be prohibited by civil law or regulations created by administrative agencies. In this respect, the tobacco
industry produces a product that kills 400,000 people a year, but its
actions are not illegal, not a substantial part of the media campaign of
the Office for National Drug Control Policy or Partnership for a Drug
Free America, or even subject to federal oversight as a drug. Similarly,
because government makes the laws, many of its own abuses of
power are not considered to be crimes. Government-sponsored genocide of Native Americans in order to secure their land and its mineral
wealth violated basic human rights and treaties, but these acts were
never subject to criminal law, nor were the victims included in the
nation's homicide rate (Barak 1998, p. 45).

One of the classic statements on this topic is a book by C. Wright
Mills called *The Power Elite* (1956), in which he argued that American
life is dominated by an elite composed of the largest corporations, the
military, and the federal government. Mills argued that these three
spheres are highly interrelated, with members of each group coming
from similar upper-class social backgrounds, attending the same private and Ivy League universities, and even belonging to the same
social or political organizations. Corporate elites also make large political donations to ensure their access to the law-making process.
Reiman (1998a) suggests that the result of these circumstances is that
law is like a carnival mirror. It distorts our understanding of the harms
that may befall us by magnifying the threat from street crime because
it criminalizes more of the conduct of poor people. At the same time
it distorts our perception about the danger from "crime in the suites"
by downplaying and not protecting people from the harms perpetrated by those above them in the class system. The criminal law, like
the operations of the criminal justice system more generally, "does

not simply *reflect* the reality of crime; it has a hand in *creating* the reality we see" (1998a, p. 57, emphasis is original).

Reiman also argues that the processing of offenders serves to "weed out the wealthy" (1998a, p. 101). Selective enforcement means that many acts will not come within the realm of criminal law, and if they are, it is unlikely they will be prosecuted, "or if prosecuted, not punished or if punished, only mildly" (1998a, p. 57). This observation is consistent with the analysis in Donald Black's highly referenced book, *The Behavior of Law* (1976). Black sought to discover a series of general rules to describe the amount of law and its behavior in response to social variables such as stratification, morphology (impersonality), culture, social organization, and other forms of social control. When it comes to issues of class, the variables of stratification and social organization are the two most relevant.

Black proposed that the law varies directly with hierarchy and privilege, so that the more inequality in a country, the more law. He also applied his proposition to disputes between two parties of unequal status or wealth. Based on a wide variety of cases, Black concluded there is likely to be "more law" in a downward direction, such as when a rich person is victimized by a poorer one. This means the use of criminal rather than civil law, for example, and a greater likelihood of a report, an investigation, arrest, prosecution, and prison sentence. In contrast, when the wealthier harms the poorer, Black predicted there would be less law—meaning civil law, monetary fines rather than jail, and therapeutic sanctions rather than punitive ones. Black argued that social organization is the potential for collective action. In the sense important here, there is likely to be "more law" in the downward direction, as when a group high in social organization—such as a corporation or the state—is victimized by an individual. Conversely, "less law" and a pattern of differential application are likely to be the result of a corporate body or the state victimizing individuals or groups of individuals.

A helpful example of these abstract ideas is a comment made by Congressman Frank Annunzio, who was Chairman of the House subcommittee on financial institutions that investigated the prosecution of criminals involved in the Savings and Loan (S & L) wrongdoings of the late 1980s. At the Congressional hearings, Annunzio's opening remarks included this statement:

> Frankly, I don't think the administration has the interest in pursuing Gucci-clad white-collar criminals. These are hard and complicated

cases, and the defendants often were rich, successful prominent members of their upper-class communities. It is far easier putting away a sneaker-clad high school dropout who tries to rob a bank of a thousand dollars with a stick-up note, than a smooth talking S & L executive who steals a million dollars with a fraudulent note. (Hearings, 1990, p. 1)

These comments highlight the difficulty and reluctance in prosecuting upper-class criminals whose crimes involve substantially greater sums of money than street crimes. Some S & L executives personally stole tens of millions of dollars, and others were responsible for the collapse of financial institutions that needed bailouts of $1 billion (Binstein and Bowden 1993; Calavita, Pontell and Tillman 1997; Pizzo, Fricker, and Muolo 1991). The total cost of the bailout has been about $500 *billion* (Day 1993), yet few S & L crooks have gone to prison (Pizzo and Muolo 1993; Reiman 1998a). The ones who have, received an average of two years compared with an average of nine years for a bank robber (Hearings 1990).

The same pattern applies to corporate crime as well. Indeed, criminologist James Coleman (1985) did an extensive study of enforcement of the Sherman Antitrust Act in the petroleum industry and identified four major strategies corporations use to prevent full application of the law. First is endurance and delay, which includes using extensive legal resources to prolong the litigation and obstruct the discovery of information by raising as many legal technicalities as possible. Second is the use of corporate wealth and largess to undermine the will of legislators and regulators to enforce the law's provisions. Third is secrecy and deception about ownership and control to prevent detection of violations and make them more difficult to prove. Fourth are threats of economic consequences to communities and the economy if regulations are fully enforced.

Coleman's observations are also consistent with Black's discussion of how law behaves in the presence of high levels of organization and high concentrations of wealth. The general patterns of selective enforcement as well as differential application have also been supported by many studies done in the wake of the 1965 President's Commission on Law Enforcement and the Administration of Justice. "Almost universally, these studies showed the presence of significant bias against lower-class suspects at every stage of criminal justice processing from arrest on," notes Reiman in the introduction to his book, *The Rich Get Richer and the Poor Get Prison* (Reiman 1998a, p. viii).

Although there is little reason or evidence to suggest that the situation has changed over the past thirty years, the topic is rarely studied and is in danger of slipping from the consciousness of many criminologists. That Reiman's book is now in its fifth edition attests to the endurance of his thesis and the importance of inequality. But the author notes that "with each subsequent edition of *The Rich Get Richer,* the number of new studies on this topic has decreased, so that now, having reviewed virtually every major journal (and many not-so-major) in the field between 1993 and 1996, I find the number of new studies has dwindled to a trickle" (Reiman 1998, p. viii).

Criminal Justice Processing

Assessing the impact of class on criminal justice is hindered by the minimal amount of information collected on the topic. The FBI's *Uniform Crime Reports,* for example, collects information only about the race, gender, and age of those arrested. The FBI collects no information about class or income to include in its yearly report. The *Sourcebook of Criminal Justice Statistics* does a little better by including a chart showing how the chance of being a victim decreases as personal income increases (see Tables 2.4 and 2.5 below). Several other charts include salary or employment information from which rough inferences about class can be drawn (see the Workers section later in this chapter). Because class data are scarce, little research and analysis are done—and government agencies that fund research are uninterested in explorations of economic bias.

As noted above, the general pattern is that those who find themselves at the first stages of criminal justice processing are disproportionately poor, and those who emerge from the other end bound for prison are poorer still. Back in 1972, one U.S. Senator observed that there are two "transmission belts": the one for the poor "is easier to ride without falling off and it gets to prison in shorter order," while the one for the rich is "slower and it passes innumerable stations where exits are temptingly convenient" (quoted in Reiman 1998a, p. 102). This comment is no less true today than it was then, but there is less interest in the topic now. Indeed, a twenty-five-year retrospective on the President's Commission devoted less than a page to a subheading on "Discrimination and Poverty" (Conley 1994, p. 66).

The remainder of this section examines how issues of economic class structure influence aspects of people's experience with crime. This analysis includes victimization, the distribution of knowledge about known offenders, and media depictions of criminal justice. It also includes more specific examples of differential application in law making and selective enforcement from the identification of criminals to the last stages of judicial processing, the sentencing to incarceration. Finally, this section looks at the economic position of those who work in the field of criminal justice.

Victimization

The main source of information about victims that criminologists use is the National Crime Survey conducted by the U.S. Bureau of the Census. Information from this survey is published by the Bureau of Justice Statistics in the annual *Sourcebook of Criminal Justice Statistics,* which includes a section on the "Nature and Distribution of Known Offenses." The *Sourcebook* is also available on the Internet, which allows the user to search all the tables and figures using keywords. A search for information relating to "income" turned up two tables related to victimization; searches using keywords "wealth" and "class" resulted in a message indicating that there was no matching information.

The information on victimization and income for 1998 is reproduced in Table 2.4, dealing with crimes of violence, and Table 2.5, dealing with property crimes. Table 2.4 clearly shows that people at the low end of the income distribution are more than twice as likely to be the victim of a violent crime than those at the upper range of this income distribution ($75,000 or more). The pattern holds for all types of violent crimes, including rape, robbery, and assault. The pattern involving higher rates of victimization for lower-income households is even more pronounced in cases where the crime of violence was completed or involved an injury.

Table 2.5 indicates that higher-income households are slightly more likely to be victims of a property crime. However, low-income households are more likely to experience burglaries—especially completed ones and involving forced entry—than upper-income households. Successful car theft and various thefts or personal larcenies that do not involve contact with the offender are the crimes that upper-income households are more likely to experience. Together, the tables

Table 2.4
Estimated Rate (per 1,000 persons age 12 and older) of Personal Victimization

By type of crime and annual household income of victim, United States, 1998

Type of Crime	Annual Household Income						
	Less than $7,500	$7,500 to $14,999	$15,000 to $24,999	$25,000 to $34,999	$35,000 to $49,999	$50,000 to $74,999	$75,000 or more
All personal crimes	65.5	51.1	40.7	43.1	33.3	33.1	34.1
Crimes of violence	63.8	49.3	39.4	42.0	31.7	32.0	33.1
Completed violence	23.7	18.5	12.4	14.0	8.9	7.3	8.7
Attempted/threatened violence	40.1	30.8	26.9	28.1	22.8	24.7	24.4
Rape/sexual assault	3.2	2.4	2.3	2.4	0.5^b	0.7^b	1.2
Rape/attempted rape	2.7	1.3^b	1.5	1.2	0.3^b	0.5^b	0.8^b
Rape	2.2^b	0.6^b	0.7^b	0.4^b	0.3^b	0.1^b	0.6^b
Attempted rape[c]	0.6^b	0.6^b	0.9^b	0.7^b	0.0^b	0.3^b	0.2^b
Sexual assault[d]	0.4^b	1.1^b	0.7^b	1.3	0.1^b	0.2^b	0.4^b
Robbery	6.5	5.8	3.6	6.9	3.1	2.8	2.9
Completed/property taken	3.3	3.9	2.7	5.6	2.1	1.3	1.6
With injury	1.6^b	0.9^b	0.8^b	1.1	0.6^b	0.7^b	0.4^b
Without injury	1.7^b	3.0	2.0	4.6	1.5	0.5^b	1.2
Attempted to take property	3.3	1.9	0.8^b	1.2	1.0	1.5	1.3
With injury	0.7^b	0.6^b	0.2^b	0.4^b	0.2^b	0.3^b	0.3^b
Without injury	2.6	1.3^b	0.7^b	0.8^b	0.8	1.2	0.9^b
Assault	54.2	41.0	33.5	32.8	28.1	28.5	29.0
Aggravated	19.6	11.8	7.9	6.3	6.2	6.2	6.2
With injury	7.7	3.9	2.4	1.3	2.3	1.5	2.0
Threatened with weapon	12.0	7.9	5.4	5.0	3.8	4.8	4.2
Simple	34.5	29.3	25.7	26.5	21.9	22.3	22.8
With minor injury	10.2	9.1	6.0	5.3	4.1	4.2	4.0
Without injury	24.3	20.1	19.7	21.2	17.9	18.1	18.7
Purse snatching/pocket picking	1.7^b	1.8	1.3	1.1	1.6	1.1	1.0
Population age 12 and older	11,724,160	21,132,940	29,783,090	28,314,520	34,039,640	33,179,460	29,414,500

Table excludes data on persons whose family income level was not ascertained
[a]Detail may not add to total because of rounding.
[b]Estimate is based on about 10 or fewer sample cases.
[c]Includes verbal threats of rape.
[d]Includes threats.

Source: U.S. Department of Justice, Bureau of Justice Statistics, *Criminal Victimization in the United States, 1998 Statistical Tables*, NCJ 181585 [Online]. Available: http://www.ojp.usdoj.gov/bjs/abstract/cvusst.htm [May 25, 2000], Table 14.

indicate that the crimes most Americans fear and regard as most serious happen disproportionately to lower-income households.

These two tables present a picture of victimization that is incomplete in several respects. For example, many harmful acts of business and government are not part of the criminal law, so differential application removes many types of injury from official data. Indeed, Reiman (1998a) recalculates figures from the FBIs *Uniform Crime Reports* on how Americans are murdered to include workplace hazards, occupational diseases, unnecessary surgery, and fatal reactions to unnecessary prescriptions. The 20,000 murders become 68,000 using the low range of estimates to produce a conservative estimate. The category of "Occupational Hazard and Disease" contributes significantly to the revised estimate, and because the victims in this category work in blue-collar manufacturing and industrial jobs, these

Table 2.5

Estimated Rate (per 1,000 persons age 12 and older) of Property Victimization

By type of crime and annual household income, United States, 1998[a]

Type of Crime	Annual Household Income						
	Less than $7,500	$7,500 to $14,999	$15,000 to $24,999	$25,000 to $34,999	$35,000 to $49,999	$50,000 to $74,999	$75,000 or more
Property crimes	209.0	229.8	211.0	233.8	221.7	248.6	248.6
Household burglary	55.4	57.8	42.6	38.2	32.7	30.1	28.0
Completed	42.0	50.3	34.7	30.1	27.1	26.3	24.3
Forcible entry	15.9	18.5	16.5	14.3	10.3	7.8	8.1
Unlawful entry without force	26.1	31.8	18.2	15.9	16.8	18.5	16.3
Attempted forcible entry	13.4	7.5	7.9	8.1	5.6	3.8	3.7
Motor vehicle theft	11.1	9.0	12.0	12.3	10.8	10.6	11.2
Completed	9.1	5.9	8.3	7.5	8.6	7.4	7.6
Attempted	2.0[b]	3.1	3.7	4.8	2.2	3.1	3.6
Theft	142.5	162.9	156.5	183.2	178.3	208.0	209.4
Completed	138.4	157.4	150.4	179.1	170.2	200.5	200.7
Less than $50	48.2	55.8	57.2	59.5	65.2	77.3	71.6
$50 to $249	54.1	59.7	51.9	66.5	58.0	68.4	70.4
$250 or more	25.5	30.5	31.1	40.0	38.1	42.8	46.9
Amount not available	10.6	11.4	10.2	13.1	8.9	11.9	11.8
Attempted	4.1	5.6	6.1	4.1	8.1	7.5	8.7
Total number of households	7,427,400	11,641,910	14,878,040	13,249,500	14,903,750	13,490,230	11,843,870

Note: Table excludes data on families whose income level was not ascertained.
[a]Detail may not add to total because of rounding.
[b]Estimate is based on about 10 or fewer sample cases.

Source: U.S. Department of Justice, Bureau of Justice Statistics, *Criminal Victimization in the United States, 1998 Statistical Tables*, NCJ 181585 [Online]. Available: http://www.ojp.usdoj.gov/bjs/abstract/cvusst.htm [May 25, 2000], Table 20.

victimizations are disproportionately located in the lower-income groups.

Further, businesses and other institutions are excluded from estimates of victimization. However, because of their concentrated wealth and social organization, businesses are able to publish supplementary statistics on the victimization they suffered from, say, employee theft or credit card fraud. Insurance companies may also produce additional information on fraud related to false claims by patients or doctors. But there is a profound lack of data in criminology about the pain and suffering experienced by the 44 million Americans who have no health insurance. Nor is there any accounting of victimization related to medical services that are denied or exceedingly difficult to obtain because of the health insurance industry's desire to secure greater profits.

Identification and Adjudication

On November 20, 1993, the front page of the *New York Times* carried two stories about crime. The first was about the United States Senate approving what would become the 1994 Omnibus Crime Bill.

That legislation provided $8.9 billion for hiring 100,000 police officers, $6 billion for prisons and boot camps, and increased federal penalties for a variety of gang-related activities. The second story carried the headline, "Anti-Drug Unit of CIA Sent Ton of Cocaine to U.S. in 1990." This pure cocaine was sold on the streets of the United States, where federal penalties are a five-year mandatory minimum for possession of 500 grams of powder cocaine or just 5 grams of even cheaper crack cocaine. There are 28 grams to an ounce, 16 ounces to a pound, and 2,000 pounds to the ton. Pure cocaine is also "cut" or adulterated as it is passed along, so the original one ton may have become twice that (or more) by the time it hit the street.

The new police officers paid for by the bill were among those out on the streets searching for gang members and busting numerous poor people with small amounts of cocaine, who ended up in the prisons built with an influx of federal money. In contrast, the CIA was not identified as a drug trafficker, nor were any officials arrested. One CIA officer resigned and a second was disciplined in what was called "a most regrettable incident" that involved "instances of poor judgment." A federal grand jury was preparing to investigate the matter and a Congressman on the House Intelligence Committee suggested that CIA antidrug activities needed closer scrutiny. But those are minimal reactions to using taxpayer money to buy cocaine and ship it into the United States, whether as part of intelligence operations or not.

This incident reflects a larger pattern in which police and law enforcement focus on acts that have officially been defined as crimes—the behaviors of the poor. Law enforcement and the larger enterprise of identifying criminals focuses on the lower economic classes. Investigative tools such as profiles tend to be done with street gangs even though studies of corporate crime regularly reveal a disturbingly high prevalence of crime and the same propensity to recidivism demonstrated by "citizen GE" in the opening narrative of this chapter. For example, Sutherland's groundbreaking work on white-collar crime included what has become a classic study based on the records of 70 of the largest 200 U.S. corporations over 40 years.

> The records reveal that every one of the seventy corporations had violated one or more of the laws, with an average of about thirteen adverse decisions per corporation and a range of from one to fifty adverse decisions per corporation. . . . The "habitual criminal" laws of some states impose severe penalties on criminals convicted the third or fourth time. If this criterion were used here, about 90 per-

cent of the large corporations studied would be considered habitual white-collar criminals. (in Reiman 1998a, p. 114)

Further studies have confirmed Sutherland's observation about the high prevalence of crime and repeat criminality in the Fortune 500. This finding is especially noteworthy because many behaviors of the corporation are not covered by the law and the government has had limited enforcement staffs to monitor and investigate corporate violations, so the figures thus represent a very conservative, minimal estimate.

A Justice Department study examining the years 1975–76 found that more than 60 percent of 600 corporations had at least one enforcement action initiated against them, and half of the companies were charged with a serious violation. A later study by *U.S. News & World Report* found that during the 1970s 20 percent of the Fortune 500 had been *convicted* of at least one major crime or paid a civil penalty for serious illegal behavior. From 1975 to 1984, almost two-thirds of the Fortune 500 "were involved in one or more incidents of corrupt behavior such as price fixing, bribery, violation of environmental regulations and tax fraud" (Etzioni 1990, p. C3).

In spite of this impressive concentration of criminality, the Reagan administration decided to get government "off the backs" of corporations while waging a war on crime against the poor. President Reagan's "tough on crime" legislation expanded the use of mandatory and minimum sentences along with federal use of the death penalty. On the other hand, the administration eliminated many federal regulators and the inspectors who acted as police in the corporate neighborhood. Some suggest that this strategy is like removing police from a high crime area because the free will of criminals is being interfered with. Rather than "get tough," deregulation permitted a broader range of activity and reduced many penalties. During the period from 1984 to 1987, the average fine imposed in corporate cases was $48,000— and 67 percent of the fines were for less than $10,000, which could easily be less than the profit gained by wrongdoing. Many companies simply entered into a consent decree stating they would not do it again but were not required to make structural or organizational changes to prevent further lapses.

One observer of corporate crime noted that the "corporate structure itself—oriented as it is toward profit and away from liability—is a standing invitation to such conduct" (in Hills 1987, p. 38). The high rates of criminality found among large corporations may be some evidence to support this claim. Yet any search for "criminal tendencies" that may help lead to the identification of criminals stays focused on street crime and the poor. Indeed, in a society that believes anyone can make it if they want to, the poor—those who have "failed"—are viewed with suspicion and contempt. There must be something wrong with them, an individual failing that reflects inferiority, "defectiveness," or moral degeneracy. In turn, this "unfitness" to be in "normal" society makes the poor a threat that needs to be controlled. At times, criminology participates in the discourse and helps identify "moral imbeciles," who are then slated for eugenic sterilization so they cannot reproduce (Rafter 1997). At other times, beliefs about the criminality of the poor mean that the search for biological and genetic factors—including the search for "born criminals"—has been confined to the poorest classes.

An accounting of the costs of crime both reflects the same class bias and helps to re-create it by focusing attention on street crime. Statistics about street crime are collected by the FBI, which compiles the *Uniform Crime Reports*, and the Bureau of the Census, which conducts the National Crime Survey. In contrast, no single agency is charged with reporting on the crimes in the suites. No annual report is issued on white-collar crime, nor are there several reports that can be easily pieced together. One of the better estimates is done by Reiman (1998a), who starts with a U.S. Chamber of Commerce publication called *A Handbook on White-Collar Crime* that was originally published in 1974 and has never been officially updated. Reiman updates figures where more current data are available and revises other numbers in light of inflation and population growth. His admittedly quite conservative estimate is $208 billion, which does not include all categories and uses only the low figure in any estimated range.

Reiman's estimate is consistent with those by other criminologists and is thirteen times higher than the total amount stolen in *all* thefts reported in the *Uniform Crime Reports*. But what is also surprising is the effort required to arrive at a respectable estimate of crimes in the suites, especially when the government is willing to spend incredible effort counting the cost of street crime. One such publication, which arrived at a cost of $450 billion, did so through a detailed accounting of the tangible and intangible losses (Miller, Cohen, and Wiersema 1996). Tangible losses include damaged and stolen property (plus costs of administering insurance claims); lifetime medical care, such as hospital and physician care, emergency services, rehabilitation, prescription drugs, and funeral expenses (plus the costs of administering insurance claims and legal fees incurred in recovering claims); mental health care such as psychiatrists and psychologists (plus insurance administration costs); police and fire services; victim services; and productivity such as "wages, fringe benefits, housework, and school days lost by victims and their families" as well as lost productivity by co-workers, "supervisors recruiting and training replacements for disabled workers, worrying about an injured co-worker, etc., and by people stuck in traffic jams caused by drunk driving crashes" (Miller et al. 1996, p. 13). The intangible losses centered on establishing monetary values for pain, suffering, and reduced quality of life, with the total being about $2.7 million per victim, out of which $1.9 million reflects the lost quality of life (Miller et al. 1996).

With street crime, the government is willing to figure in the cost of a co-worker's worry but will not spend the effort attempting to even estimate the total for crimes of the rich. While at times the problems related to corporate crime and biases from inequality seem difficult to correct, this lack of data presents a simple solution that would be a big step in the right direction: basic information. Following the example of Finland (Alvesalo 1998), additional resources should be invested into studying (and prosecuting) white-collar crime—especially the types where corporations are perpetrators rather than victims. With these data, students of criminology could study aspects of nonstreet crime. The consciousness of many citizens would be raised about this set of harms they are not likely to see on television, and they could ask their representatives for better laws or the equal application of tough-on-crime principles. Legislators and policymakers could turn their attention to some of the more serious harms in society and start to seek solutions based on more comprehensive information.

Conviction and Imprisonment

Judicial processing represents a significant exit point on the transmission belt for the rich. This chapter has pointed out how many of the analogous social harms are not criminalized, and even when harmful conduct potentially falls under the scope of existing criminal law, it is not prosecuted. Because of the division of labor in corporations and their vast resources, prosecutors frequently decide not to follow through with cases and instead dismiss them. On the other hand, the poor have fewer resources to contest charges against them, so the prisons tend to be national poorhouses.

One excellent illustration of these dynamics is the Dalkon shield case, stemming from the manufacture of a birth control device by the A. H. Robins Company. The company started selling the intrauterine device (IUD) in 1971 as a safe, modern, and effective device. Although the company had performed few tests on the device, marketing and promotion went ahead quickly, and by 1975 some 4.5 million IUDs had been distributed. Early reports indicated many problems: the tail string from the device hung outside the vagina and invited (wicked) bacteria up into the woman's body, and the device was not especially effective at preventing pregnancy. Women suffered from a variety of crippling and life-threatening infections, including some that required emergency hysterectomies; others had unwanted pregnancies that resulted in miscarriages or spontaneous abortions, or (because of infections), they gave birth to children with severe birth defects.

Conservative estimates indicate that some 200,000 women were injured (Clinard 1990). Two court-appointed examiners in 1985 found that Robins had engaged "in ongoing fraud by knowingly misrepresenting the nature, quality, safety and efficacy" of the product, and the fraud "involved the destruction and withholding of relevant evidence" (in Clinard 1990, p. 104). In spite of such facts, no prosecutor brought criminal charges against Robins or its executives. However, Judge Miles Lord, who heard some 400 civil law cases, reflected that "the man who assaults a woman from an office chair is as grave a sinner as the man who assaults a woman in an alley" (in Hills 1987, p. 40). Women were left on their own to file a variety of civil product liability suits, but Robins tried to file for bankruptcy to avoid liability. A judge required the company to establish a trust fund to compensate victims and had to reprimand it for giving substantial bonuses to top executives in violation of the bankruptcy laws.

Judge Lord, in a famous plea for corporate conscience, pointed out the class bias in the working of the judicial process:

> If some poor young man were, by some act of his—without authority or consent—to inflict such damage on one woman, he would be jailed for a good portion of the rest of his life. And yet your company, without warning to women, invaded their bodies by the millions and caused them injury by the thousands. And when the time came for these women to make claims against your company, you attacked their characters. You inquired into their sexual practices

and into the identity of their sex partners. You exposed these women—and ruined families and reputation and careers—in order to intimidate those who would raise their voice against you. You introduced issues that had no relationship whatsoever to the fact that you planted in the bodies of these women instruments of death, of mutilation, of disease." (in Hills 1987, p. 42)

Judge Lord notes that the underlying harm—inflicting harm without consent—is expressed in the street crime of assault and punishable with imprisonment, but there is no analogous crime for corporations. Prosecutors, further, are reluctant to apply the criminal law to individuals in the corporate chain of command. Even though the intention of those who harm from the office suite is different from that of a street criminal, their conduct may still fall within the statutory definition of the criminal law.

For example, the people responsible for selling quantities of contaminated food to the public do not have the same desire to injure as the mugger in the park does. But the criminal law recognizes that harms committed with other states of mind are also criminal. A premeditated and desired murder is the most serious, followed by murders that happen knowingly, recklessly, or negligently. Criminologist Nancy Frank notes that the Model Penal Code, from which many states borrow statutory language, "includes within the definition of murder any death caused by 'extreme indifference to human life'" (1988, p. 18). Such language could, for example, cover situations in which employers intentionally violated health and safety regulations—or cases where miners died because they were made to work under unsupported roofs in places where the levels of explosive gasses were falsely reported for months on end (Reiman 1998a, p. 52).

The division of labor in corporations does make it difficult at times to pin responsibility on a specific person. However, individuals in those hierarchies are routinely evaluated for promotion by examining their job responsibilities and evaluating their performance, so mechanisms exist to do better in determining accountability. Further, because of revisions in the corporate sentencing guidelines, courts have a difficult time imposing a sentence of probation that would include a corporate "self study" about how the criminal event occurred and a plan of action to "rehabilitate" it into a better citizen in the future.

Prosecutions of corporations are difficult because their financial resources give them access to significant legal expertise. In contrast, the poor are represented by a public defender who frequently has a high caseload. An article titled "You Don't Always Get Perry Mason" noted that criminal defense lawyers "lack the resources, experience or inclination to do their utmost" and as a result, "some people go to traffic court with better prepared lawyers than many murder defendants" (Lacayo 1992, p. 38). For this reason, Reiman (1998a) suggests that "we must transform the equal right to counsel into the right to equal counsel" so that the quality of legal representation—and thus the quality of justice—depends less on one's social class than it currently does.

The sum of these factors can be seen in the percentage of offenses that are officially declined for prosecution and who emerges from the process bound for prison. In 1995, federal prosecutors declined 24 percent of the drug cases but fully 67 percent of the regulatory offenses that include denial of civil rights and food and drug law violations. As Figure 2.2 shows, regulatory offenses were dropped more frequently than any other category, and drug offenses were the least likely to be dropped. The wealthy are weeded out on the way to prison. In contrast, almost half of jail inmates reported yearly incomes of less than $7,200. About one-third of jail inmates reported an income of $1,000 or more in the month before their arrest—at least $12,000 a year (see Table 2.6).

Figure 2.2
Offenses Declined for Prosecution

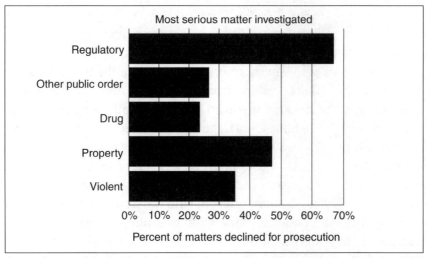

Source: Bureau of Justice Statistics. 1998. *Compendium of Federal Justice Statistics, 1995.* NCJ 168628.

Table 2.6

Employment Status and Income of Jail and Prison Inmates

Work before arrest

Employment status	Percent of jail inmates	Employment status	Percent of prison inmates 1991
Employed	64.3%	Employed	67%
Full time	49.3	Full time	55
Part time	10.4	Part time	12
Occasionally	4.6		
Not employed	35.8	Not employed	33
Looking for work	19.6	Looking for work	16
Not looking	16.2	Not looking	16

Income

Prearrest personal income	Percent of jail inmates	Annual income, for inmates free at least a year	1991
Less than $300	25.1%	No income	3%
$300–$599	20.5	Less than $3,000	19
$600–$999	18.7	$3,000–$4,999	10
$1,000–$1,999	22.2	$5,000–$9,999	21
$2,000 or more	13.5	$10,000–$14,999	17
		$15,000–$24,999	16
		$25,000 or more	15

Source: Profile of Jail Inmates 1996, NCJ 164620 April 1998. Survey of State Prison Inmates 1991, NCJ 136949 March 1993.

These forces are even more pronounced with the administration of the death penalty. Sister Helen Préjean, author of *Dead Man Walking*, says she became involved with the death penalty because her work for the Catholic Church got her involved with poor people: "The death penalty is a poor person's issue. Always remember that after all the rhetoric that goes on in the legislative assemblies, in the end, when the deck is cast out, it is the poor who are selected to die in this country" (1995). Robert Johnson, who has done an extensive and gripping study of condemned men and execution teams, concurs on this point: "In America, and indeed around the world, members of poor and otherwise marginal groups have been selected for the gallows with disturbing regularity" (1998, p.4).

Sister Préjean does note that although society is quick to execute the poor, the ultimate punishment of death is not sought when the poor are killed. She contends that "when the victim is poor, when the victim is a nobody, when the victim is homeless or a person of color—not only is the ultimate punishment not sought to avenge their death, but the case is not even seriously prosecuted" (1995). This pattern tells the poor and minorities that not only are they expendable but that their life is not worth killing for. In turn, wealthy individuals are most likely to "get away with murder" either literally or figuratively when they victimize the poor rather than someone closer to their own social class. Indeed, the Robins company may have been more harshly punished if the victims of its birth control device had included more wealthy women. Or, the consequences might have been more harsh if the Robins Corporation had injured men rather than women, who Judge Lord noted "seem through some strange quirk in our society's mores to be expected to suffer pain, shame and humiliation" (in Hills 1987, p. 42).

Further, corporate sanctions do not include the equivalent of a death penalty (something like the revocation of a corporate charter). When examining the proposed corporate sentencing guidelines (mentioned earlier in this chapter), one lobbyist remarked in horror that some of the sentences amounted to a "corporate death penalty." That is an odd argument to use in a country that widely supports the death penalty, even for juveniles who have no prior record but made a serious error. A majority of Americans indicate support for capital punishment, even when asked to assume that one in every 100 people sentenced to die are actually innocent (*U.S. Department of Justice Sourcebook* 1996, p. 413). Almost every campaign cycle since the reintroduction of capital punishment in 1976 has seen an increase in the number of crimes that are death penalty eligible and the number of jurisdictions that have capital punishment. Yet corporations that have no body, no feeling, and no soul are exempt from this sanction even if they have committed multiple deliberate and calculated (i.e., cold-blooded) murders.

Workers

In her piece on "reality television," Debra Segal noted that the police "ambush one downtrodden suspect after another in search of marijuana, and then, after a long Sisyphean day, retire into red-vinyl bars where they guzzle down beers among clientele that, to no small degree, resembles the very people they have just ambushed" (1993, p. 52). The salary information for police in Table 2.8 and the income of inmates (presented earlier) indicate that Segal is exaggerating a little but is not too far off.

Indeed, some thirty years ago, her comment would have been more accurate with respect to the police and those who worked in prisons. For example, Albert "Racehoss" Sample was an inmate in the Texas prison system in one of the plantation-style work farms. During the late 1960s, Racehoss noted that the warden had only an eighth-grade education. When one officer tried to "sign" his retirement papers, "it took him a good fifteen seconds to draw the two uncrossed streaks of lightening" (1984, p. 284). Another officer could at least make an X on the payroll. But, with the exception of one officer who had a master's degree in physical education, "the warden didn't have a single ranking officer on his immediate staff who had a high school education and none could put together a report on their operations without help" (p. 284).

Texas, like most other jurisdictions, moved to professionalize the workers in their criminal justice system during the late 1960s and early 1970s. Higher educational standards changed the hiring practices and forced many employees out because they would no longer be eligible for promotions. Along with higher job qualifications went increased salaries and occupational prestige for some criminal justice jobs. Educational requirements for criminal justice jobs were the origins of many departments of criminal justice in universities and of the establishment of majors within departments of sociology.

For more than two decades now, expenditures for criminal justice have increased and provided many job opportunities. From 1982 to 1996, expenditures on criminal justice more than tripled—from just under $36 billion to more than $120.2 billion (*Sourcebook Online*, Table 1.1). Payroll for 1995 was nearly $5.8 billion, which covered 1.9 million people (*Sourcebook Online*, Table 1.13). These figures do not include the numerous people in private security or related occupations, although, in general, officers with private security companies have a lower salary, fewer benefits, and lower requirements to qualify for their positions than public employees.

The *Sourcebook of Criminal Justice Statistics* publishes some information on employees, including sex and race breakdowns for many specific jobs. But—to repeat what is becoming a common theme—information on social class is neither collected nor published. The remainder of this section presents some of that information and tries to make inferences about social class from salary ranges and employment requirements for various positions. Many positions have a wide salary range within a state and other variations between states, so the information presented here is not definitive.

Table 2.7
Minimum Educational Requirements for Law Enforcement, 1997

	High School Diploma	Some College (nondegree requirements)	2-year College Degree	4-year College Degree
Local Police	83%	5%	8%	1%
Sheriffs' Departments	86%	3%	7%	1%

From Sourcebook Online, Tables 1.0008, 1.0020, and 1.55. Requirements vary depending on the size of the jurisdiction or college campus.

Table 2.8
Average Starting Salaries for Law Enforcement, 1997

	Entry Level	Sergeant	Chief or Sheriff
Local police	$23,300	$32,300	$38,700
Range	$18,800 to $30,600	$24,300 to $47,500	$25,700 to $100,700
Sheriffs' Departments	$21,500	$27,700	$45,100
Range	$19,400 to $30,200	$23,900 to $43,700	$31,300 to $98,900

From Sourcebook Online, Tables 1.0012 & 1.0024.

Information about police officers shown in Tables 2.7 and 2.8 reveals that many departments still do not have high educational requirements and that salaries place officers solidly within the working class. The average entry-level salary for jurisdictions of all sizes is $23,000 but varies with the size of the jurisdiction, with larger jurisdictions paying a higher salary. After one year of being an officer, the average salary is $25,600. For jurisdictions with more than 10,000 persons, the average entrance salary as of January 1999 was $29,840, with a maximum of $41,206; the number of years to reach the maximum varied from 5 to 14 years (*Sourcebook Online* Table 1.34). In general, campus police departments and officers specifically engaged in parking patrol received lower salaries and had fewer educational requirements than patrol officers in the same jurisdiction.

The *Sourcebook* has no salary or other information on correctional officers, even though this segment accounts for much of the growth in the criminal justice system. Their salary does tend to be roughly equivalent to that of police officers, but guards do not have the prestige of being "crimefighters" and have to "do time" imprisoned with the inmates (Lombardo 1989).

Highlighting the criminal justice players in Gilbert's income parade discussed earlier in this chapter is instructive. The jail inmates would be among the poor who would be in the first minutes of the parade, along with most of the prison inmates. The $32,000 salary of many police officers and guards places them right at the median and about halfway through. But, information in Table 2.9 indicates that judges would be just above the level of "not quite rich" and would appear about 50 minutes into the parade. The position of judges, however, highlights the importance of nonmonetary aspects of class. While some lawyers and many CEOs make more money than judges (see Table 2.1), a high degree of esteem, status, and prestige is attached to the position of judge.

Table 2.9
Salaries of Judges

	Trial or District Court	Appellate or Circuit Court	Highest or Supreme Court
State courts (national average)	$94,041	$103,703	$105,058
Federal courts	$136,700	$145,000	$167,900

Source: U.S. Department of Justice Sourcebook 1996, Tables 1.75 and 1.82.

More information on criminal justice careers (including law school) and salaries is available at *http://www.paulsjusticepage.com*.

Media Representations

The media offers an important lens for examining class because media's representations are "what this society tells itself about crime" (in Barak 1994, p. 9). But those who are telling society about its crime systematically distort the picture and have created a "National Entertainment State" characterized by the homogenization of news and triumph of entertainment over relevance and complexity. The term also reflects how the majority of crime images are produced by a few corporate conglomerates: General Electric, the company mentioned at the opening of this chapter, owns NBC; Disney/Cap Cities owns ABC; Westinghouse owns CBS; and Time Warner owns Turner Broadcasting, CNN, TNT, and TBS (in Barak 1998, p. 270–271). Together, they act as buffers of social reality who create a "'user friendly' Big Brother" by how they "omit the message, suppress the message, homogenize the message, sensationalize the message, or convert the message into entertainment—or worse, 'infotainment'" (p. 271).

Debra Segal, who worked for a "reality-based" show like *COPS*, illustrates this point clearly and dramatically in her description of the editing process and her commentary on what gets left on the cutting-room floor:

> By the time our 9 million viewers flip on their tubes, we've reduced fifty or sixty hours of mundane and compromising video into short, action-packed segments of tantalizing, crack-filled, dope-dealing, junkie-busting cop culture. How easily we downplay the pathos of the suspect; how cleverly we breeze past the complexities that has cast doubt on the very system that has produced the criminal activity in the first place. (1993, p. 52)

The distortions here are numerous and serious and in their totality focus attention on the street crimes of the lower classes in a way that presents crime as an individual failing and acquits the existing social order.

Stories of crime in the media tend to focus not just on street crime but on violent crime. In fact, the prevalence of crime on television is the exact opposite of its prevalence in the real world: the high volume of real-world property crime is given little time, and the less frequent violent crimes such as murder are in prominent positions in the "if it bleeds it leads" media culture. Indeed, the more odd and unusual a murder is, the more likely it is to get extensive coverage. In contrast, corporate actions that result in injury or death are not conceptualized or presented as violent crimes. White-collar and corporate crimes rarely appear on the news at all (Surette 1992), which is not surprising given corporate ownership of the news media. Corporations do appear frequently on television, however, because 90 percent of prime-time television commercials—including some of those appearing during programming about "crime"—are sponsored by the 500 largest corporations (Simon 1999, p.14).

Television tends to be interested in the lives and actions of the rich and those with high status. When these individuals are shown as engaging in crime, it tends not to be corporate wrongdoing but rather crimes like murder played out against the backdrop of a resort or some other social setting occupied by wealthy, glamorous, and beautiful people. But more frequently, and especially in what passes for "reality" or documentary "docudrama" representations, the culprit is a poor person.

In the area of drugs, for example, Drug Czar William Bennett acknowledged that the typical cocaine user is "white, male, a high-school graduate employed full-time and living in a small metropolitan area or suburb" (in Lusane 1991, p. 45). Yet the typical picture of a "bust" involves someone poor—and probably an inner-city African American. Indeed, Segal notes that the program she was involved with tended to show "hapless Hispanic families living in poverty, stashing marijuana behind tapestries of the Virgin Mary" but the omitted part was that they were selling it "to some of the same white middle-class couch potatoes who watch reality-based cop shows" (1993, p. 55).

In response to these distortions, Barak advocates a "newsmaking criminology" that seeks to "expose the underlying cultural and political-economic nature of the crime problem, and to draw the necessary connections between this nature and the way in which crime is defined as a particular type of individual pathology or social problem" (1994, p. 20–21). Academic criminologists and other activists need to create and participate in "replacement discourses" that expose what is unsaid, and, like Segal, tell the "Tales From the Cutting Room Floor" (1993). Such discourses can also take the forms like filmmaker Michael Moore's short-lived *TV Nation*, in which he introduced a corporate crime fighting chicken to give some visibility to the issue and to counter the dog McGruff, who is the mascot for the "Take a Bite Out of [Street] Crime" campaign.

Without some type of disruptive counterforce, the same distortions of crime and criminality are likely to continue in the media because they help divert attention from the actions of questionable corporate citizens like GE. Depictions of crime that focus blame on individuals rather than on society also help prevent questions about inequality and the size of corporate personas. Lastly, "reality based" shows are cheap to produce and thus turn personal suffering into profit. Segal comments on some footage of police officers busting prostitutes after watching them do a striptease. She writes of how the women—in footage that will never be part of the "reality based" show—tell stories about needing the money because there's no child support payment or how the nine-to-five job pays the rent but not food:

> One woman's misery is another man's pleasure; one man's pleasure is another man's crime; one man's crime is another man's beat; one man's beat is another man's TV show. And all of these pieces of the drama become one big paycheck for the executive producer. (1993, p. 57)

Summary and Conclusions

This chapter began by noting the reluctance in our society to discuss issues of economic class. In some less guarded moments, even leaders of white supremacy hate groups admit that class is more of a problem than race. Many of their followers are poor whites who feel that no one represents them. One leader said that their literature was derogatory to blacks, but "we just use it as a vehicle to attract possible decent people" (in Ezekiel 1995, p. 112). Apparently, decent people feel that class is a taboo topic and will respond more favorably to an incorrect analysis that fosters hate by blaming blacks or a widespread Jewish conspiracy (the Zionist Occupied Government, or ZOG) for social problems (see Ezekiel 1995; Ridgeway 1995).

While criminal justice agencies do not share all the beliefs of white supremacy groups, they too seem to feel that class is not a respectable topic and are reluctant to collect data about it. This observation did not hold for the 1960s and the first President's Commission, but it has become the current social reality. The problem of inequality and the growing gap between the rich and the poor are less frequently part of the "official knowledge" about crime, but they are important nevertheless. Indeed, a twenty-five-year retrospective on the President's Commission stated: "While evidence shows that criminal justice procedures are more evenhanded than in the past, it is also painfully obvious that the growing gap between rich and poor, and white and black, continues to make criminal justice a social battleground rather than a mechanism to increase social peace" (in Conley 1994, p. 66).

Because of the long history of racism, blacks are disproportionately poor, so issues of class and race are tied together in ways that will be explored in the following chapters. The current and evolving problem is that criminal justice is contributing to the differences between rich and poor, white and minority. Our current domestic policies of crime control operate as if "Americans have concluded that the problems of the urban poor are intractable and therefore they [apparently agreed to have their money] spent on a vast network of prisons, rather than on solutions" (in Welch 1996a, p. 101). Many taxpayers are willing to fund the construction of prisons to house the poor but are opposed to basic social and educational services for the poor. Some of these programs are cheaper than prisons and have the potential to reduce crime by preventing child abuse, enhancing the intellectual and social development of children, providing support and mentoring to vulnerable adolescents, and doing intensive work with juvenile offenders (Currie 1998, p. 81).

Irwin and Austin capture the essence of this problem, and the "enormous policy dilemma" they articulate is ultimately a problem of inequality and economic class:

> On the one hand, we are expending a greater portion of our public dollars on incarcerating, punishing, treating and controlling persons who are primarily from the lower economic classes in an effort to reduce crime. On the other hand, we have set in motion economic policies that serve to widen the gap between rich and poor, producing yet another generation of impoverished youths who will probably end up under control of the correctional system. By escalating the size of the correctional system, we are also increasing the tax burden and diverting billions of dollars from those very public services (education, health, transportation, and economic development) that would reduce poverty, unemployment, crime, drug abuse and mental illness. (1997, p. 10–11)

Increasingly, criminal justice not only reflects the class biases in society, but also helps create and reinforce them. The United States continues to enlarge its apparatus of social control against the poor in society while the rich, especially corporations, continue to grow in size.

Note

1. As the authors were preparing a final draft of this book, one of us discovered it was already listed in the offering at Internet bookseller *Amazon.com*. It was identified in two places in their system, under "Gender and Crime" and "Race and Crime," but no "Class and Crime" area exists. ✦

Chapter 3

Race

Separate but Unequal

In the case of Plessy v. Ferguson (163 U.S. 537, 1896), the Supreme Court set the precedent of "separate but equal": Separate facilities for blacks did not offend Constitutional provisions so long as they were equal to those provided for whites. Louisiana had a law requiring separate railway cars for the races—or partitions to separate the races if there was just a single car. Plessy sat in a railway car designated for use by whites only and was told by the conductor to leave. As the Court described it, upon his "refusal to comply with such order, he was, with the aid of a police officer, forcibly ejected from said coach, and hurried off to, and imprisoned in, the parish jail" in New Orleans.

The Court found that the requirement of separate accommodations was a reasonable regulation, made "with reference to the established usages, customs, and traditions of the people, and with a view to the promotion of their comfort, and the preservation of the public peace and good order." Social prejudices, said the Court, cannot be overcome by legislation, and if the races "are to meet upon terms of social equality, it must be the result of natural affinities, a mutual appreciation of each other's merits, and a voluntary consent of individuals." Although Plessy argued that enforced separation "stamps the colored race with a badge of inferiority," the majority held that it is "not by reason of anything found in the act, but solely because the colored race chooses to put that construction upon it."

What is less known about the case is that Plessy "was seven-eighths Caucasian and one-eighth African blood; that the mixture of colored blood was not discernible in him," so the suit involved a claim "that he was entitled to every right, privilege, and immunity secured to citizens of the United States of the white race." Plessy argued that "in a mixed community, the reputation of belonging to the dominant race, in this instance the white race, is 'property,' in the same sense that a right of action or of inheritance is property." The Court conceded it to be so, for the purposes of the case, but argued the statute did not take his property: either he was a white man who was entitled or a black man who was not. But who decides, and how? The train conductor seemed to have power to make racial classifications, but the Court did not see that issue as properly before it. The state legislatures should properly decide on racial classifications, but some said "any visible admixture of black blood stamps the person as belonging to the colored race; others, that it depends upon the preponderance of blood; and still others, that the predominance of white blood must only be in the proportion of three-fourths."

Justice Harlan was the sole dissenter, claiming that the decision would prove to be as "pernicious" as the Dred Scott case, which declared that escaped slaves who traveled North to freedom were still property and should be returned to their Southern masters. For him, the statute seemed inconsistent, for example, in allowing black nurses to attend white children but not an adult in bad health. The black employee of a white woman could not be in the same coach, and the statute criminalized the attendant's "exhibition of zeal in the discharge of duty." Harlan also pointed to the Chinese as being "a race so different from our own that we do not permit those belonging to it to become citizens of the United States" and "with few exceptions, absolutely excluded from our country," yet under the law "a Chinaman can ride in the same passenger coach with white citizens." Meanwhile, blacks "many of whom, perhaps, risked their lives for the preservation of the Union, who are entitled, by law, to participate in the political control of the state and nation, who are not excluded, by law or by reason of their race, from public stations of any kind, and who have all the legal rights that belong to white citizens, are yet declared to be criminals, liable to imprisonment, if they ride in a public coach occupied by citizens of the white race."

Harlan wondered whether the Court's ruling about the reasonableness of separation would allow a town to assign the races to different sides of the street or prohibit the co-mingling of Protestants and Catholics. Perhaps partitions should also be placed in courtrooms, or even jury boxes and the deliberation room to "prevent black jurors from coming too close to their brother jurors of the white race." Unlike the majority, Harlan argued the purpose of the law was to compel blacks to "keep to themselves" while traveling rather than keep whites out of black areas, and "no one would be so wanting in candor as to assert the contrary." He acknowledged that whites were the dominant race and said that while "every true man has pride of race" that can be shown in appropriate situations, the Thirteenth Amendment abolished slavery and prevented "the imposition of any burdens or disabilities that consti-

tute badges of slavery or servitude." Even though whites were the dominant race, and "will continue to be so for all time," he was clear that:

> In the view of the Constitution, in the eye of the law, there is in this country no superior, dominant, ruling class of citizens. There is no caste here. Our Constitution is color-blind, and neither knows nor tolerates classes among citizens. In respect of civil rights, all citizens are equal before the law. The humblest is the peer of the most powerful. The law regards man as man, and takes no account of his surroundings or of his color when his civil rights as guaranteed by the supreme law of the land is involved.

Introduction

A s the previous chapter indicated, economic bias undermines the ideal of equality before the law, so the poorest is not the peer of the most powerful. This chapter examines the extent to which racial and ethnic minorities are treated as equals under a criminal justice system that should be color-blind. Few would deny that progress has been made since *Plessy*, and some of Justice Harlan's concerns found expression in subsequent cases, culminating in the 1954 case of *Brown v. Board of Education*, which declared that *separate* was inherently *unequal* because it did stamp a badge of inferiority on blacks. But race still remains a contentious issue, and Harlan's vision of a color-blind legal system is still not the reality. Indeed, nearly 100 years after *Plessy*, Andrew Hacker would summarize the situation in the title of his book, *Two Nations: Black and White, Separate, Hostile, Unequal* (1995).

This chapter highlights experiences common to all minority groups within a system in which the majority population is white, while recognizing that each group also has unique experiences. Although this chapter tries to outline basic aspects of the experience of various groups, readers should remember that general terms for racial and ethnic groups conceal a great deal of internal diversity: "[J]ust as it is presumptuous to consider a Bostonian Irishman, an Anglo-California yuppie, a Jewish Greenwich Village artist, a Texas rodeo star, and a New Age Santa Fe vegetarian as all the same because they are coincidentally 'white,' it is just as unwise to render all 'Latinos' (or Asians or African Americans) as inherently alike" (Burnley, Edmunds, Gaboury, and Seymour 1998). For instance, persons of Japanese, Cambodian, Laotian, and Hmong descent are all included in the "Asian and Pacific Islander" category, masking the fact that median family income for Japanese Americans was more than twice that of the other groups in 1990 (Council of Economic Advisers 1998). Also, among Hispanics, wide variations exist, with those of Cuban background generally being better situated in terms of income, employment, health, and education than Puerto Ricans or Mexicans and Mexican Americans (Hajat, Lucas, and Kington 2000). Further, women frequently have a different experience than men of a minority group because of *gendered racism*, a term used to reflect the overlapping systems of discrimination (Essed 1991).

At the same time, members of diverse minority groups are all victims of ideological racism, in which dominant group traits are overvalued while those of other groups are devalued. While we do not agree that race is merely a function of socioeconomic class, we recognize that part of the common experiences of minorities is their overall lower economic status, which makes them vulnerable to exploitation and control by the criminal justice system.

Understanding the political economy of an era, such as the need for cheap labor or a surplus of workers, is a key factor in understanding the relationship between minority groups and criminal justice (Rusche and Kirchheimer 1939). For example, after the Civil War, the criminal justice system swept the newly freed slaves off the streets and leased them back to plantation owners for a profit (Oshinsky 1996). At other times, such as after the completion of the transcontinental railroad and the economic recession in the 1870s, the criminal justice system responded to surplus labor and white fears by passing the Chinese Exclusion Act of 1882, outlawing opium use among Chinese but not whites (Lusane 1991, p. 31).

In each case, minority group entanglement with criminal justice related to changes in the political economy and were justified by an ideology of white supremacy that devalued minority groups. In each case, too, criminal justice served to maintain white privilege by making cheap labor available, removing economic competition or other perceived social threats. The racism that criminal justice both reflects and re-creates is thus part of the "sociology of waste" that squanders the talent and potential of minority groups (Feagin and Vera 1995). People of color pay the heaviest and most direct price because of white supremacy, but "few whites realize the huge amount of energy and talent that whites themselves have dissipated in their construction of antiblack attitudes and ideologies and in their participation in racial discrimination" (Feagin and Vera 1995, p. 2). Racism diverts the attention of whites and causes them to scapegoat minority groups rather than "seeing clearly their own class exploitation and . . . organizing effectively with black and other minority workers" (p. 15).

This chapter starts by discussing how race and ethnicity are not just about biology but rather are also socially constructed. We then define key terms such as racism, stereotypes, discrimination, and prejudice before examining the status of minorities in economic, political, and social spheres. Evidence of stark inequality and disadvantage leads to a consideration of whether genocide is an appropriate term to apply to these social relations. The chapter then turns to the relationship between race and ethnicity in criminological theory and the law. We review the impact of race on various stages of criminal justice processing, examine the racial composition of the workers in the system, and analyze media images of race and crime.

One final note on terminology is necessary because so many terms are used to refer to racial groups. Of necessity, we must use the language of resources we consulted for this chapter. For example, government data and authors who follow the government classification system use "Black" and "American Indian." We are aware that many minorities prefer to identify themselves by other terms, such as "African American" and "Native American," and we use these terms as well, both when our sources do and as interchangeable with "official" terms. The designation "native American" means people of all races who were born in the U.S. and contrasts with immigrants; "Native American" refers to American Indians, and the capitalization designates their status as aborigines or First Peoples on the land before it became the United States. At times, to capture the history of discrimination or someone's prejudice, we include quotations that are intended by the original speaker to be derogatory. We do not endorse these attitudes or the use of racial epithets but believe it is important to accurately portray the attitudes that have been held.

Race and Ethnicity in Society

Definitions of Key Terms

As used here, *ethnicity* is socially defined on the bases of cultural customs such as language, religion, kinship patterns, and other characteristics. *Race* is socially defined by a constellation of traits that include physical characteristics, national origin, language, culture, and religion. Although some of these traits are linked to biology and genetics, there are no genetic markers that allow for the identification of race, and geneticists are unable to determine race from a DNA sample (Marshall 1998). Two randomly selected people from the world's population would have about 99.8 percent of their genetic material in common (Feagin and Feagin 1996). Scientists agree that "modern humans originated from a small population that emerged out of Africa and migrated around the globe," so there is a continuum of genetic variation that makes the concept of race meaningless to geneticists (Marshall 1998).

Still, many people—not just white supremacists—believe race is an objective fact; they see race as part of their essence, inherent to them, even a property of the blood flowing through them (see Box 3.1). While not denying that physical differences do exist among people, the social construction approach recognizes that selecting the number of racial categories, deciding what characteristics determine the categories, and assigning people to the categories is ultimately a social practice with political overtones. For example, the *Plessy* Court ducked the difficult issue of what makes a person black—a single drop of blood, half heritage, two-thirds? Is a Japanese person considered nonwhite, Oriental, "Other," or "Asian and Pacific Islander"?

Box 3.1

Race and Blood

Hans Serelman was a doctor in Germany in 1935. His patient needed a blood transfusion, which at the time was done by finding a live donor ("donor-on-the-hoof") rather than using stored blood. Unable to find a suitable donor quickly enough, the doctor opened his own artery and donated his own blood. Rather than receiving praise, the Jewish doctor was sent to a concentration camp for defiling the blood of the German race.

In the succeeding years, Germany moved to eliminate the "Jewish influence" from medicine by limiting access to patients and medical school. To bolster claims of Aryan supremacy, the study of blood became a focus for distinguishing Aryans from Jews. The combined effects of these initiatives dealt a self-inflicted wound on the Nazi war effort. The more than 8,000 Jewish doctors barred from practice were replaced by hastily trained and inexperienced paramedics. The infusion of mythology and misapplied anthropology set back serious scientific research on blood. The Nuremberg Blood Protection Laws severely limited the availability of blood for transfusions because of the possibility of being charged with "an attack on German blood" if the donor could not prove it was pure Aryan blood (Starr 1998, p. 26).

In the U.S., the topic of "colored" versus "white" blood also stirred up controversy during World War II. The Red Cross knew that "blood was blood" and did not differ by race, but followed the wishes of the military and refused to collect blood from African Americans. Following the attack on Pearl Harbor and the large demand for blood to treat many wounded soldiers, the Red Cross collected blood from blacks but labeled and processed it separately. As historian Douglas Starr notes, "The policy proved offensive to many Americans because the country was, after all, fighting a racist enemy" (1998, p. 108). A *New York Times* editorial commented that "the prejudice against Negro blood for transfusions is all the more difficult to understand because many a Southerner was nursed at the breast of a Negro nanny. . . . Sometimes we wonder whether this is really an age of science" (in Starr 1998, p. 108).

In the late 1950s, Arkansas passed a law requiring the segregation of blood. Louisiana, home of the Plessy case, "went so far as to make it a misdemeanor for physicians to give a white person black blood without asking permission" (Starr 1998, p. 170). The segregation of blood ended during the 1960s, more because of the civil rights movement than further advances in science.

The "mixed race" option in the 2000 Census is an excellent example of the social construction of race. The 1980 and 1990 forms told people to choose one race only and asked them to choose from: white, black, Asian/Pacific Islander, American Indian, and "other." With the question about Hispanic origin, the racial and ethnic categories totaled 10. The 2000 census has greatly expanded categories and includes a fill-in-the-blank "some other race," so that when combined with the question on whether the person is also "Spanish/Hispanic/ Latino"—an ethnicity, not a race—there are 126 possibilities for racial and ethnic identity.[1]

Even though people of mixed race now have additional options for reporting, only some will exercise it. One man who said he would describe himself as black has a white Jewish father and an African-Bermudan mother. He is married to a woman whose background includes Caribbean, African, and Indian influences; their family celebrates Passover with an "African-American Latino seder" (Schemo 2000). "Checking more than one race, he contends, would undermine the influence of blacks by reducing their number as a distinct

group and so most likely diluting public policies addressing their concerns" (Schemo 2000; see also Brune 1999). Other Americans are
likely to mark the same single box as in the past out of habit.

As these examples illustrate, people are not assigned to racial
groups on the basis of genetics. Rather, people are assigned to racial
groups by either visual observation or self-identification, both of
which are subject to numerous social influences. People's willingness
to claim a racial identity changes over time, further undermining any
claim that race has to being an objective, fixed status. For example,
Census Bureau figures indicate that between 1960 and 1990, the
Native American population tripled. Birth rates are less a factor than
improved data collection and increased self-identification because "it
has become trendy, and economically beneficial, to claim Indian
ancestry" (in Lynch and Patterson 1991, p. 110). Stereotypes about
the "drunken savage" remain, but the environmental movement and
movies like *Dances With Wolves* have removed the perceived "taint" of
being Native American and have replaced it with pride (Brune 1999).

Stating that race and ethnicity are socially constructed does not
deny that some differences exist among people, nor that people experience very real oppression based on race and ethnicity. In other
words, certain differences between people are seized on as reflecting
inherent or essential racial identities. These racial categories reflect
the social, economic, and political dynamics of the society that creates
them, so there is a hierarchical ordering. Power and privilege are
reflected in the schema of racial classification, which shapes people's
lives and identities through stereotypes, racism, prejudice, and discrimination.

Stereotypes build on the dynamics of categorizing people, but they
have the property of being fixed and largely negative generalizations
about a group of people. Many definitions stress the inadequate or
problematic basis of stereotypes in personal experience—such as
when people have stereotypes about groups they have never personally encountered but "know" about the group because of friends, the
media, or social institutions that reflect prevailing beliefs. Stereotypes
build on people's tendency to look for examples that confirm their
beliefs and dismiss those contrary to how they see the world ("that's
the exception that proves the rule"). Many Asians, for example, are
stereotyped as the "model minority." Although this seems like a positive rather than negative evaluation, it has destructive consequences

for Asians since being "a paragon of hard work and docility carries a negative undercurrent" (Feagin and Feagin 1996, p. 404).

Individual racism describes the situation in which the stereotypes favor a race to such an extent that the person has the "excessive pride of race" discussed in *Plessy*. Racism has conventionally been defined as a set of beliefs or attitudes—even a doctrine or dogma—in which "one ethnic group is condemned by nature to congenital inferiority and another group is destined to congenital superiority" (in Bonilla-Silva 1997, p. 20). In this perspective, racism is an irrational or flawed ideology. The term *institutional racism* acknowledges that racism may have structural aspects that stratify society and shape identity. For example, Stokely Carmichael and Charles Hamilton observed that

> When white terrorists bomb a black church and kill five black children, that is an act of individual racism, widely deplored by most segments of the society. But when in that same city—Birmingham, Alabama—five hundred black babies die each year because of the lack of proper food, shelter and medical facilities, and thousands more are destroyed and maimed physically, emotionally, and intellectually because of conditions of poverty and discrimination, that is a function of institutional racism. (1967, p. 65)

Bonilla-Silva expands on the notion of institutional racism by proposing the notion of *racialized social systems*, which "refers to societies in which economic, political, social and ideological levels are partially structured by the placement of actors in racial categories" (1997, p. 132). This concept includes ideological beliefs as a component but also shows how the hierarchy of racial categories and the placement of people in them produce social relationships between the races.

Prejudice refers to a negative or hostile attitude toward another (usually racially defined) social group. Psychologically, people project onto the minority group many of the negative attributes they wish to deny in themselves or the group with which they want to identify. While prejudice is a thought or attitude, discrimination is an action or expression of that thought or attitude. *Discrimination* occurs when people act on the basis of stereotypes and prejudice.

Because whites still have the vast majority of the power in society, they have the greatest ability to discriminate, so this chapter will focus mostly on the problems of white prejudice and discrimination. People of all races can have prejudices or excessive pride of race (racism), but generally speaking, members of racial and ethnic minorities do not have the institutional backing that permits them to inflict substantial and recurring discrimination on whites in areas such as employment, business contracts, classrooms, department stores, and housing (Feagin and Feagin 1996).

A lack of understanding about race is perpetuated through the belief that race is about people of color and that whites do not have race. Being white or Caucasian involves having a race that affects identity and opportunity, even if whites are less conscious about this trait and have little race consciousness: "In the same way that both men's and women's lives are shaped by their gender, and that both heterosexual and lesbian women's experiences are shaped by their sexuality, white people *and* people of color live racially structured lives. In other words, any system of differentiation shapes those on whom it bestows privilege as well as those it oppresses" (Frankenberg 1993, p. 1).

Because whites are the dominant group, this social position and its privileges are naturalized through ideology so that being white seems neither privileged nor socially constructed. Ideology serves to naturalize the racial hierarchies and the racist views that re-create them. Because the majority group position is naturalized, members do not think of themselves as privileged and have few occasions to reflect on the "property interest" they have in being white.

Box 3.2 contains a series of questions to provoke thoughts about naturalized or unrecognized privilege. Also, Frankenberg's work on white women (1993) explores the social construction of whiteness through interviews with women who have had to confront their whiteness through a variety of life experiences (including interracial relationships). For one woman who liked to read, the breakthrough came when she discovered black writers such as Toni Morrison and Alice Walker: "What came as a shock to me was that I could have grown up without thinking about it, believing that Black people were less educated than I was. I found *that* more shocking than that there *were* intelligent Black people around" (1993, p. 163, emphasis in original). Understanding whiteness involves asking many difficult questions, as indicated by another woman interviewed by Frankenberg:

> I have an identity that doesn't have to do with my volition, but I've been profiting from it from birth. So what does that make me, and where does my responsibility lie? And where does my blame lie? And do I have a right to be angry because I did not create this society, but I am paying for it? And do I have a right to be pissed because my friendships are crippled because of something that I came into

the world not knowing anything about, but benefiting by? (1993, p. 175)

Box 3.2

You Know You're Privileged When . . . (Part 1)

In 1988, Peggy McIntosh's frustration with men who would not recognize their male privilege prompted her to examine her own life and identify ordinary ways in which she experienced white privilege. "I think whites are carefully taught not to recognize white privilege, as males are taught not to recognize male privilege" (1997[1988], p. 292). Her list of 46 forms of privilege included the following:

- When I am told about our national heritage or about "civilization," I am shown that people of my color made it what it is.
- I can go into a music shop and count on finding the music of my race represented, into a supermarket and find the staple foods which fit with my cultural traditions, into a hairdresser's shop and find someone who can cut my hair.
- Whether I use checks, credit cards, or cash, I can count on my skin color not to work against the appearance of financial reliability.
- I can talk with my mouth full and not have people put this down to my color.
- I can swear, or dress in secondhand clothes, or not answer letters, without having people attribute these choices to the bad morals, the poverty, or the illiteracy of my race.
- I can do well in a challenging situation without being called a credit to my race.
- I can be pretty sure that if I ask to talk to "the person in charge," I will be facing a person of my race.
- If I declare there is a racial issue at hand, or there isn't a racial issue at hand, my race will lend me more credibility for either position than a person of color will have.
- I can worry about racism without being seen as self-interested or self-seeking.
- I can take a job with an affirmative action employer without having my co-workers on the job suspect that I got it because of my race.

A few years later, Stephanie M. Wildman (1997, p. 325) suggested some additional conditions specific to dominant cultural white privilege, made with respect to her Latina/o friends, acquaintances, and colleagues. These included:

- People will not be surprised if I speak English well.
- People seeing me will assume I am a citizen of the United States. . . . People will never assume that I or my children are illegal immigrants.

> - People will not comment about my sense of time if I am prompt or late, unless I am unusually late. Then people will assume that I have an individual, personal reason for being late. My lateness will not be dismissed as a joke about white time.
> - People will pronounce my name correctly or politely ask about the correct pronunciation. They will not behave as if it is an enormous imposition to get my name right.

Andrew Hacker (1995) has created a class exercise to help students understand the value of being white. In "The Visit," an embarrassed official comes to a white person to say he (or she) was supposed to have been born to black parents. At midnight, he will become black and will have the features associated with African ancestry, so he will not be recognizable to current friends but inside he will be the same person he is now. The white man is scheduled to live another 50 years as a black, and the official's organization is willing to offer financial compensation, as the mistake is their fault.

Hacker notes that white students do not feel it out of place asking for $50 million, or a million a year, which is a good indication of the value—the property interest mentioned in *Plessy*—of being white. Students who say that because of affirmative action they would be better off as a black still come up with a figure to "buy protections from the discriminations and dangers white people know they would face once they were perceived to be black" (Hacker 1995, pp. 31–32).

The discriminations of the criminal justice system are discussed later in the chapter, where we note that social indicators of well-being reveal none in which African Americans or Hispanics occupy a favored position (Council of Economic Advisers 1998; Johnson and Leighton 1999). Indeed, Tonry summarizes the situation as one in which "mountains of social welfare, health, employment, and educational data make it clear that black Americans experience material conditions of life that, on average, are far worse than those faced by white Americans" (1995, p. 128).

Economic Sphere

Chapter 2 provided some data indicating blacks have substantially less wealth than whites, for example. Table 3.1 illustrates the large gap in median income and the disproportionate number of blacks and Hispanics in poverty. Income and wealth are important indicators because they relate to political power (see Chapter 2) and the ability to shield oneself from hardships such as cold and hunger. Money allows people to buy more food and better nutrition, as well as gain access to medical care (Reiman 1998a). Among the many manifestations of these differences is an infant mortality rate that is twice as high for blacks as whites (U.S. Census Bureau 1999).

Table 3.1
Median Family Income and Individual Poverty Rate by Race and Hispanic Origin, 1996

	Median Family Income	Percent Below Poverty Line
White (non-Hispanic)	$47,023	8.6%
Black	26,522	28.4
Asian	49,105	14.5
Hispanic	26,179	29.4

Source: Council of Economic Advisers (1998), Chapter 5, Tables 1, 2.

Table 3.2
Distributions of Selected Demographic Characteristics by Hispanic Origin Subgroup and Race

Selected Demographic Characteristic	Puerto Rican	Cuban	Mexican/ Mexican American	Other Hispanic	Non-Hispanic Black	Non-Hispanic White
All persons (in thousands)	3,128	1,361	14,747	6,021	31,535	188,940
65 years or older (%)	5.0	17.2	3.8	5.3	8.1	14.1
Less than high school graduate (%)	42.1	31.2	55.3	34.7	30.6	16.2
Currently employed (%)	49.2	63.4	57.3	59.6	57.3	65.8
Below poverty (%)	27.8	12.0	26.6	18.0	24.5	7.7

Source: Hajat, Lucas, and Kington (2000), Table 2.

As shown in Table 3.1, Asian and non-Hispanic white families have much higher median incomes than black or Hispanic families. This reflects, in part, the differences in educational attainment, unemployment rates, and wage rates reported in Table 3.2. The poverty rate for Asians, blacks, and Hispanics remains well above that of non-Hispanic whites. Since 1994, the poverty rate for Hispanics has been higher than that for blacks, partly as a result of the lower educational and economic attainment of many Hispanic immigrants. Census figures for 1990 found that the poverty rate for American Indians was the highest among the five racial and ethnic groups (Council of Economic Advisers 1998). One study found that 57 percent of Hispanics and non-Hispanic blacks were currently employed, compared to nearly two-thirds of all non-Hispanic whites. Among Hispanics, however, wide variation can be found in employment status; nearly two-thirds of all Cubans and 57 percent of Mexicans and Mexican-Americans were employed compared to less than half of Puerto Ricans. Interestingly, while Mexicans and Mexican-Americans were more likely than Puerto Ricans to report employment, about 27 percent of both groups were reportedly living below poverty level (Hajat, Lucas, and Kington 2000).

As shown in Table 3.3, Hispanics, African Americans, and American Indians are more likely than non-Hispanic whites or Asians to work in semi-skilled jobs (e.g., transportation workers, equipment cleaners, helpers, and laborers) or as service workers (e.g., private household workers). They are less likely to hold white-collar jobs, and when they do hold such positions, they are more likely than whites or Asians to work as typists, clerks, or salespeople (Pollard and O'Hare 1999).

Table 3.3
Occupational Distribution by Race and Ethnicity, 1998

	Percent of Employed Persons, Ages 16+				
		Non-Hispanic			
Occupation	White	African American	Asian	American Indian	Hispanic
Total (thousands)	97,162	14,028	4,942	892	12,983
White Collar					
Managerial and professional	33%	20%	34%	20%	15%
Technical and administrative	30	30	31	31	23
Blue Collar					
Skilled labor	11	8	8	12	13
Semi-skilled and unskilled labor	12	20	11	17	22
Services	12	21	15	17	21
Farming, fishing, and forestry	2	1	1	2	5

Source: Population Reference Bureau analysis of the March 1998 *Current Population Survey.* *www.prb.org/pubs/bulletin/bu54-3/part6.htm.*

Political Sphere

Racial and ethnic minorities continue to be underrepresented in politics, although the situation has improved (Pollard and O'Hare 1999). A 1992 survey by the Census Bureau found that less than 5 percent of local elected officials were black, Hispanic, Asian, or American Indian. African Americans were 3 percent of all local elected officials, Hispanics were 1 percent, American Indians and Alaska Natives and Asians and Pacific Islanders were less than 1 percent. According to a *Population Bulletin* report, the number of African American elected officials jumped from 4,890 in 1980 to 8,658 in 1997, and the number of Hispanic public officials rose from 3,147 in 1985 to 5,459 in 1994. Among the 535 voting members of the 106th Congress were 37 African Americans, 18 Hispanics, and 3 Asians and Pacific Islanders in the U.S. House of Representatives; two Asians and Pacific Islanders and one American Indian were serving in the U.S. Senate. Statistics for 1996 indicate that around two-thirds of whites and blacks are registered to vote, compared to only around 36 percent of Hispanics (who may be of any race).

Social Sphere

Educational attainment influences economic status and health. Since 1980, all racial and ethnic groups have experienced increases in their level of educational attainment; increases for blacks have been the most marked, while increases for Hispanics have been relatively small. Non-Hispanic whites and Asians are more likely than blacks, Hispanics, and American Indians to have completed education beyond high school. The level of educational achievement varies by race and ethnicity. For example, roughly one in five of all Cubans and one in four of non-Hispanic whites are college graduates compared to fewer than one in seven Puerto Ricans, Mexicans and Mexican-Americans, and non-Hispanic blacks (Council of Economic Advisers 1998).

According to the 1998 *Changing America* report authored by the Council of Economic Advisers for the President's Initiative on Race, "Poor housing may contribute to a number of adverse health and educational outcomes, particularly in children. For example, severe crowding, indoor air pollution, or deteriorating lead paint may cause or exacerbate diseases such as asthma or lead poisoning, sometimes with long-term effects" (1998, p. 60). The Council concluded that non-Hispanic white households have the best housing conditions relative to non-Hispanic black, Hispanic, Asian, and American Indian households, although the relative position of the other groups varies depending on the measure. For instance, non-Hispanic black households are more likely than members of other groups to live in units with moderate or serious physical problems (e.g., lack of indoor plumbing, inadequate heating, lack of a kitchen sink or refrigerator). Non-Hispanic black, Hispanic, Asian, and American Indian households are nearly *twice* as likely as non-Hispanic whites to spend 50 percent or more of their income on housing. About 15 percent of black households and 12 percent of Hispanic households reported that crime was a problem in their neighborhood, compared to 6 percent of non-Hispanic white households.

Black Americans are also more likely than whites or any other minority group to live in toxic physical environments. "In 1987 the Commission for Racial Justice of the United Church of Christ reported that three of every five black and Hispanic Americans live in a community with uncontrolled toxic-waste sites" (Austin and Schill 1991, p. 69; Lee 1992). Although poverty is an important factor, "the racial composition of a community was found to be the single variable best able to explain the existence or nonexistence of commercial hazardous waste facilities in a given community area" (Bullard 1990; Lee 1992, p. 14). Another recent survey indicated that, although attention has been focused on the problem of environmental racism, the concentration of toxic waste in low-income communities is *growing*, especially for low-income black Americans. Hazardous wastes were examined because nationally comprehensive data were easily available: "Many other problems in minority communities, such as air pollution, workplace exposure, pesticides, lead poisoning, asbestos, municipal waste and others, are equally or more serious" but not subject to ready assessment (Lee 1992, p. 16; see also Bullard 1994; Kozol 1991; Lynch and Stretesky 1998).

Such living conditions may help us understand findings that non-Hispanic blacks, Mexicans and Mexican-Americans, and Puerto Ricans are less likely than Cubans and non-Hispanic whites to describe their health as "excellent." According to a Centers for Disease Control report, Puerto Ricans in the mainland U.S. fare significantly worse than other U.S. Hispanics on a number of health indicators. For instance, nearly one in five Puerto Ricans reported being in fair or poor health, compared with 14 percent of Cubans and 12 percent of "other Hispanic" groups (e.g., persons of Central and South American descent, Dominicans, and European Spaniards) (Hajat et al. 2000). The authors of the study acknowledged that some of the difference in health status and other outcomes may be attributable to socioeconomic status and acculturation, although how acculturation differentially affects different racial and ethnic groups remains to be determined. Given that the Asian population in the United States is also diverse and rapidly growing, understanding subgroup heterogeneity is becoming increasingly important.

The *Changing America* report observes that much research into health differences between racial and ethnic groups has focused largely on differences in socioeconomic status. But the report does not rule out stress caused by discrimination and racism against members of racial minority groups; for example, the higher prevalence of hypertension among blacks relative to whites has been linked to personal experiences of discrimination.

Is It Genocide?

Because the deprivations of minorities are so extensive and so profound, some argue that the conditions amount to genocide—a powerful word used to describe extreme cases of mass violence. It comes from the Greek work *genos* (race or tribe) and the Latin *cide* (kill), so the underlying concept involves an attempt to exterminate a group that shares common characteristics and a common identity. Charging genocide is thus claiming great victimization that confers a moral authority on the victims to be heard and to demand change. Also, it is a powerful indictment of a group that it is committing, or standing by in the face of, mass violence. Compounding the problems of studying genocide is a long and pervasive history of denial (Chalk and Jonassohn 1990). For example, criminology takes great interest in the issue of serial killers and mass murder but typically excludes genocide—and human rights—as part of the accepted disciplinary issues. Denial and exclusion are good reasons to review the claims that the majority population of the U.S. has committed genocide involving Native Americans and blacks.

Many Americans consider charges of genocide made by minority populations to be overstated at best. They tend to associate genocide with the Holocaust in Nazi Germany, which creates a distorted standard because it is an extreme case rather than a more typical one. The core concept, however, is "an attempt to exterminate a racial, ethnic, religious, cultural, or political group, either directly through murder or indirectly by creating conditions that lead to the group's destruction" (Staub 1989, p. 8). Such destruction encompasses "not only killing but creation of conditions that materially or psychologically destroy or diminish people's dignity, happiness, and capacity to fulfill basic material needs" (Staub 1989, p. 25).

On Columbus Day of every year, readers might notice signs protesting "500 years of genocide." Like many claims of genocide, this one is met with much denial. Indeed, for the 500th anniversary of Columbus arriving in North America, the National Endowment for the Humanities refused to fund any film that "proposed to use the word 'genocide,' even in passing to explain the subsequent liquidation of America's indigenous population" (Churchill 1997, p. 5). Similar thinking has precluded much discussion about charges that Columbus himself was an agent of genocide and that the colonization process he set in motion has resulted in genocidal processes.

Columbus understood his own life "in apocalyptic terms" and even "announced that he himself was the Messiah prophesied by Joachim, a twelfth-century Italian mystic" (Lamy 1996, p. 47). He believed that "his own divinely inspired mission to open up a new path to Asia" was part of heralding in "an age of universal conversion that would precede the End of the World" by helping to liberate Jerusalem from the Muslims (in Lamy 1996, p. 48). When he set sail in 1492, "Columbus confided to his regal patrons that he would bring gold from the East Indies for that future epic venture" (Lamy 1996, p. 46). Churchill makes the implications of this mind set clear in his book, *A Little Matter of Genocide: Holocaust and Denial in the Americas 1492 to the Present* (1997). He states that the diaries and letters of Columbus show that he was expecting to encounter wealth belonging to others, and his stated purpose was "to seize this wealth, by whatever means necessary and available, in order to enrich both his sponsors and himself" (1997, p. 85) Thus, Columbus "not only symbolizes the process of conquest and genocide which eventually consumed the indigenous people of America, but bears the personal responsibility of having participated in it" (p. 85).

Evidence about whether genocide is a fair characterization of the next 500 years relates to Staub's definition of genocide as involving direct murder and the creation of conditions leading to the group's destruction. Lemkin, the man who coined the term genocide, under-stood genocide to be in the "destruction of the essential foundations of the life" of the group and undermining the integrity of the group's basic institutions, which produces the "destruction of the personal security, liberty, health, dignity, and even the lives of the individuals belonging to such groups" (in Kuper 1985, p. 9). Few instances of mass murder that are acknowledged to be genocide involve the actual elimination of a group, so the presence of Jews today and the state of Israel does not undermine a claim the Holocaust was genocide.

With Native Americans, at its low point the population was down 90 percent from the level before the time Columbus arrived (Churchill 1997). Over the course of several centuries, some population fluctuation was inevitable, but the drastic decline here is related to a number of practices that involved direct murder as well as attacks on the well-being and cultural integrity of Native Americans. Consider, for instance, the aggressive appropriation (theft) of land that included forced marches—such as the Trail of Tears—that had a high death toll because hunger, exhaustion, and exposure to inclement weather killed many women, children, and the elderly. The removal of Native Americans from land that was sacred and had cultural significance eroded their cultural integrity, and their placement on desolate land further undermined the essential foundations of life. This process of forced relocation recurred multiple times with the expansion in the population of white settlers or the discovery of mineral wealth on what was thought to be wasteland given to Native Americans (Churchill 1997; Lazarus 1991; Weyler 1992). Today, there are still substan-tial problems with reservations being located on inhospitable land, which can also be a site for toxic and radioactive materials (Eichstaedt 1994).

To control the Native American population, settlers in the 1800s intentionally gave them disease-infested blankets that would kill large numbers who did not have immunity to European diseases (Churchill 1997). In addition, children were taken—sometimes at gunpoint—and put into boarding and reform schools where they were deprived of access to their culture and native language. Indeed, children were punished for doing anything "Indian" and were taught to be ashamed of their heritage. Even today, many Native Americans in prison are denied access to culturally appropriate practices such as the sweatlodge and are coerced into programs such as Alcoholics Anonymous that have Christian foundations, thus further eroding their cultural integrity (Little Rock 1989).

The U.S. government—the representative of the American people—has broken every treaty it has made with the Native Americans (Lazarus 1991). The refusal to honor treaties negotiated in good faith by the native peoples has denied them rights to land, resources, and sovereignty in many ways that have imposed, both historically and currently, hardship and have destroyed their personal security, liberty, health, and dignity. Although several cases involving broken treaties have resulted in symbolic reparations for Native Americans, the ongoing problems remain. Indeed, most tribes, even on reservations, have little in the way of sovereignty and are subject to state and federal control. The tribal decision-making bodies recognized by tribal members are often not the same as the leaders officially recognized by the federal government. In addition, the Bureau of Indian Affairs has come under scathing criticism for being corrupt and not having the best interest of Native Americans at heart in administering their affairs (Churchill 1997; Lazarus 1991; Weyler 1992). Activism on the part of Native Americans, such as the American Indian Movement, has met with illegal surveillance and at times violent repression by the Federal Bureau of Investigation and other law enforcement agencies (Churchill and Wall 1990a, 1990b).

Although most of the direct killing of Native Americans is part of the past, the place accorded them by the white majority is one that destroys the essential foundations of their life. Spirited and creative acts of resistance to domination and colonialism have highlighted the ongoing effort to undermine the integrity of Native Americans' basic institutions. What the National Advisory Commission on Civil Disorders noted about inner-city ghettos applies equally well to reservations:

> What white Americans have never fully understood—but what the Negro can never forget—is that white society is deeply implicated in the ghetto. White institutions created it, white institutions maintain it, and white society condones it. (quoted in Pinkney 1984, p. 78)

In each case, whatever the intentions or consciousness of white society, both the inner city and reservations are places of extreme social deprivation and violence. Indeed, as Wilhelm noted, "as the races pull apart into lifestyles with greater polarity, the Black ghetto evolves into the equivalent of the Indian reservation" (1970, p. 334).

Questions thus arise as to whether the history or current conditions of blacks can be described as genocide as well.

Charges related to the genocide of blacks start with slavery and the forced removal of blacks from Africa to work in involuntary servitude on Southern plantations; the experiences of black Americans with the institution of slavery produced deaths totaling between 50 and 100 million (Anderson 1995; Gorman 1997; Oshinsky 1996; Tolnay and Beck 1995). In 1951, black scholar William Patterson wrote a 240-page indictment against the United States called "We Charge Genocide" that he deposited with the United Nations (see Patterson 1970, 1971). Interestingly, U.S. delegates argued that what was being done to poor blacks happened because they were poor and that the issue was one of social class. Because it was an economic issue rather than a racial dynamic, the genocide convention did not apply (Churchill 1997, p. 376).

Although the class dynamic is in operation with blacks, it is also racism that keeps blacks disproportionately in poverty. Further, class does not explain the history of lynchings or of segregation that consistently condemned blacks to inferior accommodations. Blacks have certainly made gains since the 1950s, in terms of civil rights, income, and political representation. Despite these gains, the "mountains" of data mentioned in the earlier section of this chapter demonstrate pervasive social, economic, and political disadvantage. Blacks are still much more likely to live in poverty and in inner-city neighborhoods that are places of concentrated poverty (Mandel 1978, 1992; Massey and Denton 1993; Wilson 1987).

This concentrated poverty and social disorganization function to compromise many essential foundations of life and the integrity of institutions. The consequences of this racial stratification can be seen in a study of life expectancy done by Johnson and Leighton (1999) that compares the observed number of deaths for a race with what would be expected if it had the death rate of the other race. If blacks had the same death rate as whites in 1991, the expected figure would be 78,951 *fewer* untimely deaths of blacks that year (45,693 men and 33,258 women). If whites had the death rate of blacks, the expected figure would be 647,575 *more* premature deaths each year (376,992 men and 270,583 women). These figures are for a single year, and such excess deaths continue to accumulate over the years.

These shortened black lives are not always the result of direct intervention by whites but also reflect black-on-black violence and self-destructive behavior. The debate about genocide does not deny the personal responsibility blacks have for their actions, although it does take note that such behavior reflects adaptations to a broader social context marked by a "socioeconomic predicament which is itself profoundly antisocial" (Rubenstein 1987, p. 206; see also Braithwaite 1992). Indeed, Williams, in his classic *The Destruction of Black Civilization*, writes of genocide emanating from within the black community:

> They, the so-called criminals and their youthful followers, expect nothing beneficial from the white world, and they see no reason for hope in their own. Hence, like caged animals, they strike at what is nearest them—their own people. They are actually trying to *kill a situation* they hate, unaware that even in this, they are serving the white man well. For the whites need not go all out for "genocide" schemes, for which they are often charged, when blacks are killing themselves off daily on such a large scale. (1987, p. 325, emphasis in original)

In the case of both blacks and Native Americans, white society has created conditions that undermine the essential life foundations and integrity of the group. Genocide still entails a certain—and unspecified—level of destruction and white involvement in those destructive processes. These elements are very much a subject of contention and cannot be resolved in this chapter. The goal here has been to overview the claim of genocide and indicate why it should not be dismissed as "mumbo jumbo" or the paranoia of "wild-eyed conspiracy mongers" (White 1990, p. 20). Beyond the specific debate about genocide, Hacker raises questions and logic that deserve further consideration:

> Can this nation have an unstated strategy for annihilation of [black] people? How else, you ask yourself, can one explain the incidence of death and debilitation from drugs and disease, the incarceration of a whole generation of [black] men, the consignment of millions of women and children to half-lives of poverty and dependency? Each of these conditions has its causes. Yet the fact that they so centrally impinge on a single race makes one wonder why the larger society has allowed them to happen. (1995, p. 54)

Further, the issue of genocide should lead the way into asking about the future of marginal groups, who are prime targets for genocide and are by definition expendable (Rubenstein 1987, p. 1). Wilhelm raised the disturbing question in his 1970 book, *Who Needs the Negro?* That question assumes a new salience and urgency in our increasingly technological society, one where intellectual and well-paying work figures as a privilege of the educated and raw labor is of sharply decreasing value (Aronowitz and DiFazio 1994; Rifkin 1995; Wilson, 1996). Impersonal processes such as automation make the unskilled, uneducated poor expendable—even the raw materials of what Dyer (2000) calls "the perpetual prisoner machine" and Christie (1993) discusses as the crime control industry. Thus, even those who do not believe genocide is currently happening might be able to see the vulnerability blacks feel. The relevant question is "whether the bonds of community between Americans would be sufficiently strong to protect the poor in a crisis" (Rubenstein 1987, p. 213).

Race and Ethnicity in Criminology

Chapter 2 noted that class bias means that the poor are disproportionately under the control of the criminal justice system. Minorities are disproportionately poor and vastly overrepresented in the criminal justice system in comparison with their numbers in the population. Critics charge that disproportionate rates of arrest and incarceration reflect higher rates of involvement in crime, not the operation of racial bias. The remainder of this chapter explores these issues. The current section examines theorizing about race, ethnicity, and crime, followed by a review of race, crime, and law. The next section reviews the effect race has on many aspects of current criminal justice, as well as methodological issues involved in studying racial bias.

Race has been a consistent correlate of crime, but researchers debate whether there is a causal link. The higher rates of involvement of minorities can be interpreted as evidence of discrimination, the result of criminogenic social context, or the product of some inherent (biological or genetic) racial differences. The study of these issues cannot be a search for an objective truth because both "crime" and "race" are socially constructed. Research on race and crime thus both reflects prevailing racial attitudes and is a site for resistance to the conscious or unconscious reproduction of racism in scholarship.

For example, Lombroso, the "father of criminology," wrote that "The white races represented the triumph of the human species, its hitherto most perfect advancement" (quoted in Miller 1997, p. 185). This belief influenced his criminal anthropology and the implications of his belief that criminality was related to atavistic or evolutionary throwbacks. Many texts do not mention his racism and the understanding it might help provide about how social and historical context influences the ideas developed during that epoch. In contrast, Bonger's 1943 study, *Race and Crime,* was written as a critique against the growing fascist movement in Europe and arguments about the superiority of Nordic peoples (Hawkins 1995, p. 23).

American criminology and social science has generally been characterized by "liberal political tone and assumptions" that document black disadvantage and attribute it to white prejudice rather than biological notions of black inferiority (Hawkins 1995). Hawkins starts his analysis with W. E. B. DuBois (1868–1963), a prominent black intellectual and writer who is typically omitted from criminology texts. He is an important figure because "many of the most virulently racist, social Darwinist critiques of black life were published during the period in which he wrote [and] DuBois was among the first to provide a retort to their argument" (Hawkins 1995, p. 13). DuBois seemed to accept the truth about higher rates of black criminality and ascribed them to the urban migration that occurred after the end of slavery as well as the social disruption and degradation of slavery.

Some of DuBois' analysis is shared by criminologists such as Sutherland and Sellin, although they both urged much more caution in concluding that blacks had a higher crime rate than whites from official statistics. Still, Sellin (1928, p. 64) recognized that black crime rates might still be higher than whites, but he argued this was not a condemnation of blacks because "it would be extraordinary, indeed if this group were to prove more law-abiding than the white, which enjoys more fully the advantages of a civilization the Negro has helped to create." Sutherland and Sellin did recognize the importance of *culture* as relevant to criminality but argued that culture is somewhat different from nationality (based on political boundaries) and race. Important data for them included the observation that immigrants from the same culture would have different rates of criminality depending on the age at which they arrived in the U.S. and the number of generations their family had been here—data that cannot be explained by reference to biology or genetics.

Shaw and McKay's study of social ecology in Chicago neighborhoods also raised questions about the importance of biology and genetics because "no racial, national or nativity group exhibits a uniform, characteristic rate of delinquents in all parts of Chicago" (Shaw and McKay 1942, p. 153). The key factor for them was social disorganization and delinquency related to community attributes rather than racial traits. Wolfgang and Cohen (1970) later elaborated on the persistence of high rates of criminality among blacks while other immigrant groups had moved out of socially disorganized communities and zones of transition. In particular, they noted that blacks faced more blocked opportunities because of racism than white immigrants and that the legacy of racial oppression might make blacks less ambitious than immigrants more optimistic about achieving the American dream.

Wolfgang and Cohen (1970) also explicitly addressed flaws in the logic of biological determinism. They noted that there could not be a genetic predetermination to general criminality because "the definition of crime is not stable in time or place" and "most criminals obey most laws—indeed are extremely careful to do so to avoid drawing police attention." Like Bonger, they argued that criminality is not a specific trait like eye color:

> According to Mendel's rule of inheritance of specific traits, if criminality were genetically determined, we should inherit specific tendencies for embezzlement, burglary, forgery, etc. And if we inherited specific *criminal* forms of behavior, and some of us were genetically destined to be burglars or stock embezzlers, rapists or check forgers, we would also have to inherit specific *noncriminal* occupations, which would mean some of us would be genetically destined to become police officers or truck drivers or school teachers, as to have red hair. (1970, p. 92)

Biology, physiology, and genetics are appropriate disciplines to include in a comprehensive and integrative study of crime (Barak 1998). The caution here is that there is no genetic basis for race; the physical differences used to create racial categories are socially constructed and do not correlate with general criminality or specific kinds of criminality.

Hawkins concludes his thoughtful overview of literature on race and crime by noting that the liberal tradition tries to balance a recognition that racial bias inflates the official criminality of minorities with an awareness that minorities frequently live in criminogenic conditions. He is skeptical of efforts to find the "real" rate of crime and of attempts to get more accurate counts of real misconduct. Instead, he argues for the development of a conflict perspective, which examines official records of minority crime as an index of social control and an understanding of "how the criminal justice system is used by the dominant ethnic and racial groups to maintain their status" (Hawkins 1995, p. 34). This perspective, reviewed in the next section, views contact with the criminal justice system as less a result of criminal conduct than of social standing.

Race, Crime, and the Law

The type of analysis suggested by Hawkins cuts across lines of race and class. The analysis starts with examining how the criminal justice system functions to control the "surplus population," which includes the poor of all races and ethnicities. Minorities are disproportionately poor and thus most vulnerable to entanglement in systems of control. In addition, racism and racist assumptions are frequently involved in creating moral panics or other situations thought to justify increased social control (e.g., drug laws). More fundamentally, Rusche and Kirchheimer (1968/1939) examined how the amount and type of punishment in society related to changes in the political economy, including the amount of surplus labor and changing modes of production. These principles were clearly shown in the rise of black imprisonment following the Civil War, which illustrates the distinctive racial dynamic in operation.

The Civil War abolished involuntary servitude and freed the slaves, although "the transition from bondage to freedom was more theoretical than real" (Gorman 1997, p. 447). Millions of blacks were "suddenly transformed from personal property to potential competitors" (Tolnay and Beck 1995, p. 57). Whites now had to compete with blacks for jobs, and plantation owners would now have to compete with one another in the form of high wages for good help. In addition, many whites feared "domination" by newly freed blacks, and others "believed that blacks would perish in freedom, like fish on the land. The Negro's 'incompetence,' after all, had been essential to the understanding—and defense—of slavery itself" (Oshinsky 1996, p. 19). One Southerner summed up the situation:

> I think God intended the niggers to be slaves. Now since man has deranged God's plan, I think the best we can do is keep 'em as near to a state of bondage as possible. My theory is, feed 'em well, clothe 'em well, and then, if they don't work whip 'em well. (Oshinsky 1996, p. 11)

Actual imprisonment was not an option because there were few prisons, and the Civil War had destroyed many buildings. The solution lay in leasing inmates out to the plantations from which they had just been freed. The plantation owners had cheap labor, the blacks were back under control, and—as a bonus—many agents of the criminal justice system took a share of money involved in the leases. Blacks were the ultimate losers of the new system, and many were returned to the plantation so quickly they hardly noticed Emancipation. The threat of plantation prisons kept many other blacks in servitude under labor contracts that re-created the conditions of slavery: "the horror of the ball and chain is ever before [blacks], and their future is bright with no hope" (in Gorman 1997, p. 450).

Worse still, now that owners no longer had the same economic interest in blacks as property, further restraints against brutality were removed. If a slave died, the owner had to buy another, but leased blacks who died were easily and cheaply replaced. The system was indeed worse than slavery, and in Mississippi in the 1880s not one leased convict lived long enough to serve a sentence of ten years or more (Oshinsky 1996, p. 46). However because of the social control, cheap labor, and fees generated by the leases, the system expanded. Blacks were put to work not just on plantations but in a variety of grueling and dangerous jobs that included mining, building roads, clearing swamps, and making turpentine.

The nominal basis for arrests was laws based on slave codes: "the slave codes of the antebellum period were the basis of the black codes of 1865–66 and later were resurrected as the segregation statutes of the period after 1877" (in Gorman 1997, p. 447). When able-bodied black men had not actually done anything wrong, the police would falsely charge them with crimes. When the men could not pay off the court fees, they were forced to go to work (Gorman 1997). These bogus arrests were sometimes orchestrated by "employers working hand-in-glove with local officials to keep their [work] camps well stocked with able-bodied blacks" (Oshinsky 1996, p. 71).

The picture that emerges is of black convicts as slaves and the state functioning as slave master (Gorman 1997). Understanding black "criminality" at this juncture involves the perspective Hawkins described where arrest is "less a product of their conduct than their social standing" (Hawkins 1995, p. 34). The folk song, "Standin' On De Corner" captures this dynamic:

Standin' on de corner, weren't doin' no hahm,

Up come a 'liceman an' he grab me by d' ahm.

Blow a little whistle an ring a little bell;

Heah come 'rol wagon a-runnin' like hell.

Judge he call me up an' ast mah name

Ah tol' him fo' sho' Ah weren't to blame.

He wink at 'liceman, 'liceman wink too;

Judge he say, "Nigger, you got some work to do."

Workin' on ol' road bank, shackle boun'.

Long, long time fo' six months roll aroun'.

Miserin' fo' my honey, she miserin' fo' me,

But, Lawd, white folks won't let go holdin' me.

(Franklin 1989, p. 104–105)

Variations on this pattern occur for minorities at various points in history. For example, after the transcontinental railroad was completed, Asian labor was no longer needed. To control this population, the U.S. either passed laws that selectively prohibited "Orientals" from possessing drugs or selectively enforced drug laws against them. However, moral panics and the criminalization of minorities could occur for reasons other than political economy. What did remain constant was the use of racism and drug laws to further the social control of minorities. Lusane, for example, discusses a 1910 report that detailed "the supposed superhuman strength and extreme madness experienced by Blacks on cocaine, and explained that cocaine drove Black men to rape" (1991, p. 33). Rumors circulated that cocaine made blacks bulletproof, and an article in the *New York Times* ("Negro Cocaine 'Fiends' Are a New Southern Menace") reported that Southern police were switching to larger caliber weapons to protect themselves from drug-empowered blacks (Lusane 1991, p. 34).

In his *Plessy* dissent, Justice Harlan argued that the Constitution and the law of the land should be color-blind. For much of the nation's history, laws like the one at issue in *Plessy* explicitly required differential treatment for minorities. At times, it required them to have separate accommodations or excluded them from certain occupations. In Georgia before the Civil War a black man faced capital punishment when convicted of the rape or attempted rape of a white woman; for white men convicted of raping black women, on the other hand, the penalty was a fine, prison, or both (Scully 1990). As noted early in this chapter, the Chinese Exclusion Act of 1882 outlawed opium use among Chinese but not whites (Lusane 1991, p. 31).

Even statutes that are "facially neutral" can still have a disproportionate impact on minorities. These laws may not be racist in intention, but they are in their effect. One example is the federal sentencing guidelines that penalize the possession of crack cocaine more heavily than powdered cocaine in a 100 to 1 ratio. Possession of a mere 5 grams of crack cocaine means a mandatory minimum in prison, while it takes 500 grams of powder cocaine for the same sentence. About 85 percent of those sent to prison under the crack provisions of this law are black, so this sentencing pattern contributes directly to problems of disproportionate minority confinement (Bureau of Justice Statistics 1997b). The inference of racist intent is problematic because if arrests had been in proportion to the percentage of crack cocaine users, fewer minorities would have been affected. According to the National Institute on Drug Abuse, 50 percent of crack users are white as compared with 36 percent black (Bureau of Justice Statistics 1992). Indeed, former drug czar William Bennett acknowledged that the typical crack smoker is a white suburbanite (Lusane 1991).

In many ways, establishing actual racist intent should not be necessary for remedial action. In the areas of employment and housing discrimination, for example, evidence of patterns of discrimination is sufficient. Further, Congress knew the impact of this law from protests, reports, and a recommendation from the Sentencing Guidelines Commission itself to end the disparate penalties. The awareness of the consequences, coupled with a lack of action to change it, does not prove legislators directly intended the racial disparity, although there is an obvious degree of complacency with disproportionate minority imprisonment. The moral philosopher R. M. Hare (1990) articulates the moral status of such actions in his distinction between direct and oblique intention:

> To intend some consequence directly one has to desire it. To intend it obliquely one has only to foresee it. . . . We have the duty to avoid bringing about consequences that we ought not bring about, even if we do not desire those consequences in themselves, provided only that we know they will be consequences. I am to blame if I knowingly bring about someone's death in the course of some plan of mine, even if I do not desire his death in itself—that is, even if I intend

the death only obliquely and not directly. As we shall see, this is very relevant to the decisions of legislators (many of whose intentions are oblique), in that they have a duty to consider consequences of their legislation that they can foresee, and not merely those that they desire. (p. 186)

Legislators argue that they cannot foresee all the implications of their proposed laws. To help them, one suggestion for reform is a "racial impact statement" modeled after current environmental and financial impact statements. This analysis would collect relevant data and project the likely impact of the legislation on current levels of minority confinement. Certainly the dangers posed by disproportionate levels of minorities in prison are at least as severe as the environmental problems and financial crises that justify the need for other impact statements. Law makers could still enact legislation that would worsen the situation, but they could no longer say they did not know the potential consequences. Moreover, they would have to answer to a community empowered to ask questions about the racial impact of legislation.

As a final note, the quest for color-blind laws that live up to the promise of equal protection is not inconsistent with greater cultural sensitivity within the criminal justice system. The laws and law enforcement officers should treat everyone equally and not be more willing to arrest minorities; cases should be prosecuted and decided without reference to the race of defendant or victim. But crime prevention programs need to take cultural beliefs of the neighborhood into account if they are to be effective. Victim counseling needs to be sensitive to cultural values through which the victimization experience is interpreted. Rehabilitation and intervention programs likewise need to build on cultural values for maximum effectiveness.

Laws are written in categorical language that calls for arrest and charging of persons engaging in legally prohibited acts, but police officers exercise a certain amount of discretion in deciding whether to arrest or charge individuals who in fact violate the law (Reiman 1998a, 1998b). The question is to what extent discretion is exercised in ways that reflect racial bias against nonwhites, over and above any bias created by enforcing laws that have a disproportionate impact on minorities. After reviewing an extensive number of studies, the *Harvard Law Review* stated: "The argument that police behavior is undistorted by racial discrimination flatly contradicts most studies, which reveal what many police officers freely admit: that police use race as an independently significant, if not determinative, factor in deciding whom to follow, detain, search, or arrest" (1988, p. 1496). Because most people violate the law at some points during their lives, this heightened scrutiny results in higher levels of arrest and creates a picture of the "typical criminal" as being young, black, and inner-city (Reiman 1998a). The racially based profile of the typical criminal is then used to justify that belief that "race itself provides a legitimate basis on which to base a categorically higher level of suspicion" (Harvard Law Review 1988, p. 1496).

Since the *Harvard Law Review* surveyed the research, attention has been focused on the issue of "driving while black" (see also Box 3.3 on "Breathing While a Black Man"). The first data were anecdotal but indicated that police targeted black and minority drivers, frequently for minor violations—no seat belt, tilted license plates, or illegible (dirty) plates. These stops were a pretext for searching for drugs or weapons, but the Supreme Court upheld their validity in *Whren v. U.S.* (1996), saying that as long as the police saw a violation for which they could stop a car, it did not matter that the stop was a pretext. Critics feared the decision invited discriminatory enforcement (Harris 1999).

Concern over driving while black continued because many stops involved extensive searches. Police would start by looking under seats and in the trunk but continued by deflating tires, prying off door panels, and taking apart sun roofs. In at least one instance, officers handed the driver a screwdriver, saying "you're going to need this" to put the car back together (Harris 1999). On occasion, the belongings of blacks were strewn on the highways, blown around by passing trucks, and urinated on by dogs sniffing for drugs. Other stops involved a disproportionate number of officers who were quick to unholster firearms. Some of these stops happened to rich or famous blacks, including local politicians.

Box 3.3

Breathing While a Black Man

In October, 1999 the U.S. Court of Appeals for the Second Circuit ruled that police officers in Oneonta, N.Y., did not violate the Constitution when they tried to stop every black man in town in 1992 after a woman said she had been robbed in her home by a young black man. The case involved a 77-year-old white woman in the mostly white town who was attacked by a black man in her home near the college campus. The woman told police that while she had not seen her assailant's face, she knew that he was black (by looking at his hands) and young (by watching how he crossed her room). She also thought her attacker had cut his hand.

The police proceeded to obtain a list of the approximately 125 black male students from a college administrator, then tried to locate and question everyone on it. When that approach failed, the police swept the town, stopping almost every black man they saw (and at least one black woman) and examining their hands for cuts. Fewer than 300 blacks live in the town, and over 200 persons were questioned. The police never did find the man they were looking for.

"This went far beyond the problem of driving while black," syndicated columnist Bob Herbert (1999) observed:

> **People were being stopped in Oneonta for breathing while black. Trust me, if some poor guy had innocently cut his finger while slicing a tomato for dinner he would have landed in jail. . . . With this ruling, cops are free to harass any and all black people as long as they have in hand a complaint that a black person has committed a crime. If you are black, you are a suspect.**

Herbert concluded his column with a statement from Eliot Spitzer, the State Attorney General who was statutorily obligated to defend the state in the suit. "I read the circuit opinion. And I said: 'You know what? We won the case but it makes your skin crawl.'"

As part of the settlement to lawsuits charging discrimination, several jurisdictions started requiring data collection on police stops. Other studies were undertaken directly on behalf of minority groups and still others were done pro-actively by localities concerned about discrimination. The overall results confirm the experience of minorities that they are disproportionately targets of police power and "vulnerable to the whims of anyone holding a criminal justice commission" (Doyle 1992, p. 75). The results of statistical analysis do not lead to direct conclusions about the intentions of the conduct, but the results are consistent with the *Harvard Law Review's* statement that the criminal justice system appears to operate on stereotypes and profiles that define some groups "as having a propensity to be morally depraved, thus endorsing a view of those who share in that culture as unworthy of equal respect" (1988, p. 1514).

The more quantitative studies do not include the detailed qualitative descriptions of the stops, but they can illustrate how disproportionate the stops are relative to the minority population, the amount they drive, and the frequency with which they violate traffic laws. For example, a 1988 study of vehicles on the New Jersey turnpike showed that African- American motorists with out-of-state plates accounted for fewer than 5 percent of the vehicles but 80 percent of the stops. In Illinois, Hispanics make up less than 8 percent of the population and take fewer than 3 percent of the personal vehicle trips, but they make up approximately 30 percent of the motorists stopped for discretionary offenses, such as the failure to signal a lane change or driving one to four miles over the speed limit (Harris 1999).

One of two more recent comprehensive studies involved observers who watched an Interstate near Baltimore and recorded information on 5,741 cars over 42 hours. They reported that 93.3 percent were violating traffic laws and thus were eligible to be stopped by Maryland State Police. Of the violators seen by the study's observers, 17.5 percent were black and 74.7 percent were white. However, the State Police reported that 72.9 percent of the vehicles they stopped had black drivers (Harris 1999).

A second study looked at the New York Police Department's "Stop and Frisk" practices more generally, rather than just issues of driving (New York State Office of the Attorney General 1999). Data came from 175,000 "UF-250" forms—paperwork that police officers are required to complete—after a wide variety of "stop" encounters from 1998 and the first three months of 1999. Under *Terry v. Ohio* (392 U.S. 1 1968), a police officer can detain a civilian if the officer can articulate a "reasonable suspicion" that criminal activity is "afoot." (Even without "reasonable suspicion," the police may lawfully approach civilians, but to "stop" people means detaining them against their will and requires "reasonable suspicion.") The report found that minorities were stopped in numbers that were disproportionate to their numbers in the population:

> Blacks comprise 25.6 percent of the city's population, yet 50.6 percent of all persons "stopped" during the period were black. Hispanics comprise 23.7 percent of the city's population, yet 33.0 percent of all "stops" were of Hispanics. By contrast, whites are 43.4 percent of the city's population, but accounted for only 12.9 percent of all "stops." (NYSOAG 1999)

Analysis revealed that the disparity in stop rates was particularly high in areas that are predominantly white. In precincts where blacks and Hispanics each represent less than 10 percent of the total population, they accounted for more than half of the total stops. This finding seems consistent with the *Harvard Law Review* suggestion that an officer's sense that someone was "'out of place' may be more a product of conscious or subconscious resistance to racial integration than an empirically true description" (1988, p. 1510).

Another finding was that in precincts with the highest overall rates of "stop and frisk" activity, people of color made up the majority of the population. The Office of the Attorney General, with the aid of Columbia University's Center for Violence Research and Prevention, also performed a regression analysis indicating that differing crime rates alone cannot fully explain the increased rate of stops of minorities. After accounting for the effect of differing crime rates, the analysis showed blacks were stopped 23 percent more often than whites and Hispanics were stopped 39 percent more often (NYSOAG 1999). Finally, the report examined the number of stops that resulted in an arrest. They found that "the NYPD 'stopped' 9.5 blacks for every one 'stop' which resulted in the arrest of a black, 8.8 Hispanics for every one 'stop' that resulted in the arrest of an Hispanic, and 7.9 whites for every one 'stop' that resulted in the arrest of one white" (NYSOAG 1999).

Excessive identification of minorities is not only a problem of local law enforcement agencies; it extends to the elite federal agencies as well. The National Narcotics Intelligence Consumers Committee (NNICC) consisted of representatives of the Central Intelligence Agency, U.S. Coast Guard, U.S. Customs Service, Department of Defense, Drug Enforcement Administration, Federal Bureau of investigation, Immigration and Naturalization Service, Internal Revenue Service, National Institute on Drug Abuse, Department of State, and Department of Treasury. Their report on the supply of illicit drugs to the United States mentions Colombian drug mafias, Mexicans, African American street gangs, Dominicans, Cubans, Haitians, Jamaicans, and Puerto Rican criminal groups, Chinese, Nigerian, and West African groups, Middle Eastern traffickers, Lebanese, Israelis, Pakistanis, Turks, Afghans, Burmese, Thai, Laotian, Cambodian, Russian, Filipino, Taiwanese, and Korean.

There are a few references to domestic production, but only one specific reference to whites, the market for LSD being white college students. Although whites own planes and boats, they seem to be one of the few groups in the world not involved in drug smuggling according to the NNICC. Given low levels of minority wealth and ownership of the economy (see Chapter 2), one would expect that whites might make an appearance as money launderers, but the report mentions only casinos and notes that Native Americans operate them in almost every state. Money laundering also involves Pakistanis and Southwest Asia's underground banking system as well as Russians in the U.S. Technology generally, but apparently not whites specifically, also appear to facilitate the laundering of drug money.

The New York Office of the Attorney General reported that "Civil Rights without personal safety is a mirage; policing without respect for the rule of law is not policing at all" (1999). Bias undermines the legitimacy of the use of coercive power and can make the criminal justice system no better than the criminals it pursues (Reiman 1998a). It is in this vein that pretextual stops based on racial bias erode trust in the system of justice and create the cynicism and hostility Clear spoke of in his "truth and sentencing." Harris agrees that "pretext stops capture some who are guilty but at an unacceptably high societal cost," because they "undermine public confidence in law enforcement, erode the legitimacy of the criminal justice system, and make police work that much more difficult and dangerous" (1999). In addition, "pretextual traffic stops fuel the belief that the police are not only unfair and biased, but untruthful as well" because if the stop was about enforcement of the traffic code, there would be no need for a drug search:

> Stopping a driver for a traffic offense when the officer's real purpose is drug interdiction is a lie—a legally sanctioned one, to be sure, but a lie nonetheless. It should surprise no one that those who are the victims of police discrimination regard the testimony and statements of police with suspicion. If jurors don't believe truthful police testimony, crimes are left unpunished, law enforcement becomes much less effective, and the very people who need the police most are left less protected. (Harris 1999)

Although the Court upheld pretextual stops (Blast 1997) in *Whren*, it did not decide any racial discrimination issues raised under an equal protection challenge. The challenge could prevail under other precedents, such as *Yick Wo v. Hopkins*, in which the Court held that even if "the law itself be fair on its face and impartial in appearance, yet if it is applied and administered by public authority with an evil eye and an unequal hand the denial of equal justice is still within the prohibition of the Constitution" (118 US 356 1886). Such a challenge would need to have much more data than are available at the present time, but an increasing number of jurisdictions are starting to collect data on traffic stops. A further move in the right direction would be passage of a federal Traffic Stops Statistics Act, which would require the widespread collection of racial data on police stops.

Criminal Justice Processing

As part of sentencing reform, many jurisdictions are enacting "truth in sentencing" laws, which require offenders to serve at least 85 percent of their sentence. Criminologist Todd Clear notes that the length of sentence is a small part of the "truth" about the irrationality behind the sentence. He imagines a judge telling the full truth:

> For the crime of selling drugs, I sentence you to 10 years in prison. I am doing so even though we know that this sentence will not prevent any more drugs from being sold, and that it will probably result in someone not now involved in the drug trade being recruited to take your place while you are locked up. I impose this sentence knowing that the main reason you have been caught and convicted is that we have concentrated our police presence in the community where you live, and that had you lived where I live, your drug use and sales would probably have gone undetected. I impose this sentence knowing it will cost the taxpayers over a quarter of a million dollars to carry it out, money we desperately need for the schools and health care in the area where you live, but instead it will go into the pockets of corrections officers and prison builders who live miles away from here and have no interest in the quality of life in your neighborhood. I impose this sentence knowing it will most likely make you a worse citizen, not a better one, leaving you embittered toward the law and damaged by your years spent behind bars. You think you have trouble making it now? Wait until after you have served a decade of your life wasting in a prison cell. And I impose this sentence knowing that it will make your children, your cousins, and your nephews have even less respect for the law, since they will come to see you as having been singled out for this special punishment, largely due to the color of your skin and the amount of money in your pocket. I impose this sentence knowing that its only purpose is to respond to an angry public and a few rhetorically excited politicians, even though I know this sentence will not calm either of them down in the slightest. This is the truth of my sentence. (in Welch 1999, p. x)

In this paragraph, Clear identifies a range of problems in the criminal justice system that relate to race—the drug laws, selective enforcement, the destruction of communities, and growing disrespect for the law. The bias against minorities is seen as so strong that it feeds into perceptions about genocide discussed above.

The conclusion that the criminal justice system is "out to get" minorities might strike some as exaggerated. However, an extensive report by the *Harvard Law Review* noted that there was "substantial underenforcement of antidiscrimination norms" and that "increasingly sophisticated empirical studies indicate disparities in the treatment of criminal suspects and defendants that are difficult to explain by reference to decisional factors other than racial discrimination" (1988, p. 1476). Identifying the extent to which discrimination does exist is complicated by methodological issues that can suppress findings of discrimination. First, research that examines one stage—say sentencing—may not reveal patterns of discrimination that accumulate through multiple stages of criminal justice processing. (Indeed, reforms like mandatory sentencing do not ensure equality if they simply push the discretion to an earlier part of the system.) Even multistage studies may not go far enough, given that criminal code statutes, prosecutorial charging practices, jury-pool eligibility, how judges are selected, and unofficial processes (such as being questioned by the police) can also influence treatment in the criminal justice system.

Second, research that does not perform separate analysis by the race of the victim runs the risk of two separate biases canceling each other out. Research has typically found that a black-on-white crime is treated as more serious than a black-on-black crime, and the average outcome for these two black offenders may be similar to the outcome for white offenders. Third, another major limitation in assessing the extent to which discrimination occurs is that reliable national data on criminal justice system involvement are available only for blacks, whites, and "others," limiting discussion mainly to black-white differences. For instance, when Hispanics are categorized as white—a frequent practice when data are dichotomized as black/white and ethnicity is not reported separately—the level of discrimination is suppressed. In addition, discrimination against Hispanics becomes invisible and impossible to document.

Studies can also exaggerate the level of discrimination when they fail to control for many of the legally relevant variables (type of crime, strength of evidence, etc). However, to the extent racism is present in decision making, statistical control for prior record of an offender will suppress the effects of discrimination (because one is controlling for the effects of previous discrimination that resulted in the prior conviction). Although few data sets or studies are perfect because potential variables are missing, the key factor is whether the study includes the major variables. Formulas exist for examining the potential effect of omitted variables (Gastwirth and Nayak 1997).

Finally, disproportionate offending and discrimination are frequently presented as if they are mutually exclusive, competing phenomena. Even if, for example, blacks do disproportionately offend, this does not mean they are not discriminated against. Blumstein (1995) found that 20–25 percent of the black incarceration rate (representing about 10,000 black inmates) is not explained by disproportionate offending.

Victimization

Chapter 2 noted that crime victims are disproportionately from the lower economic classes. Minorities are disproportionately poor, so it follows that they are also disproportionately victims of crime. The figures that follow illustrate the racial differences, but official statistics capture only part of the violence present in the lives of minorities. If one accepts Brown's (1987) definition of violence as any act that violates, infringes upon, disregards, abuses, or denies another (whether or not physical harm is involved), minority life can be seen as a continuing state of structural violence because of poverty and racism, punctuated by officially recorded direct acts of violence.

Figure 3.1 presents a breakdown of victimization rates for American Indians and all races. The graph clearly illustrates that Native Americans have a substantially higher likelihood of victimization for all crimes except homicide. The victimization rate for all the crimes listed is about twice as high for Native Americans as the combined rate for all races. Figure 3.2 contains a more comprehensive racial breakdown for victims of violent crimes, and Figure 3.3 shows the more detailed homicide rates by race. Overall, American Indians experience violent victimization at more than twice the rate of any other group, although blacks are *by far* the most likely to experience homicide (Bureau of Justice Statistics 1999a, p. v). Table 3.4 reports victimization rates for the same crimes by ethnicity rather than race. The general finding is that Hispanics have a higher victimization rate than non-Hispanics, with the exception being the crime of simple assault. Within this category of simple assault, however, Hispanics have a higher rate of simple assault with a minor injury, but non-Hispanics have greater levels of simple assault without injury.

Table 3.4
Rates of Victimization by Ethnicity
(Rates per 1,000 persons age 12 and older)

	Hispanic	Non-Hispanic
Violent victimizations	43.0	38.3
Rape and sexual assault	1.5	1.4
Aggravated assault	10.4	8.3
Simple assault	24.0	24.7

Source: U.S. Department of Justice 1998, Table 3.8, p 177.

Figure 3.1
Average Annual Number of Violent Victimizations per 1,000
Persons Age 12 or Older*, 1992–96

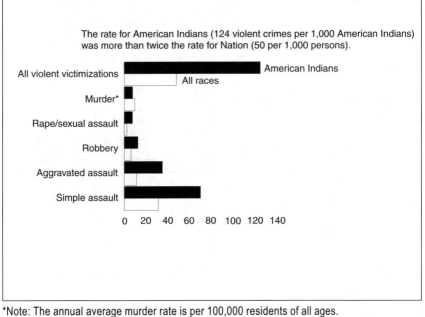

*Note: The annual average murder rate is per 100,000 residents of all ages.
Source: Bureau of Justice Statistics, 1999.

Figure 3.2
Violent Victimizations, Average Annual Rate, 1992–96
(Number per 100,000 persons age 12 or older)

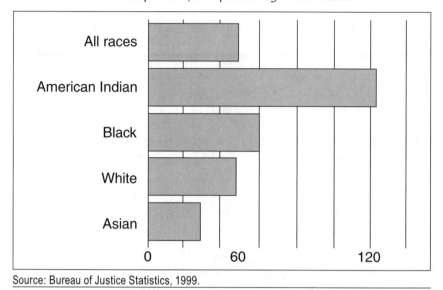

Source: Bureau of Justice Statistics, 1999.

Figure 3.3
Murder, Average Annual Rate, 1992–96
(Number per 100,000 persons)

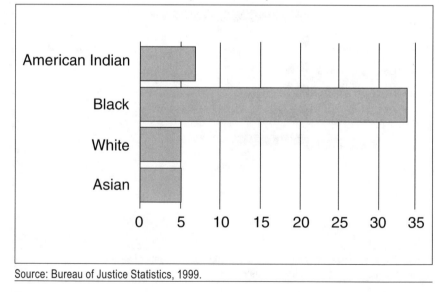

Source: Bureau of Justice Statistics, 1999.

Most victimizations are perpetrated by an offender of the same race and are thus *intra*racial crimes, although American Indians are the most likely of any racial group to experience a violent victimization by someone of a different race (Bureau of Justice Statistics 1999, p. iii). The pattern of intraracial offending is consistent with strong patterns of racial segregation (Massey and Denton 1993). One subset of crimes involving different races or *inter*racial crimes, is hate crimes, or bias-motivated offenses. The FBI defines hate crimes or bias crimes as involving crimes against person or property motivated at least in part by the perpetrator's bias against a "race, religion, disability, sexual orientation, or ethnicity/national origin" (UCR 1997, p. 59). This definition excludes gender and thus does not include any violence against women, including rape, as a hate crime. (The purpose and controversy over sentencing enhancement for these crimes is discussed in Box 3.4).

Box 3.4

Hate Crime Legislation

As the United States strives to be a more tolerant and inclusive society, legislators have attempted to deal with the problems posed by hate crimes and hate speech. Many legislators do not believe that existing assault and harassment laws are a sufficient response to expressions of hatred that involve an extra harm related to intimidation or terrorism. In *R.A.V. v. St Paul* (507 US 377, 1992), the U.S. Supreme Court invalidated a law making it a crime to display objects such as a burning cross that "arouses anger, alarm or resentment in others on the basis of race, color, creed, religion or gender." In addition to other problems with the ordinance, the majority of the court found it was an impermissible regulation on the content of speech. Such regulation is impermissible under the First Amendment's guarantee of free speech, which applies even to offensive speech.

R.A.V. did not resolve questions about sentencing enhancements for bias-motivated assaults—harsher sentences for hate crimes (rather than prohibitions on offensive speech). The Supreme Court unanimously upheld such laws in *Wisconsin v. Mitchell* (508 US 476, 1993). In that case, Mitchell, a black teenager, had been watching the civil rights film *Mississippi Burning* with friends. When they were outside later, the group saw a young white boy and Mitchell asked the group if they felt "hyped up to move on some white people." He added: "You all want to fuck somebody up? There goes a white boy; go get him" (quoted in *State v. Mitchell* 485 NW 2d 807, 809 1992). The Court held that the Wisconsin statute was not aimed at punishing protected speech or expression and that motive could be a consideration of the sentencing judge. Likewise, previous speech and utterances by defendants are frequently admitted into evidence in court to establish motive. The Court found that the state provided an adequate basis for singling out bias crimes for enhanced penalties because they are "more likely to provoke retaliatory crimes, inflict distinct emotional harms on their victims, and incite community unrest" (508 US 476, 1993).

For more information about hate crimes, including the best practices for dealing with them and teaching tolerance, see the hate crimes resources at *http://www.stopviolence.com*.

For 1997, race and ethnicity combined accounted for 70 percent of bias crime incidents, with religion and sexual orientation contributing 15 percent each (UCR 1997, pp. 60–61). Of the offenders for whom race was known, 71 percent were white, 23 percent black, 0.1 percent American Indian/Alaskan Native, 2 percent Asian/Pacific Islander; the remainder were multiracial (UCR 1997, p. 62). Not all crimes by minorities involve antiwhite bias, because members of some minorities have prejudice and antipathy toward other minorities, even though we tend to dichotomize race into "white" and "minority" (or just "black"). Hate crime statistics should be interpreted with caution, because any biases present in the police force will affect the likelihood of officers being willing to record the offense as bias motivated and fill out the additional paperwork. Also, future increases in the number of reported hate crimes may well be due to more complete reporting practices and greater sensitivity on the part of police.

Identification and Adjudication

In 1998, 8.4 million persons age 18 years or older were arrested. Of these, 67.3 percent were white, 30.5 percent were black, and around 2 percent were American Indian/Alaskan Native or Asian/Pacific Islander. By contrast, about 83 percent of the U.S. population is white, 13 percent is black, and other racial categories make up 5 percent of the total population. The only arrest categories in which whites are overrepresented are driving under the influence and drunkenness. Blacks are overrepresented in nearly all other arrest categories. Their overrepresentation is most noticeable in the categories for gambling, robbery, and murder and nonnegligent manslaughter, where they make up over 50 percent of all arrestees. By contrast,

Asians or Pacific Islanders are underrepresented in every arrest category with the exception of gambling (U.S. Department of Justice, 1999).

Compared to blacks, a greater percentage of whites and members of "other" racial groups are convicted of felony property offenses and a smaller percentage are convicted of felony drug offenses. In 1996, whites were most often convicted in state courts of property offenses (34 percent) and drug offenses (30 percent) followed by violent offenses (16 percent). By contrast, blacks were most often convicted of drug offenses (42 percent), followed by property offenses (26 percent), and violent offenses (18 percent). Members of "other" racial groups were most likely to be convicted of property offenses (36 percent), followed by drug offenses (28 percent) and violent offenses (20 percent) (Levin, Langan, and Brown 2000).

Prosecutors have wide discretion about which cases to pursue and what bargains to offer in exchange for guilty pleas. These decisions become all the more important with sentencing guidelines, which effectively remove discretion from sentencing judges and make prosecutorial decisions, more important. Unfortunately, there is little independent review of prosecutorial decisions as there can be with judicial decisions, so bias is less likely to be scrutinized. When it comes to black defendants, "statistical studies indicate that prosecutors are more likely to pursue full prosecution, file more severe charges and seek more stringent penalties than in cases involving nonminority defendants" (*Harvard Law Review* 1988, p. 1520).

Decisions about the severity of a crime can easily reflect conscious or unconscious racism and stereotypes that relate to dangerousness, moral depravity, and so on. For example, Native Americans receive harsher treatment related to stereotypes of "drunken Indians" or "savages." They may be seen as "outsiders" to the community, and court decisions may reflect paternalistic attitudes that "locking up the drunken Indians was the best thing they could do for them" (in Lynch and Patterson 1991, p. 108). Also with Native Americans, cultural factors can hinder communication of important aspects of the case and of Anglo legal concepts or procedures (Welch 1996a, p. 284).

A variety of studies indicate that black-on-white crime is most likely to be seen as serious in contrast to white-on-black or black-on-black crime (*Harvard Law Review* 1988). For example, Radalet (1989) reviewed the records of almost 16,000 executions that had occurred in the U.S. between 1608 and 1989 to look for cases in which whites had been executed for killing blacks. He was able to find only 30 cases—fewer than two-tenths of 1 percent. Some of these cases occurred during slavery, indicating that the important dynamic was class, not race. In remaining cases, Radalet found examples where defendants had killed whites but could not be prosecuted because of lack of evidence, when defendants had long records or previous sentences to life imprisonment, and where the occupational status of blacks "clearly surpassed that of the white assailant," including cases "in which the defendants were marginal members of the community, perhaps being labeled as 'white trash'" (1989, 534–535).

More recently, Bernhard Goetz, the New York subway vigilante, was acquitted of attempted murder charges after he shot four young black men he claimed were trying to rob him. They looked and sounded menacing when they asked him for $5, he said, and the defense played the "racial fear" card by invoking the image of "innocent whiteness surrounded by threatening blackness" (in Levine 1997, p. 540). As one commentator suggested, "Just try to imagine whether a pistol-toting black man would have had such sweeping vindication [from the jury] had he shot four white teenagers because two of them approached him and one of them had a 'shine' in his eyes and a 'funny' smile" (p. 540).

Further, both empirical data and mock trial experiments indicate that minority defendants face a greater risk of receiving unjust verdicts when their jury does not adequately represent minorities (*Harvard Law Review* 1988). When the defendant is a minority, "white jurors are less likely to show compassion, and are less likely to be influenced by group discussion," so the defendant is more likely to be "found guilty and to be punished severely" (p. 1560). Race matters more than any other personal characteristic of the defendant, and a survey of "experimental research led one writer to state that there is a tendency among white jurors to convict black defendants in situations where whites would be acquitted" (Levine 1997, pp. 528–529). Also, nonminority defendants who have minority attorneys to represent them do not fare as well as those who have nonminority attorneys (*Harvard Law Review* 1988).

Juries with more black and Hispanic representation tend to acquit more, but this pattern may or may not be based on jury nullification, in which a jury acquits an obviously guilty person as a protest or expression of solidarity with the defendant. One observer notes that "even when cases entail heart-wrenching mitigating circumstances or absurd laws, jurors are reluctant to acquit those whose guilt is indisputable" (Levine 1997, p. 537). Rather, their experiences with racism and greater distrust of police, based partly on "driving while black" and racial profiling, make minorities more suspicious of the prosecution's case, especially when based substantially on police testimony. In contrast, whites' interactions with police may be more benign and lead to less skepticism about the testimony, which is accorded greater weight.

Punishment and Imprisonment

The United States is a world leader in the rate at which it incarcerates its citizens (Dyer 2000). Over 5.5 million people are under control of the correctional system—in jail, in prison, on probation, or on parole—which amounts to about 3 percent of the nation's population (U.S. Department of Justice 1998, Table 6.2, p. 462). As indicated in Figures 3.4 and 3.5, control over minorities is much higher, with 2 percent of whites and 9 percent of minorities under control of the correctional system. The disparities are glaring because they reflect

Figure 3.4
Adults Under Correctional Control, 1997
(Total per 100,000 adults)

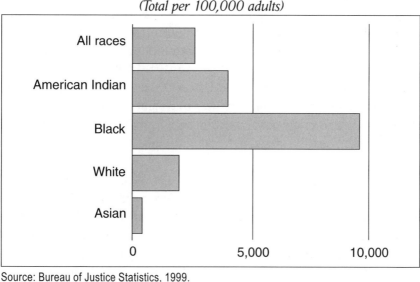

Source: Bureau of Justice Statistics, 1999.

the cumulative biases from all stages of criminal justice administration and additional outside factors, as indicated in Figure 3.6.

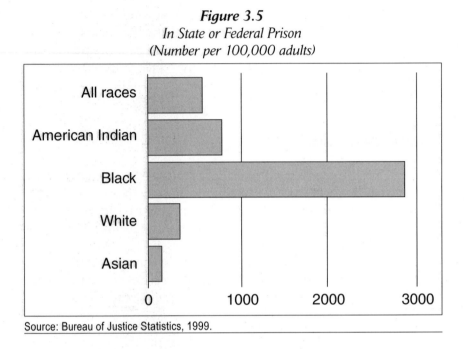

Figure 3.5
In State or Federal Prison
(Number per 100,000 adults)

Source: Bureau of Justice Statistics, 1999.

In 1998, blacks accounted for 35 percent of the almost 3.5 million adults on probation and 44 percent of the 700,000 adults on parole (BJS 1999b). In 1997, they accounted for 50 percent of the 1.2 million adults in state or federal prison (BJS 1999c). White men are incarcerated at a rate of 491 per 100,000 while black men are incarcerated at a rate more than *six* times that figure—3,235 per 100,000. The incarceration figures for women show similar discrepancies, with black women as the category showing the highest rates of increase in recent years.

The numbers presented are for a single year, and the Bureau of Justice Statistics recently calculated the *lifetime* likelihood of going to state and federal prison (Bureau of Justice Statistics 1997b), which is presented in Table 3.5. Their calculations were based on constant 1991 rates of incarceration, and thus produce an understated magnitude of both the likelihood and the racial disparity (both incarceration rates and minority overrepresentation continued to increase). Even

Figure 3.6
Underlying Factors That Contribute to Minority Overrepresentation

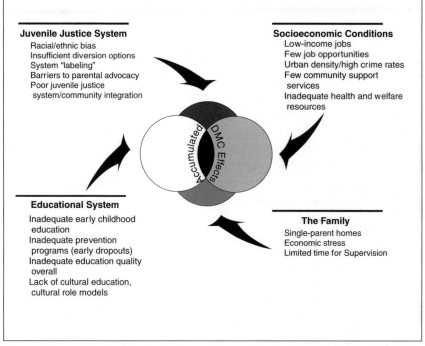

Source: "Disproportionate Minority Confinement Lesson Learned from Five States" by Devine, Wolbaugh, and Jenkins. Office of Juvenile and Delinquency Prevention, Dec. 1998. See http://www.ncjrs.org/94612.pdf.

with these conservative assumptions, BJS concluded that "a black male in the United States today has greater than a 1 in 4 chance of going to prison during his lifetime, while a Hispanic male has a 1 in 6 chance and a white male has a 1 in 23 chance of serving time" (Bureau of Justice Statistics 1997b). The lifetime likelihood for women is overall lower, but reflects the same general pattern of disparity: 0.5 percent for white women, 1.5 percent for Hispanic women, and 3.6 percent for black women (p. 3).

An important but frequently neglected aspect of the racial justice of incarceration is Immigration and Naturalization Service "processing centers." But as one INS official noted, "It is a jail, albeit a minimum security jail. The sign outside may say it's a processing center, but that's just semantics" (in Welch 1996b, p. 180). Such centers hold a variety of undocumented, disproportionately nonwhite immigrants while their status and case are decided. Despite complaints about food, poor medical care, lack of access to lawyers and human rights violations, few watchdog groups are admitted (Welch 1996a, 1996b, 2000).

As a nation, we are "trapped somewhere between the Statue of Liberty's welcome and the unwanted nonstop flood of poor people who, by land and sea—seldom by air—will pay almost any price, take any risk, to enter the United States" (National Catholic Reporter 1999, p. 28). Recent changes in immigration law have served to tighten restrictions on who can enter and who can stay. As a result, INS facilities have become increasingly crowded, and criticism of their conditions has mounted. As with regular prisons, the INS has started contracting with the private prison industry for additional facilities to relieve overcrowding. In New York, one

> 200-bed facility—operated by the Wackenhut Corrections Corpora-
> tion, the self-described "global leader in privatized corrections," in a
> five-year, $49 million contract with the INS—is also a harsh symbol
> of how America protects its wealth. Such prisons stand at the cross-
> roads of anti-immigrant anxiety and the roaring economy of incar-
> ceration, raking in profits and, at the same time, barring the
> supposed threat of teeming masses coming to snatch those profits
> away. In emblematic terms, INS detention is a veritable fortress of
> the new American prosperity. (Solomon 1999, p. 47)

Table 3.5
Percentage of Males Likely to Ever Go to Prison

Not Yet incarcerated by age	Males Likely to Ever Go to Prison		
	All persons	White men	Black men
Birth	5.1%	4.4%	28.5%
20	4.5	4.1	25.3
25	3.1	3.0	17.3
30	2.1	2.1	10.8
35	1.4	1.5	6.5
40	.9	1.1	3.6
45	.6	.8	2.1

Source: Bureau of Justice Statistics (1997).

Workers

Compared to the Segregation Era (1890s–1960s), some progress has been made in employing racial and ethnic minorities in the criminal justice system. Between 1960 and 1990, African American representation on police forces nearly tripled, from 3.6 percent to 10 percent (Walker, Spohn, and DeLone 1995). In 1997, non-Hispanic whites constituted 78.5 percent of all full-time sworn personnel in local police departments, while non-Hispanic blacks and Hispanics (of any race) made up the remaining 11.7 percent and 7.8 percent respectively.

These figures indicate that whites continue to be overrepresented in police work, while Hispanics in particular tend to be underrepresented, and blacks are more or less proportionately represented. (As discussed in Chapters 4 and 5, women of all races continue to be grossly underrepresented in police work.) Larger departments are more likely to employ a greater percentage of non-white employees. For example, around one-third of full-time personnel in departments serving 250,000 people or more are nonwhite, compared to only around 10 percent in departments serving populations less than 50,000. Needless to say, minorities are more underrepresented in the positions of police chief (Bureau of Justice Statistics 2000b).

Whites continue to be overrepresented among Presidential appointees to U.S. court judgeships. Around 90 percent of those appointed by Presidents Johnson, Nixon, Ford, Reagan, and Bush were white, as were 80 percent of those appointed by President Carter. By contrast, around 74 percent of President Clinton's 248 appointees were white, 20 percent were black, and 5 percent were Hispanic (Bureau of Justice Statistics 2000a). In correctional work, whites and Hispanics are slightly underrepresented as correctional officers (making up only around 68 percent and 6.4 percent, respectively), while blacks are overrepresented. Although only around 12 percent of the United States population, blacks are nearly 24 percent of all correctional officers (Bureau of the Census 1990). According to 1998 data collected by the American Correctional Association (1999), approximately 73 percent of the wardens and superintendents in adult facilities are white, 21 percent are black, and 6 percent are Hispanic.

The implication of these figures is that criminal justice is a dispro-portionately white male occupation. Although non-Hispanic whites make up only around 70 percent of the U.S. population, they make up around 80 percent or more of all police officers, judges, attorneys, and stenographers. As is also discussed in the next chapters, the pro-portionate representation of racial and ethnic minority groups is important for several reasons. First, employment discrimination based on race or ethnicity is illegal and must be eliminated. Also, it is impor-tant to have a system that reflects the composition of the United States. Members of a variety of races and ethnicities have diverse experiences and insights that can and should be incorporated into how the criminal justice system does business.

Affirmative action programs have been undertaken in an effort to remedy the effects of past discrimination on the basis of race, gender, ethnicity, religion, and age. Affirmative action is needed because atti-tudes and habits of prejudice in some cases undermine common sense. In 1950, William H. Parker almost did not become police chief of Los Angeles because he was a Catholic. During the 1960s, Parker described Latinos as "not far removed from the wild tribes of Mex-ico." And being African American would have denied LAPD Chief Bernard C. Parks his current job (Carmona 2000, p. B9).

Stemming from the civil rights movement of the 1960s, affirma-tive action is set up to give special consideration to women and minority men in employment, education, and contracting decisions. Walker, Spohn, and DeLone (1996) describe the process by which affirmative action programs are implemented. These include taking a census of employees to identify whether areas exist in which racial minorities and women are underutilized. If underutilization does exist, the employer must develop a plan to eliminate it. For example, a police department may undertake active outreach to increase the number of racial minority applicants.

It is important to recognize, however, that not all recruiting efforts are created equal. The New York City Police Department (NYPD) is 67.4 percent white in a city that's nearly 60 percent racial or ethnic minorities. Hiring data and a recent city audit indicate that affirmative action efforts were set back dramatically after Mayor Rudy Giuliani took office in 1994 (White 1999). For example, an audit carried out by the Equal Employment Practices Commission (EEPC) reviewed hires from July 1992 to February 1997. The audit cited the NYPD with repeatedly failing to comply with New York City's official affirmative action guidelines. Consider the following:

- The 1996 recruitment drive spent far less money and covered only a two-month period compared to the 1993 drive, which lasted eight months.

- The NYPD's EEO office was "minimally involved" in the 1996 recruitment drive, and the Deputy Commission in charge of the EEO officer was "kept out of the loop" on important issues related to hiring practices.

- Though the NYPD claimed it routinely advertised positions in minority neighborhoods, only one position was so advertised.

- The audit was supposed to review hires from July 1992 to December 1994; however, NYPD did not submit some critical data until December 1996—19 months after the audit began.

- After the EEPC audit concluded, the Giuliani administration cut funding for a program that encouraged students at City University's John Jay College of Criminal Justice to join the NYPD by helping pay their tuition. Sixty-five percent of the students placed under the program were minorities.

Although numeric representation of racial and ethnic minorities in an occupation is important, it still represents only one aspect of the social reality. With a more diverse police force in impoverished ethnic communities, black and Hispanic officers may find that their community loyalty is questioned. Blacks and Hispanics hostile to the police may challenge officers' "racial pride." The complexities of race have been highlighted in the discussion of police work perhaps more than any other occupation. Two examples are illustrative. In July 2000, a black man, Thomas Jones, was stopped in north Philadelphia for driving a stolen car. He crashed the car and fled on foot but was tackled by the police. During the scuffle, Jones grabbed an officer's gun and began shooting before jumping into a nearby empty patrol car. Although police shot him several times, he managed to commandeer a police patrol car and stage another getaway. He drove the police car about a mile before being cornered by police. Videotape from a local helicopter television news crew shows that after an officer pulled Jones from the car onto the street, about two dozen officers surrounded Jones. For a half minute, four black and six white officers punched or kicked Jones. Most of the punches or kicks were delivered by three officers, two of whom were black.

Some individuals point to the fact that black as well as white officers threw punches as evidence that the incident was about brutality and excessive force, not race. Others observe that brutality occurs in minority officers as well as white ones. Also, black officers are capable of holding prejudices about black offenders. Ronald Hampton of the National Black Police Association observes, "Success [in a department] is defined in white male terms. So these guys internalize the racist, oppressive culture of the police department in order to succeed" (Ripley 2000).

Further, a *New York Times* article, "Why Harlem Drug Cops Don't Discuss Race," describes the influence of race in the lives of undercover narcotics officers (Winerip 2000). Undercover work requires the involvement of detectives whose dark skin permits them to blend into certain neighborhoods, a fact readily acknowledged by one of the supervisors, Sergeant Brogli, a five-foot-tall white woman. For example, all undercover officers fear mistakenly shooting an unarmed person in no small part because it could destroy his or her career. But dark-skinned officers have an additional fear: that a white officer will accidentally shoot them.

Undercover officers are also concerned about racial profiling. Sergeant Brogli and a dozen undercover black and Hispanic undercover officers recognize, however, that racial profiling (e.g., going "cold" into a corner full of young black and brown men and trying to buy drugs) is not only poor police work, but dangerous. Detective Gonzalez, a Dominican, says that he does not attempt to make a buy unless investigators have gathered information such as what dealer is operating; whether the dealer is selling in grams or ounces, crack, coke, or heroin; the brand name being sold, and other information that will permit him to know what he is asking for. That is where Detective Gonzalez draws the line between good police work and racial profiling. "It's insulting to walk up to a guy just because he's black or Dominican standing on a corner and say, 'Who's working?'" When white sergeants have ordered Gonzales and other black and Hispanic officers to do just that, they report that they go up, walk past, and tell the sergeant nothing is going on.

These two examples illustrate the limitations of essentializing or oversimplifying race relations in an occupational setting. Statements such as "All white officers engage in racial profiling" or "Black officers would never engage in police brutality" are too simplistic. The social reality is that people are influenced not only by their personal attitudes and experiences but also by the context in which they live and work. Whites are capable of recognizing the problems of racial profiling and brutality, and racial and ethnic minority officers are capable of succumbing to them. To suggest otherwise is to diminish everyone by treating people as if their actions are solely dictated by their racial categorization rather than by a variety of occupational, organizational, situational, and larger social contexts.

Media Presentations

In September 1989, President George Bush gave a televised speech about the drug problem in the United States. To dramatize the point, he held up a bag of crack cocaine that he said had been purchased right across the street from the White House. Media coverage of drug issues increased and public concern about drugs skyrocketed. Following the speech, the Gallup Poll recorded its highest ever response to the question about whether drug abuse is the most important problem facing the United States (Bureau of Justice Statistics 1992). Congress and state legislators responded with another round of tougher mandatory sentences. And Keith Jackson, an 18-year-old black high school student, was indicted for drugs.

The story behind the "political theater" of the prop in Bush's speech was not well covered in the media. Jackson had no previous record and was a student in good standing; he only occasionally sold drugs for extra money because the area of Washington, D.C. in which he lived had severely limited job opportunities. His drug sale pattern did not normally take him near the White House, and he did not know where it was. Drug Enforcement Administration agents had to drive him there so he could make the sale. The DEA's special agent in charge of D.C. admitted in court, "We had to manipulate him to get him down there. It wasn't easy" (Thompson 1989, p. C1; Thompson and Isikoff 1989, p. D6). Worse still, a DEA agent charged with videotaping the transaction was attacked by a homeless woman in the park because she thought he was taping her. The jury chuckled and the presiding judge likened the event to the slapstick "Keystone cops."

The reality for Jackson was not so funny. He was held without bail and faced a mandatory 12-year sentence in prison. The first trial ended in a hung jury, but the second one convicted him of drug charges stemming from drug sales other than the one near the White House. Judge Sporkin—a former CIA general counsel appointed to the bench by Reagan—imposed a 10-year sentence without the possibility of parole under mandatory sentencing guidelines for crack cocaine (Thompson 1990b, p. B11). The judge said he regretted having to impose a sentence of 10 years (at a cost to the taxpayers of $175,000) and hoped Bush would commute the sentence (he didn't).

The image on the television screen was of another black man in handcuffs for selling drugs. What was covered was the rhetorically excited politicians calling for more and harsher penalties. What went uncovered and unsaid was the truth about sentencing discussed by Clear earlier in this chapter—the lack of jobs and opportunities, the need for money to go to schools rather than prisons, that most of the crack users and dealers are white, the perception that Jackson was singled out, that he will emerge from prison worse, and that those who know him will have less respect for the law.

Television coverage seamlessly re-creates an array of stereotypical images of a drug-plagued America and of the ongoing struggle for law and order, rather than exposing or examining the politics of "whose law and what order." The association of crime with race is re-created rather than challenged. Even "reality television" constructs distorted pictures. Segal, in her discussion of what gets left on the cutting room floor, notes the case of a police chief who hassled a man arrested for marijuana distribution. The chief threatened to seize the man's car and house, then take away his child. The defendant asserted his right to an attorney and in response to threats of asset forfeiture asked if this is Mexico or the United States. After getting no concessions, the chief walked away saying: "That's the first white guy I've ever felt like beating the fucking shit out of" (Segal 1993, p. 55). Segal notes that this footage is too much reality for "reality based" television. However, if more examples like this one were on prime time rather than on the cutting room floor, the country would be less surprised by racial incidents like the beating of Rodney King and the differing perceptions whites and blacks have of the criminal justice system. Instead, when the episode airs, Segal says the chief will be portrayed as a hero protecting society from dangerous drug dealers.

The repeated presentation of these images and the telling of these stories provide the audience with shared frameworks for understanding ideas like "crime" and "criminal." Such understandings, in turn, support "sincere fictions" that help people discriminate while keeping their self-image of being good, even tolerant, persons. Although some Americans still sincerely endorse beliefs about black inferiority, low intelligence, or laziness, sincere fictions in modern racism take a different form: "What many whites with modern racist tendencies do consciously feel is some amalgam of negative affect (especially fear and resentment), rejection of the political agenda commonly endorsed by black leaders, and denial that racism is still a problem" (in Barlow 1998, p. 151). Whites thus talk about the crime problem rather than race problem and about "getting tough" on crime rather than repressing blacks. Advocating a "war on crime" has disturbing, if unspoken implications, when "talking about crime *is* talking about race" (Barlow 1998, p. 151, emphasis in original).

Summary and Conclusions

Part of the ideology of racism makes it difficult for whites to understand the vulnerability minorities feel, which seems exaggerated to whites who have had few occasions to think about the privileges conferred on them by their racial classification. Even whites who would demand a large sum for a visitor telling them they had to live as a black are aware that being white does give them some protections, but it is a large step to internalizing the sense of marginality that comes from living every day as a minority in a white country.

Unfortunately, even in the face of history and a mountain of social indicators that all illustrate minority disadvantage, many whites are still unable to grasp their racial privilege. In spite of a wide variety of data about inequality in the administration of criminal justice, politicians clamor for more of the same practices that are causing the problem. Indeed, there are even calls to bring back the chain gang in spite of its long and obvious symbol as a tool of racial oppression (Gorman 1997). Meanwhile, communities are being destroyed, and the experience of incarceration makes it harder for inmates to be productive community members upon release. Even though released inmates have "done their time," the government is developing increasingly sophisticated computerized records that will help ensure the stigma does not fade. Thus, "It is not fanciful to worry about the emergence of a sophisticated computer quarantine that has profound implications for social structure" because it isolates and further marginalizes the poor, especially the black poor (Gordon 1990, p. 89; Gandy 1993).

All of the foregoing should help clarify why many minorities picture themselves as profoundly marginal and expendable, leaving them with a sense of alienation perhaps best captured in Derrick Bell's "Chronicle of the Space Traders" (1990). In this story, blacks as a group are sacrificed to aliens for gold to retire the national debt, a chemical to clean up pollution, and a limitless source of clean energy. Following a national referendum and a Supreme Court decision, blacks are lined up and turned over to the aliens—in chains, just as they entered the country hundreds of years ago. The moral of this story for Bell is that we have made no racial progress; whites would sacrifice blacks for their own gain today just as they did 400 years ago with the institution of slavery. Among blacks, the chronicle "captures an uneasy intuition" that black Americans "live at the sufferance of whites—that as soon as our [black] welfare conflicts with something they [whites] consider essential, all our gains, all our progress, will turn out to be illusory" (Delgado and Stefancic 1991, p. 321).

Note

1. May 31, 2000 population projections indicate that 11.7 percent of the U.S. population is made up of Hispanics, who may be of any race. The rest of the population is made up of non-Hispanic whites (71.5 percent), blacks (12.2 percent), Asian and Pacific Islanders (3.8 percent), and American Indians (.7 percent). According to the Council of Economic Advisers (1998) around the year 2005 Hispanics (of any race) will be the largest of the minority groups in the United States. If recent demographic trends continue, Hispanics, non-Hispanic blacks, Asians, and American Indians combined will approach half the population by the year 2050. ✦

Chapter 4

Gender

Equality With a Vengeance

In 1990 Bobbi Brandt pleaded guilty to a one-count indictment charging her with distribution of 2 grams of cocaine (there are 28 grams in 1 ounce). Federal Sentencing Guidelines stated an applicable range of 10 to 16 months of incarceration. The sentencing court, however, took into account that she had two children, ages seven and one and a half, whom she would lose in a custody battle because she was separating from her husband. The children would not be raised by their father. Instead, the court noted, "Strangers will be taking care of your children" (United States v. Brandt 907 F2d 31 1990). The court considered that Brandt had been a teen mother and had dropped out of high school but was trying to stay employed and be a good mother: "The carrying forward of the guideline range of imprisonment . . . would have a devastating impact upon the emotions, mind and the physical well-being, just every aspect, of the two innocent youngsters to be separated from you."

The court imposed a sentence of five years' probation and a $5,000 fine. The state of West Virginia appealed the downward departure because the Sentencing Guidelines Commission had included wording that "family ties and responsibilities and community ties are not ordinarily relevant in determining whether a sentence should be outside the guidelines" (see also Nagel and Johnson 1994, p. 201). The appeals court framed the question as to whether Brandt's family responsibilities were "extraordinary" and concluded that "the district court's implicit finding that the situation was extraordinary was clearly erroneous . . . Mrs. Brandt's situation, though unfortunate, is simply not out of the ordinary."

The court did comment that having Brandt's children placed with strangers "would have been perfectly relevant before the advent of the Sentencing Guidelines and, obviously, quite sufficient even if there had been sentence review." But under the wording of the Sentencing Guidelines, they had to decide whether the family responsibilities were extraordinary and "a sole, custodial parent is not a rarity in today's society, and imprisoning such a parent will by definition separate the parent from the children." Indeed, other federal courts have concluded that "it is not uncommon for innocent young children . . . to suffer as a result of a parent's incarceration" (in United States v. Mogel 956 F2d 1555 at 1565). Under this same reasoning, other courts have denied a downward departure for lack of extraordinary circumstances to a single mother of five (United States v. Headley 923 F2d 313 1989); a single mother of a two-year-old and a sixteen-year-old daughter, who herself also had a two-year-old (United States v. Pena 930 F2d 1486 1991); the sole caretaker of three children, one of whom was mentally disabled (United States v. Brown 29 F. 3d 953 1994); and a single mother of four young children, one of whom was born after sentencing (United States v. Chestna 962 F.2d 103 1992).

Another federal court likewise did not grant a downward departure for a father even though he had three children and his wife was totally disabled, thus requiring care and being unable to help raise the children. The dissent likened this situation to a single-parent family, "which, unbelievably to me, we have held to be absolutely ordinary, apparently without exception." Judge Heaney's dissent continued by remarking that "Congress did not intend to make calculating machines out of our district judges, yet time and time again this court has seen fit to . . . transfer that discretion to prosecutors whose actions remain utterly unreviewable." The dissent said the majority was "mandating that [judges] swim in the sea of the guidelines, instructing them that any attempt to reach higher ground and exercise their informed judgment about the facts of the defendant's life will be frustrated by this court" (United States v. Goff 20 F3d 918 1994).

The primary goal of the Federal Sentencing Guidelines was to eliminate unwarranted sentencing disparity (U.S. Sentencing Commission 1992). In the mid-1980s, Congress directed the U.S. Sentencing Commission to create sentencing guidelines and policies that would be entirely neutral with respect to the offender's race, sex, national origin, creed, and socioeconomic status. Also, as part of the shift from making the punishment fit the criminal (rehabilitation model) to making the punishment fit the crime (the "just deserts" model), Congress directed the Commission to downplay "individualizing" factors such as ties to family and community, occupation, and education.

The courts interpreted this charge as meaning that the lack of consideration given to whether a man has children should be extended into women's sentencing so there would be no consideration of sex, and thus no unwarranted sentencing disparities. However, because women are more frequently the caretakers of children, the incarceration of single mothers causes more of a disruption in children's lives. Yet defenders of the Guidelines express concern that permitting women's primary child-care responsibilities to be used to justify a reduced sentence may reinforce gender stereotypes. But taking primary parenting responsibilities into account is a problem only if the consideration is extended just to women primary parents. Instead of defining the source of the problem as an unwillingness to incarcerate mothers, as the authors of the Guidelines have done, perhaps consideration should be given to the relative ease with which fathers (particularly black fathers) are incarcerated and the impact this situation has on families, especially minority households and communities.[1]

In her objection to the Guidelines, Raeder (1993) observes that adopting a model of women's decarceration for sentencing men may be more humane for both men and women. Instead, the reverse has occurred, with a result that has been described as "equality with a vengeance" (1993, p. 925). Raeder proposes that sentencing policy distinguish between single parenting and primary parenting responsibilities. Although both should be considered as mitigating circumstances that justify giving a lower sentence than the Guidelines recommend (a downward departure), single parenting downward departures should become the norm rather than the exception. In this way, gender-linked roles such as child-care provider can be considered fairly in sentencing both women and men.

Raeder (1993) cautions against equating equality (represented by longer or more severe sentences for women) with justice. She argues that the "gender-neutral"/"equal treatment" approach to sentencing has harmed women, as the current sentencing model is not neutral at all but actually is based on the punishment of violent male offenders and major drug dealers. Moreover, gender bias in sentencing cannot be eliminated simply by legislating gender neutrality because society is not gender neutral. Offense type and severity, prior record, and indicators of stability such as family and employment all reflect gendered patterns. The effect of downplaying or ignoring the influence of family ties has been to sentence women more severely than previously. If in the past women have disproportionately and justifiably benefited from being sentenced less severely because of their family responsibilities, they are now disproportionately harmed when the considerations are withdrawn. The result is anything but neutral.

Introduction

As with class and race, discussions of gender raise controversy. There's the "f" word—*feminism*—which many men and women resist even as they endorse basic tenets of equal rights for women. Discussing sex and gender means exploring what we mean by equality when men and women are different biologically. This problem is most evident in issues around pregnancy, but is also present in debates about whether men and women are "similarly situated" and thus deserve equal treatment as a matter of law. Should equality be based on what men were getting? Are both sexes to be treated equally based on what women are getting? For that matter, is gender equality possible, or even desirable?

Some of the discussion has an apparent paradoxical quality: Women are 51 percent of the population but are considered a "minority" group for many purposes. Within the criminal justice system, men are the majority of offenders and victims, but theoretical understandings of violence frequently omit any discussion of masculinity or consider why men have such a high rate of crime relative to women.

This chapter examines the treatment of men and women victims, offenders, and workers in the criminal justice system. In particular, it considers how women have been ignored by or misrepresented in the criminal justice field and the consequences of this deficient treatment. Although this chapter focuses almost exclusively on gender, it is important to note that women's and men's experiences within the system are not homogeneous but vary with a number of factors, including race, ethnicity, and class, as well as age and sexual orientation.

Because people's treatment within the criminal justice system is shaped by what takes place outside the criminal justice system, this chapter begins by comparing how men and women are situated in larger economic, political, and social spheres. Next, we summarize the process by which the fields of criminal justice and criminology are beginning to recognize the relevance of gender, focusing on the groundwork laid and contributions made by feminist perspectives. We then turn to the definition of crime, the practices of criminal justice, and the ways in which our laws reflect the gendered interests of the lawmakers. In particular, we look at how violence against women, such as intimate violence, marital rape, and stalking, are relatively new crimes of violence, having previously been accorded the status of familiar and private rather than public affairs. From there, we explore how gender shapes the nature of victimization and criminalization. We consider gender differences in the likelihood and experiences of being arrested, charged, convicted, and punished. We also address criminal justice workers' experiences and focus on how the male-dominated nature of most criminal justice professions shapes work experiences. Finally, this chapter concludes by considering media images of women in the criminal justice system.

Gender in Society

Key Terms

Many of the terms defined in the previous chapter are relevant here, with the idea of "otherness" constructed around gender rather than race. (Race, ethnicity, class, and sexual orientation help construct otherness within the category of women, whereas white, middle-class, heterosexual women are seen as the "real" women.) The idea of social construction applies here even though sex is biological: "One is not born, but rather becomes, a woman" is Simone de Beauvoir's reminder that people are born male or female but learn gender roles through interactions with others and the larger society. The process of learning gender roles can be as obvious as when a girl is told that swearing is "unladylike" and a boy is instructed to "be a man; boys don't cry." Gender roles for men and women reflect society's heterosexism, such as when men (young and old) are told not to act like "sissies" or "faggots" and women are warned not to be "tomboys" or "dykes."

Gender thus has a wide range of variability and is not a fixed characteristic; it is a social process, something that is negotiated and "accomplished" through routine interactions with other people. Both men and women "do gender,"—that is, handle situations in such a way that the outcome is considered gender appropriate. The process can be seen most visibly when a woman fixes her own car, studies computer science, or undertakes competitive bodybuilding but still wants to be seen as feminine or "a real woman." Males face similar challenges as they take on extensive childcare responsibilities, learn how to cook, or explore their own feelings but still want to be seen as masculine or "manly." These examples also indicate that gender is never accomplished once and for all; rather, people must constantly "do gender" as they work their way through new situations and stages of life. Studying how men and women accomplish masculinity and femininity entails a consideration of how social structures constrain and channel behavior, which, in turn, may influence a person's criminal or law-abiding behavior or his or her actions in the workplace (Martin and Jurik 1996; Messerschmidt 1997; West and Zimmerman 1987).

Gender roles are the socially approved or appropriate behaviors for males and females, and they are usually assigned based on patriarchal values that reserve for men public power and control of women—for example; women should be nurses and secretaries while men are managers and doctors (see Box 4.1). Gender roles for women include values and attitudes "labeled 'women on a pedestal,' which represent the idea that women need male protection and that they should be more virtuous than men, for example by not telling dirty jokes, getting drunk, or paying their share of the cost of a date" (Scully 1990, p. 79). Women who fall off the pedestal are seen as "legitimate victims" who deserve hostility and contempt, whether in the form of harassment, domestic violence, or rape.

Box 4.1

You Know You Are Privileged When . . . (Part II)

a poem for men who don't understand what we mean when we say they have it

privilege is simple:
going for a pleasant stroll after dark,
not checking the back of your car as you get in, sleeping soundly,
speaking without interruption, and not remembering
dreams of rape, that follow you all day, that woke you crying, and
privilege
is not seeing your stripped, humiliated body
plastered in celebration across every magazine rack, privilege
is going to the movies and not seeing yourself
terrorized, defamed, battered, butchered
seeing something else
privilege is

riding your bicycle across town without being screamed at or
run off the road, not needing an abortion, taking off your shirt
on a hot day, in a crowd, not wishing you could type better
just in case, not shaving your legs, having a decent job and
expecting to keep it, not feeling the boss's hand up your crotch,
dozing off on late-night buses, privilege
is being the hero in the TV show not the dumb broad,
living where your genitals are totemized not denied,
knowing your doctor won't rape you
privilege is being
smiled at all day by nice helpful women, it is
the way you pass judgement on their appearance with magisterial
authority,
the way you face a judge of your own sex in court and
are overrepresented in Congress and are not strip searched for a traffic
ticket
or used as a dart board by your friendly mechanic, privilege
is seeing your bearded face reflected through the history texts
not only of your high school days but all your life, not being
relegated to a paragraph
every other chapter, the way you occupy
entire volumes of poetry and more of your share of the couch
unchallenged,
it is your mouthing smug, atrocious insults at women
who blink and change the subject politely-privilege
is how seldom the rapist's name appears in the papers
and the way you smirk over your PLAYBOY
it's simple really, privilege
means someone else's pain, your wealth
is my terror, your uniform
is a woman raped to death here or in Cambodia or wherever
wherever your obscene privilege
writes your name in my blood, it's that simple,
you've always had it, that's why it doesn't
seem to make you sick at stomach,
you have it, we pay for it, now
do you understand

Source: Copyright 1981 by D. A. Clark, from her book *Banshee* (Peregrine Press).

Patriarchy is the totality of oppressive and exploitative uses of male authority and varies in form depending on whether the society is capitalist, socialist, feudal, or technological. *Sexism*, which can be present both at the individual and institutional level, describes the beliefs and social relations holding that men are superior to women. Sexism includes *paternalism*, the view that women need protection and are not fully responsible for their actions, and *chivalry*, the reluctance to inflict harm on a woman accompanied by an unwillingness to believe that a woman could really be criminal (Moulds 1980). The devaluation, hatred, and fear of women underlies sexual violence against women; "Adrienne Rich has characterized misogyny as organized, institutionalized, normalized hostility and violence against women" (Humm 1990, p. 139). *Phallocentrism* is not to be confused with the biological penis but refers to social constructs that make men the focus of law and meaning (Gamble 1999).

Feminism comprises both a basic doctrine of equal rights for women and an ideology for women's liberation from patriarchy. Feminism's basic task is consciousness raising about oppression and encouraging actions that undo the exclusions of women's opinions, experiences, and accomplishments. As discussed below, a wide diversity of perspectives are contained under this umbrella term, indicating that *feminisms* might be more appropriate by not suggesting a singular woman's point of view. Under the particular definition we are using, men can be feminists by contributing to the analysis of women's oppression—including their own participation in it—but should not try to speak for women (Gamble 1999).

Sexuality is an important basis for gender identity and patriarchal control because it relates to men's control over female reproduction, standards of beauty and body image, the objectification of female bodies, and attempts to ensure sexual access or availability. Lesbianism has strong resonance for feminism because it represents a relationship in which a woman can be "woman identified" and not have aspects of her person defined by her relationship to men. It is also a relationship in which a woman can be free of sexual domination by men although she has forsaken some of the privileges that accrue to heterosexual women and is vulnerable to hate crimes based on her sexual orientation.[2]

Economic Sphere

Women make up slightly more than half of the total U.S. resident population and are thus a numeric majority in the United States. However, they are still considered a "minority group" on par with minority racial and ethnic groups—and thus deserving of consideration under programs such as affirmative action—because of their unequal position in the economic, political, and social spheres of American life. In their thoroughly researched book, *The Cost of Being Female*, Headlee and Elfin (1996) state that women were paid 71 cents for every dollar men made. In addition to this quantifiable economic cost are social and political costs. The authors note that women

> are excluded from many good jobs. We are discriminated against in pay. More and more of us are supporting ourselves and our children with or without a husband's help. If we try to climb the corporate ladder, we bump our heads on a "glass ceiling," beyond which we cannot climb. (p. xiv)

In addition to glass ceilings, a large amount of occupational segregation with "sticky floors" keeps women in low-paying occupations like secretaries and typists—jobs that are seen as "women's work," and devalued accordingly (Headlee and Elfin 1996). Even women in higher-level jobs and professions earn less than their male counterparts. A common explanation for this discrepancy is that women have less education and work experience than men. However, "Women in their thirties actually have more education than men in that age group, and are still paid less" (p. 7). Other studies show that additional years of experience do not have the same rate of salary return for women as they do for men.

Although women have made gains in the last 30 years, they remain severely overrepresented in clerical and service occupations, making up over 90 percent of those employed as registered nurses and licensed practical nurses, secretaries and receptionists, kindergarten teachers, and childcare workers. Meanwhile, men are disproportionately employed in craft and laborer jobs; around 90 percent of all mechanics, construction workers, metalworkers, truck drivers, and other motor vehicle workers are men, as are about 90 percent of all architects and engineers, clergy, airplane pilots, police officers, and firefighters (Bureau of Labor Statistics 1999b). White men are only 43 percent of the Fortune 2000 workforce, yet they hold 95 percent of the senior management jobs. White men make up only 35 percent of the U.S. population, but they are 65 percent of physicians, 71 percent of lawyers, 80 percent of tenured professors, and 94 percent of school superintendents. In 1997, women held only 671 of the total 6,064 board seats (11.1 percent) on Fortune 500 companies (American Association of University Women 1997; Catalyst 1998).

According to the Bureau of the Census, in 1995 the annual real median earnings of workers on the job year-round and full time was $22,497 for women, while it was $31,496 for men. Women's concentration in jobs that pay below-average wages contribute to their lower earnings, yet even within an occupation men typically earn more than women. As we have noted, in 1997 women earned an average of 74 cents for every dollar men earned. The pattern of women earning less than men holds for 99 percent of occupations for which data are available. Many economists predict that women's and men's pay will become more equal as their education, experience, and choice of occupations become more similar. A Department of Labor study, however, suggests that if men and women were equally likely to study the same subjects and enter the same occupations at roughly the same age, women could still expect to make only 82 percent of what men earn.

Women are overrepresented among the poor. In 1998, approximately 15 percent of women lived below the poverty level compared to 12 percent of men. By the time a woman is 65 years old, she is almost twice as likely to live in poverty as her male counterpart. The economic situation of single female-headed families with children under age 18 is particularly grim. Overall, nearly half of all such households live below the poverty line, compared to less than one-quarter of single male-headed households. One in three single female-headed families own a home, compared to more than half of single male-headed families. These findings hold for white, black, or Hispanic families, although white families generally are better situated than black or Hispanic families. For example, around 60 percent of all black and Hispanic single female-headed households with children live in poverty, compared to 40 percent of comparable white families (Costello and Krimgold 1996).

Political Sphere

In 1986 the historical pattern of higher voter turnout rates for men than for women was reversed. Ever since then, the proportion of eligible female adults who voted has exceeded the proportion of eligible male adults who voted. In recent elections, voter turnout rates for women have equaled or exceeded voter turnout rates for men, with women casting between four and seven million more votes than men. But voting is only one aspect of political participation. Women are woefully underrepresented in elected positions (Headlee and Elfin 1996). In 1998 women held only 11.8 percent of the 535 seats in the U.S. Congress (a record high), 25.7 percent of the statewide elective executive positions, and 21.8 percent of the 7,424 state legislator positions (Center for the American Woman and Politics 1998b). The shortage of women involved in national politics hinders attempts to alter the status quo and effect lasting change in criminal justice legislation and policy. As of this writing, only two women serve on the nine-member Supreme Court.

Social Sphere

Historically, women have been less educated than men. In 1997, however, the educational attainment levels of women ages 25 to 29 exceeded those of men in the same age group. Young women were more likely than men to have high school diplomas and to complete college (Bureau of the Census 1998d). According to a 1997 study conducted by the Frederick D. Patterson Research Institute, among blacks, women are almost a quarter more likely to go to college than men and twice as likely to obtain a bachelor's and master's degree.

In terms of life expectancy women have a 7 to 9 year advantage, and the gap is greater for blacks than for whites. Part of this difference can be explained by gender roles, which encourage men to be aggressive and to take risks. Also, findings that men are more likely than women to die of stress-related conditions such as heart attack and stroke suggest that men cope less well with stress than women do. Although women have longer life expectancies, a study by the Society for the Advancement of Women's Health Research showed that women fare worse than men when it comes to several leading ailments (Brody 1998b). For example, three out of four victims of autoimmune diseases (e.g., multiple sclerosis, rheumatoid arthritis, diabetes, and lupus) are women. Women are twice as likely as men to contract a sexually transmitted disease and are ten times as likely to become infected with HIV during unprotected sex with an infected partner. Women smokers are at a greater risk of developing lung cancer than men smokers. Cardiovascular disease actually kills 43,000 more women than men each year, yet virtually all randomized controlled trials on risk and treatment have focused on men. Heart disease in women often goes undetected and untreated until the disease has become severe. Consequently, 44 percent of women who have heart attacks die within one year, compared to 27 percent of men. In sum, gaps in our understanding of women's health exist and may impede efforts to identify effective preventive methods, treatments, and cures.

Reviewing the evidence, it is apparent that most power is concentrated in the hands of men; the United States is a male-dominated society. Men (particularly white men) control key institutions such as "the military, industry, technology, universities, science, political office, and finance—in short, every avenue of power within the society" (Millett 1970, p. 25). The remainder of this chapter focuses on how male domination influences the treatment of men and women victims, offenders, and workers in the criminal justice system, typically to the disadvantage of women.

Gender in Criminology

Men historically have dominated the government, the judiciary, the legal profession, and the criminal justice system. Women historically have made up a small percentage of offenders and have tended to commit less serious crimes than men. These and other factors contribute to the lack of interest in women in the criminal justice system. Until the mid-1970s, the field of criminology showed only a passing interest in explaining the offending and treatment of women in the criminal justice system. Since then, however, gender has come to be incorporated into the study of criminology and criminal justice with various degrees of thoughtfulness and thoroughness. A five-stage framework developed by McIntosh (1984) and others (Anderson 1988; Daly 1995; Goodstein 1992) describes the ongoing process by which the fields of criminology and criminal justice have evolved to consider women (Flavin 2001).

Stage One: The Intellectual Falklands

The earliest days of criminology were marked by the free will orientation of the Classical school. People were presumed to rationally choose whether or not to act criminally. Over time, however, emphasis came to be placed on the influence of personal characteristics (such as biological and psychological defects) on criminality, rather than free will. During these periods, women's criminality was ignored by most researchers. The study of female criminality was considered "an intellectual Falklands," that is, "remote, unvisited and embarrassing" (Heidensohn 1995, p. 124). Theorists who did consider women saw them as being particularly determined by their biology.

Lombroso, for example, studied female offenders to support his theory that criminals were physically anomalous. His methodology involved extensive measurements of criminals to isolate the "born criminal." He found that female criminals were not significantly different from other women, a fact that he attributed to a lack of external differentiation in women generally. Lombroso concluded that the female born offender was closer to a normal man than woman, but,

> unlike the "semi-masculine, tyrannical and selfish" born criminal who wants only to satisfy her own passions, the occasional offender puts trust in her male protectors and regains confidence in men—especially her lawyer, and in some cases that Lombroso is fond of relating, her executioner. (Hart 1994, p. 23)

Other theorists subsequently perceived women's deviance as peculiarly sexual. For example, Pollak (1950) argued that women's tendency toward deceit stemmed from their physiological ability to hide their true sexual feelings and the social expectation that they will conceal menstruation and menopause.

Stage Two: 'Add Women And Stir'

In the twentieth century, criminologists moved away from viewing deviant behavior as inherently abnormal and pathological and toward seeing deviance as normal. Thus, models based on internal sources of crime (i.e., free will, biology, psychology) were gradually replaced by models that examined external sources of crime, such as poverty, social structure, and racial discrimination. Up until the 1970s, most studies of crime continued to look exclusively at men and boys. In the mid-1970s, however, women insisted they be included in research and analysis about criminology and the criminal justice system. Unfortunately, the result was simply to "add-women-and-stir" them into existing research rather than reconsider and challenge what is "known" about crime.

Eileen Leonard's work (1982, 1995) provides perhaps the most comprehensive attempt at using traditional theories of crime such as anomie theory, labeling theory, differential association, subcultural theory, and Marxism to explain women's low involvement in crime. Because these theories excluded consideration of women's criminality, Leonard developed hypotheses that the theorists might have constructed had they been so inclined. To take but one example, Merton's anomie theory holds that when people lack legitimate means (e.g., a job, a savings account) to achieve socially accepted goals (e.g., material and monetary success), they innovate (e.g., steal, write bad checks). Leonard points out that although women are overrepresented among the poor and thus arguably are subjected to more strain than men, women are less likely to deviate. Leonard also challenged whether monetary success is as salient a goal for women as it is for men. She criticized Merton for assuming that women's goals (and men's too, for that matter) are shared across class, race, and ethnicity. Following her systematic review and analysis of traditional theories, Leonard concluded that traditional theories are unsuited for explaining female patterns of crime. She called upon scholars not to develop a "criminology of women" but to reconsider the understanding of women's *and* men's criminal behavior.

In spite of the challenge raised by Leonard and others, much of criminology seems content to remain in the "add-and-stir" stage. Evidence of this is found in many typical criminal justice textbooks or journals that ignore feminist perspectives completely or lump them together as one theory. The male-centered nature of the discipline in major criminology journals is demonstrated by a study showing that fewer than one-third of the articles analyzing individuals published between 1992 and 1996 included at least half a page of discussion of gender differences or analyzed men and women separately (Hannon and Dufour 1998).

Stage Three: Enter Feminism

The third stage—the first of the feminist stages—reflects some scholars' realization that women have been excluded from crime theories or that when women *are* discussed, their behavior is distorted. This stage focuses more attention on crimes that adversely affect women more than they affect men, such as domestic violence. Also, increasing attention is paid to the ways in which women's experiences differ not just from men's but from each other's based on characteristics such as race, ethnicity, class, age, and sexual orientation.

While this stage is a marked improvement over ignoring women altogether or "adding-and-stirring," it still has its shortcomings. Most notably, this stage reflects a tendency to treat men as the normative and women as the anomalies. The situation can be likened to that in professional basketball. The all-male National Basketball Association (NBA) was formed in 1949. Nearly fifty years later, in 1997, the first game of the Women's National Basketball Association (WNBA) was played. Referring to the women's league as the WNBA and the men's league as the NBA (rather than the MNBA) implies that the male basketball player is the norm against which women players are to be compared and suggests that women are second-class athletes. Considering a men's athletic program as the "real" sport makes it easier, for example, to justify the median $431,282 spent on personnel for women's Division 1-A programs compared to the $1.9 million spent on men's programs (Naughton 1997). It also helps make it easier to justify paying men's head coaches twice as much as women's head coaches. This way of thinking both reflects and re-creates the situation in which women make up 53 percent of all college students but account for only a third of all student athletes.

Labeling one sex the "anomalies" and relegating them to a marginalized status is incompatible with aims to achieve more equal opportunities for men and women on the basketball court as well as in a court of law. The implications of male-centered (or androcentric) thinking for criminal justice are significant. If an entire field has been shaped by a male norm, we must seriously question whether the issues considered important include those that are important for women. For example, delays in recognizing marital rape and stalking as crimes, providing vocational programs for women prisoners, and addressing sexual harassment in the workplace as issues worthy of attention can be traced to the historically male-centered nature of the criminal justice system.

The development of feminism has helped raise consciousness about the male bias reflected in criminology and has re-created its theoretical understandings and actual operation. Feminism attempts to describe gendered oppression, to identify and explain its causes and consequences, and to prescribe strategies for the political, economic, and social equality of the sexes (Rice 1990; Tong 1989). Misconceptions of feminism abound, including the somewhat understandable one that feminism is interested only in women. Feminism does try to correct the exclusion or silences about women's beliefs, experiences, and achievements, but feminists generally agree that a full understanding of women's lives requires consideration of masculinity and male sex-role expectations. Feminist analysis thus does include men, but does not make them the center of the analysis. One important contribution of feminists has been the attention drawn to the fact that men have a gender, whites have a race, the wealthy have a class, and straight people have a sexual orientation.

Some people lump all varieties of feminist thought together and assume that there is only one feminist perspective. As discussed later in this chapter, although feminists agree that gender inequalities exist in society and that these inequalities should be addressed, they differ in where they locate the source of the problem and what measures they think should be pursued to rectify the situation. There is no One and True Feminist Theory but instead many feminist perspectives (see Daly and Chesney-Lind 1988; Tong 1989). The various feminist perspectives have led some to criticize feminism for having too many "factions" and for lacking consensus. The same charge, however, could be leveled against the plethora of nonfeminist criminological theories or a group of "liberals" or a group of "conservatives."

Stages Four and Five: 'A Whole New Pie'

The current literature reflects a growing willingness to reconsider what is "known" about women and crime and to examine racial and ethnic differences among women as theoretical and political issues rather than as "problems" or "anomalies." The fourth and fifth stages exist primarily on a conceptual level because women (and minority men) do not currently form part of our basis of knowledge. In the fourth stage, scholars will not only locate women with men at the center of research but study women on their own terms without reference to a male norm. An established body of feminist theory and research will already exist. It will thus be possible to build on feminist knowledge rather than dedicate time and attention to critiquing and evaluating traditional criminological theories and research.

Rather than addressing how the study of crime and criminal justice contributes to our understanding of women's criminality, research in the fourth stage will emphasize how feminist insights contribute to our understanding of crime and of men's high incidence of criminality. Knowledge at this stage will be better integrated than the current, somewhat haphazard borrowing of ideas for understanding and trying to develop programs for, say, men who batter women. Although feminist insights are included in most interventions, there are shortcomings both with theories and with their translation into programming and their seamlessly including information from other theoretical perspectives. This issue is explored further in Box 4.2.

Box 4.2

Why Men Batter and Intervention Strategies

As defined by many intervention providers, battering comprises a constellation of physical, sexual, and psychological abuses that may include physical violence, intimidation, threats, emotional abuse, isolation, sexual abuse, manipulation, the using of children, economic coercion, and the assertion of male privilege (such as making all major family decisions or expecting the woman to perform all household duties). Three theoretical approaches dominate the field of batterer intervention; however, in practice, most interventions draw on several explanations for domestic violence in their work.

Feminist View

According to the feminist view batterers feel that they should be in charge of the family—making decisions, laying down rules, and disciplining disobedient wives and children. As men, batterers feel entitled to gender-based respect and obedience; therefore, what they perceive to be disrespect and disobedience infuriates them. Batterers often rationalize their violence on the grounds that their partner's actions provoked or caused it and that they simply reacted as any man would.

Feminist programs attempt to raise consciousness about gender-role conditioning and how it constrains men's emotions and behavior (through education around sexism, male privilege, and male socialization). Programs with a feminist philosophy present a model of egalitarian relationships along with the benefits of nonviolence and of building relationships based on trust instead of fear. Most feminist approaches support confronting men over their power and control tactics, including verbal and psychological abuse, isolation, undermining of the victim's self-confidence, and sexual coercion.

Support for the feminist analysis of domestic violence comes from the observation that most batterers are able to control their anger when "provoked" by someone more powerful, such as their work supervisors, police officers, or judges. Further, research shows that batterers are less secure in their masculinity than nonbatterers and need to assert their masculinity more forcefully to compensate for their sense of inadequacy. Other studies have documented the sense of entitlement batterers feel in controlling their partners' behavior and in justifying violence if these women deviate from the female gender role.

Critics have claimed that the feminist perspective overemphasizes sociocultural factors, such as patriarchy, to the exclusion of individual factors, such as growing up abused. Other criticisms center on the translation of that theory into programming: that feminist educational interventions are too confrontational in tone, thereby alienating batterers, increasing their hostility, and making them less likely to become engaged in treatment.

Family Systems Model

The Family Systems Model regards individual problem behaviors as a manifestation of a dysfunctional family unit, with each family member contributing to the problem. Rather than identifying one individual as the cause of the violence, the model advocates working with the family or couple together, providing support with the goal of keeping the family intact. Both partners may contribute to the escalation of conflict, with each striving to dominate the other. Interactions produce violence, so no one is considered to be the perpetrator or victim, even if only one person is physically violent. Family systems therapists criticize psychological approaches that focus on individual deficits (low self-esteem, dependence, anger) while neglecting to teach interpersonal skills that could promote safety. Family systems theory leads to treatment that involves improving communication and conflict resolution skills. Both members of the couple can develop these skills through "solution-focused brief therapy" that: (1) locates the problem in the interaction rather than in the pathology of one individual; (2) focuses on solving the problem rather than on looking for causes; and (3) accentuates the positive—for example, examining occasions when the couple avoided violence.

Proponents of both feminist and cognitive-behavioral approaches feel that batterers bear full responsibility for the violence and victims play no causal role. Both are concerned about the format of couples counseling: encouraging each partner to discuss problems openly with the other can put the victim at risk after the session if the woman expresses complaints (for this reason, family-based therapy is prohibited by law in many states). Further, honest exchanges about abuse are unlikely in the presence of the batterer, and the format is conducive to victim blaming.

Psychological Approaches

Psychological approaches hold that personality disorders or early experiences of trauma predispose some individuals to violence. Being physically abusive is seen as a symptom of an underlying emotional problem. Parental abuse, rejection, and failure to have dependence needs met can be the psychological source of battering. People with these underlying problems may choose partners with whom they can reenact the dysfunctional relationship they had with their parents. Two forms of batterer intervention have evolved from this perspective.

Psychodynamic counseling involves uncovering the batterer's unconscious problem and resolving it consciously. Proponents believe that other interventions are superficial because they are unable to eliminate the abuser's deep-rooted and unconscious motive for aggression. Long-term change requires exposing and resolving the root cause of the violent behavior. Feminists argue that labeling batterers as having psychological problems not only exonerates them in their own eyes but ignores the cultural acceptability of male dominance in the family and how it serves to keep the batterer in control of his partner.

Cognitive-behavioral therapy is intended to help individuals function better by modifying how they think and behave in current situations. This method maintains that behaviors are learned as a result of rewards and punishments (e.g., parental pride or praise for aggressive behavior). Behavior is also influenced by how people mentally construct and interpret their environment and experiences—that is, the way they think about themselves, other people, and their relationships. Cognitive-behavioral theory postulates that men batter because (1) they are imitating examples of abuse they have witnessed during childhood or in the media; (2) abuse is rewarded; (3) it enables the batterer to get what he wants; and (4) abuse is reinforced through victim compliance and submission.

Interventions focus on "cognitive restructuring" and skill building. Counselors focus on identifying the chain of events that lead each batterer to violence, starting with beliefs and "self-talk"—the way people talk to themselves in their minds. For example, a batterer whose partner is ten minutes late may tell himself, "She's out with her boyfriend" or "She can't be trusted." The programs attempt to restructure the beliefs and "self-talk" that lead to violence; for example, "I don't know why she's late, but I'm sure she's trying to get here." The programs help batterers to analyze the thought patterns underlying violent reactions (e.g., "Dinner isn't ready because my wife doesn't respect me") and learn new ways of understanding situations that trigger violence (e.g., "Dinner isn't ready because my wife had a busy day"). The program teaches nonviolent alternative behaviors, such as conflict-resolution tactics, relaxation techniques, and communication skills.

The feminist perspective criticizes the cognitive-behavioral approach for failing to explain why many men with thought patterns or skills deficits that allegedly explain their domestic violence are not violent in other relationships, how culture or subcultures influence patterns of violence, and

> why some men continue to abuse women even when the behavior is not rewarded.
>
> Information excerpted from Kerry Healey, Christine Smith, with Chris O'Sullivan, *Batterer Intervention: Program Approaches and Criminal Justice Strategies* (February 1998) NCJ 168638, *http://www.ncjrs.org/txtfiles/168638.txt*.

In the fifth stage, our knowledge base is fully transformed and feminist and includes a theoretical and analytical focus on multiple relations of class, race, and gender. Kathleen Daly (1995) identifies a number of challenges to be addressed in the process of reaching this stage, which will be discussed in greater detail in Chapter 5. Among these challenges is the fact that our inherited ways of thinking obstruct our ability to imagine alternative ways of viewing crime and punishment. Not too many years ago, it was laughable to contemplate that the Soviet Union and other European countries would come to be open, "free market" economies without being forced to do so after losing a major war. Similarly, the biases built into our existing knowledge make it difficult to imagine what a fully inclusive and transformed body of knowledge will be like. The challenge remains to recognize the failings of past research and to theorize without permitting these to limit our imaginations. While this stage is difficult to envision, one thing is certain: Developing new theories of inequality will be a more inclusive endeavor than those stages that have preceded it.

Gender, Crime, and the Law

Feminist perspectives differ in where they locate the sources of inequality, privilege, and discrimination, and consequently, in what they see as the solution to unequal social relationships. The most obvious differences involve the extent to which women's oppression is linked to racism (because women and minorities are both the "other"), capitalism and classism, or heterosexism. Solutions thus differ on the extent to which women's liberation involves also fighting racism, capitalism, and homophobia. Several of the main strands are discussed below, but readers should be aware that many other varieties exist.

Feminist Perspectives

Liberal feminists focus on discrimination and consider legal and customary restraints to be the main barriers to women's getting their piece of the pie. Thus, the goal is to ensure that men and women have equal civil rights and economic opportunities. Liberal feminists focus on discrimination against female offenders, prisoners, and workers as well as the criminalization of deviance among women for behaviors such as vice crime. Their program for change revolves around achieving greater gender equality via affirmative action and other equal opportunity programs.

Marxist, socialist, radical, cultural, and postmodern feminists differ in the emphasis they place on economic, biological, racial, and sexual sources of oppression (or some combination thereof). Critical feminists object to liberal approaches not only for failing to question the existing system but for wanting equality in it. As Colette Price framed the issue over twenty years ago, "'Do we really want equality with men in this nasty competitive capitalist system?' 'Do we want to be equally exploited with men?' 'Do we want a piece of the pie or a whole different pie?'" (Redstockings 1978, p. 94).

Marxist feminists are concerned with the way the criminal justice system under capitalism serves the interests of the ruling class at the expense of the lower class. Marxist feminists view the oppression of women as an extension of the oppression of the working class. It is impossible for anyone to obtain genuine equal opportunity in a class society in which the wealth produced by the powerless mainly ends up in the hands of the powerful few. These relatively few powerful are disproportionately male, which makes it even harder for women, as the powerful have a vested interested in maintaining their privileged position. In terms of criminology, the powerful in the society define what the laws are, what is considered a crime, and what the punishments are. In short, laws reflect the interest of powerful males. Because women are less likely to be the attorneys, the judges, and the lawmakers, they have less access to the structures of power and operate at a disadvantage. Also, because capitalism renders women powerless, they are under pressure to commit less-serious, nonviolent, self-destructive crimes, such as using illegal drugs. For instance, women drug couriers who are dependent on a man for economic support have less freedom to decline to participate in illegal activity than women who are economically independent.

Women are locked out of many criminal occupations. For example, it is hard for individuals to be major embezzlers if they do not have a high-ranking position in a corporation. It is difficult for women to use trucks to traffic in large quantities of drugs when not many women are truck drivers. If *all* women are to be liberated—not just the relatively privileged or exceptional ones—the capitalist system must be replaced by a socialist one in which the means of production belong to one and all. Under socialism, no one would be economically dependent on anyone else; women would be economically freed from men and therefore equal to them.

Socialist feminists extend Marxism to argue that women are oppressed not only because of their subordinate economic position but because of their "class" as women. Socialist feminists were among the first of the feminist theorists to recognize exploitation rooted in racism, ageism, and heterosexism. Like Marxist feminism, socialist feminism clarifies how economic conditions alter labor market demands for women. Socialist feminism also highlights how sexist ideology legitimates women's exclusion from higher-paying men's jobs and their confinement to the domestic sphere. Patriarchal ideologies and exclusionary practices produce pools of women who resort to shoplifting, transporting or packaging drugs, or exchanging sex for money or other goods and services as a means of survival. Socialist feminists call for widespread economic and cultural changes to dismantle the twin evils of capitalism and patriarchy. They place special emphasis on the needs of poor and working women—women who suffer the consequences of a system that not only exalts men over women, but those who "have" over those who do not, especially the poor. They advocate equal work opportunities for men and women, as well as policies that would alleviate women's "second shift" by increasing childcare and family-leave programs while increasing men's involvement in domestic work.

Radical feminists tend to focus on female victims, particularly survivors of male violence. They criticize liberal or Marxist feminists for not going far enough. For radical feminists, the source of the problem is the male-dominated nature of society. It is not sufficient to overturn society's male-dominated legal and political structures (as Marxist and socialist feminists assert); we must change society's social and cultural institutions (such as the family, the church and the educational system) that emphasize women's role as childbearers and mothers. The solution is to liberate women by permitting each woman to choose for herself when to use or not use reproduction-controlling technologies (i.e., contraception, sterilization, abortion) and reproduction-aiding technologies (i.e., artificial insemination, in vitro fertilization, surrogate/contract motherhood). Each women should determine for herself how and how not to rear the children she bears. The focus of radical feminists tends to be on how men attempt to control females sexually. Radical feminists frequently study sex-related crimes such as rape, stalking, obscene phone calls, sexual assault, and domestic violence, including marital rape. They call attention to the fact that a woman is at equal or greater risk of assault in her own home as she is on the street. Radical feminists also examine how exploitation at a young age may contribute to a young girl's running away, cutting school, and dropping out and consequently being labeled as deviant, even though she is a victim. Along with Marxists, radical feminists have been active in the domestic violence arena.

While positivists and other "modernists" (including many feminists) claim that we can determine the truth provided we all agree on responsible ways of going about it, *postmodern feminists* argue for multiple truths that take context into account. Many criminologists recognize that "knowledge" or "truth" (e.g., definitions of what actions are considered illegal, what constitutes a fair punishment) often reflects the perspective of those with more power. Postmodernists take this idea further, questioning whether *any* knowledge is knowable and rejecting the belief in a universal definition of justice—i.e., one that would be true for all people, all of the time (DeKeseredy and Schwartz 1996; Wonders 1999). Toward this end, postmodernism emphasizes the importance of alternative accounts and frequently takes the form of examining the effects of language and symbolic representation—for example, how legal discourse constructs different "types of Woman" such as "prostitute" or "bad mother" (Smart 1995).

Some charge that postmodernism basically amounts to a "call to inaction" (Tong 1989, p. 232). If justice is different for everyone depending on one's perspective, then what is the point of trying to pursue it? If what are called "facts," "truth," and "knowledge" are no different from "opinion" and "belief," then, as one student asked, "Why not just sit by the pool?" (Smart 1995, p. 212). In this respect, it is helpful to separate the skeptical from the affirmative types of postmodernism. *Skeptical postmodernists* embrace a more extreme relativism, in which there is no basis or valid standards for determining truth or objectivity. They focus on deconstruction, which reveals the underlying assumptions of a claim and disrupts its acceptance as a fact by revealing the bias in its construction. Skeptical postmodernists "do not believe in suggesting alternatives because to do so would then also be making truth claims and be subject to their own criticism (hence skeptics are also called *nihilists*)" (Henry and Milovanovic 1999, p. 6, emphasis in original).

In contrast, *affirmative postmodernism* addresses the possibilities of rebuilding based on contingent truths. With deconstruction, "affirmative postmodernists show how humans actively build their social world, rather than being passive subjects of external forces" and in doing so "show how people could invest their energies to build new social worlds" (Henry and Milovanovic 1999, p. 6). Postmodern feminist scholars tend to recognize a responsibility to build bridges across diverse groups in order to work collectively—not to arrive at a universal understanding of justice, but "to do our best to make judgments that make the world a good place to be" for everyone (Wonders 1999, p. 122).

Approaches to Gender Equality

In addition to the varying positions regarding the reasons for inequality, privilege, and discrimination, another debate revolves around how to achieve gender equality, whether in responses to victimization, the sentencing of men and women offenders, the conditions of incarceration, the treatment of men and women on the job, or so forth. During the course of debate, three approaches have arisen: the sameness perspective, the difference perspective, and, more recently, the dominance perspective.

Advocates of the *sameness perspective* (sometimes referred to as the "gender-neutral" or "equal treatment" perspective) support a single standard governing the treatment of women and men. Take, for instance, the lack of vocational and educational programs in women's prisons relative to what's found in men's prisons. One solution is to give women the same programs that men have. If men have programs designed to rehabilitate sex offenders, then these programs should be available to women prisoners as well. There's just one problem: relatively few women prisoners (less than 2 percent) are rape and sexual assault offenders (Greenfeld 1997). Women prisoners on the whole do not have the same need for sex offender programs as men prisoners do.

This analysis suggests caution in equating equality with justice. The sameness approach may actually harm women, as the approach is not neutral at all but is actually based on the treatment of men. As the narrative at the beginning of this chapter illustrates, gender bias in sentencing cannot be eliminated simply by stipulating (as is done in the federal Sentencing Guidelines) that gender is not to be considered. Gender neutrality cannot be legislated because society is not gender neutral. Similarly, in terms of employment, the gender-neutral framework is most likely to benefit those women whose biographies (at least on paper) resemble a male norm in terms of education and experience. Yet another example is the purportedly gender-neutral nature of training. For example, Britton (1997) observed that the rhetoric of correctional officer training in her study was explicitly gender neutral, yet closer examination revealed that the training model was based on the experiences of male officers, particularly those working in male-dominated institutions.

Given the flaws of the sameness approach, the logical conclusion seems to be to treat women differently from men, which is the *difference perspective*. After all, some very real differences exist in the situation of men and women, such as women's capacity to bear children. MacKinnon (1991) criticizes the difference approach because it runs the risk of being "seen as patronizing but necessary [and] exists to value or compensate women" for the ways in which women are or may be different from men under existing conditions (p. 82). Women can be seen as getting "special treatment" or "special rights"; and other critics express concern that the difference approach may reinforce gender stereotypes. For example, a policy of permitting single parenthood to receive a "downward departure" from sentencing guidelines discriminates against both men and women who do not have children. Such a policy would effectively use the criminal law to reward women for their status as mothers (or, alternatively, to punish women for not having children). It would say in effect, "You have violated the criminal law, but we'll overlook that so you can do what you are supposed to do—care for your children" (Nagel and Johnson 1994, p. 208).

Both the sameness and the difference approaches exhibit two problems. First, they both assume a male norm: "Gender neutrality is thus simply the male standard, and the special protection rule is simply the female standard, but do not be deceived: masculinity, or maleness, is the referent for both" (MacKinnon 1991, p. 83). Second, both approaches reflect a preoccupation with gender differences while ignoring the role of power and domination. To address this oversight, MacKinnon and others advocate a third position: the dominance approach.

The *dominance approach* focuses on gender differences in *power*. The dominance approach reminds us that while men are as different from women as women are from men, the sexes are not equally powerful. Most differences between men and women can be attributed to a society in which women are subordinate and men are dominant. The answer is not to create a single standard (the sameness approach) or a double standard (the difference approach) but to address the inequality in power between the sexes. For example, proponents of the dominance approach have been instrumental in pressuring the legal system to abandon its "hands-off" attitude toward domestic violence and to define wife battering and marital rape as crimes. By contrast, they have been much less successful in their struggle to outlaw pornography.

The dominance approach is not perfect either and has been criticized for its overconfidence in legal recognition and its failure to acknowledge that "legal rights are sometimes overshadowed by social realities" (Chesney-Lind and Pollock 1995, p. 157). For instance, while women in most states have the legal right to be treated like any other assault victim and to have their battering husband arrested and punished, the reality is that they face social, economic, and cultural barriers that may prevent them from taking full advantage of their legal rights (see Box 4.3).

Box 4.3

Why Some Battered Women Sometimes Stay

Why women stay in abusive relationships is the wrong question. The questions we should be asking are: Why do men terrorize their partners? Why does the community allow battering to continue? How can we be helpful to women in the process of leaving? A common mistake in understanding domestic violence is to scrutinize the survivor and avoid looking at the perpetrator. People believe that if battered women *really* wanted to leave, they could just get up and go. Many people overlook the environmental barriers that prevent women from leaving and too often focus on psychological "characteristics" of women instead. Although men's violence is the crucial question, many people wonder why women stay—and advocates of battered women have made the following suggestions.

Some battered women are held prisoner in their own homes. Batterers use psychological terrorism and abuse to break down the victims' will to resist and bring them under control. A worthwhile model is the "Stockholm syndrome," which describes how those who are taken hostage begin to identify with, become attached to, and take the side of their captors as survival reactions to life-threatening situations. Batterers use knowledge gained in an intimate relationship to attack the woman's spirit and her sense of self-worth, and thus her ability to resist. Sexual abuse and domination are particularly degrading to the spirit and weaken the capacity to resist. Torture and murder of pets—particularly those special to the woman—are also not unusual.

Some battered women stay because they believe that therapy will help their batterers stop being violent. Having the assailant enter counseling bolsters the woman's hope about the relationship: if he can be cured, she reasons (and her reasoning is supported by the therapist who is doing the counseling, whom she sees as the expert), the violence will end and their relationship can resume. All women want the violence to end; many do not want the relationship to end.

Some battered women are forced to stay because they can't afford justice. Getting a personal protection or restraining order may require getting a lawyer—which usually requires money. Legal aid offices may not necessarily handle divorce, and many do not have the resources to handle divorce and custody cases when domestic violence is involved. Major cuts to legal services have hindered the limited options for legal redress. The husband may have told the victim that he will use his income to hire a more skilled attorney who will take her children.

Battered women sometimes stay for their children, so their abusive partner will not get custody. Some survivors reason that they will sacrifice themselves so their children can have a father, good schools, a safe neighborhood, or financial security.

Some battered women stay because there is no place for them to go. Shelters do not exist everywhere, or are full. Their funding is in constant danger, vulnerable to attacks from groups believing the shelters are "destroying the family" or are "anti-male." Women face discrimination in the rental market, and landlords are often reluctant to rent to formerly battered women, believing that their assailant will show up and cause property damage or physical harm. The assailant often deliberately sabotages his partner's credit rating (or prevents her from establishing one at all).

Some battered women stay because they are not given accurate information about battering. They are told by professionals, family, friends, and the batterer that alcohol or drugs causes battering. They are told that they are codependent or enablers of his behavior—if they would change, their assailant would. Women then endlessly attempt to modify their behavior, only to watch the violence worsen and find themselves blamed for not trying hard enough.

Some battered women stay because they believe what most people in our society think about battered women: that they imagine or exaggerate the violence; that they provoke or are to blame for the violence; that battered women all come from poor, uneducated, or minority backgrounds; that their partner just has a problem controlling his anger or stress; or that unemployment problems have caused the battering. If the woman goes for help to family, friends, or professionals who believe these myths, these people will suggest ideas that will not work and make it harder for her to escape.

Some battered women stay because their assailants deliberately and systematically isolate them from support. People who are in trouble need the aid of family, friends, co-workers, and professionals to weather the crisis and make the best decisions for themselves. Many assailants are extremely jealous and possessive; they constantly accuse their partner of affairs, demand that their partner speak to no one, and accuse the partner of infidelity every time she does speak to someone. Assailants force their partner to account for every minute of her time. One assailant marked the tires of his girlfriend's car to monitor her use of it. Another nailed the windows shut and put a lock on the outside of the door. Many take car keys, disable cars, and unplug or break telephones. Assailants methodically drive friends and family away.

Some battered women stay because they believe in love and they still love their partners. This phenomenon is hard for people who have not been battered to understand. However, many people have been in difficult relationships (or jobs) that they knew they should leave but couldn't, or needed time to be able to depart. Love is glorified in our culture. Popular songs and movies reinforce the idea that love is the most important thing in life and that people (especially women) should do anything for it. Women may love their partners and at the same time hate their violent and abusive actions. Battered women need to be reminded that they do not have to stop loving their partner in order to leave. Some women may be troubled about making it on their own and being lonely. Leaving a batterer may mean enduring feelings of grief and loss from abandoning a circle of friends, a family, a neighborhood, and a community.

Some battered women stay because they believe what their assailant is telling them:

- "You're crazy and stupid. No one will believe you." Or, "You're the one that's sick. You need help. You're hysterical."
- "I know the judge; he won't put me in jail." Or, "The police will never arrest me."
- "If you leave, I'll get custody because you'll have abandoned me and the kids."

- "If you leave, I'll find you and kill you. I'll kill your family, your kids, and your pets. You'll never escape me."

Assailants deliberately supply their partners with false information about the civil or criminal justice system. At the same time, they often play on their partner's concern for their well-being through threats of suicide or exaggerating the devastating effects of prison. (In fact, convictions are rare, and usually for misdemeanors that carry a sentence of counseling.) Assailants may tell their partners that shelters are lesbian recruiting stations, are staffed by lesbians, or are places where she will be attacked by lesbians or become one.

Some battered women stay because they are addicted and their addiction prevents them from taking action. Their assailant encourages or coerces the woman into using alcohol or drugs, or sabotages recovery by preventing her from going to meetings. Some women consume alcohol or other drugs to numb the psychic, emotional, or physical pain caused by the violence. Doctors may prescribe tranquilizers for a battered woman's "nerves." Few women know or are told that minor tranquilizers can be seriously and quickly addictive. They make the woman less able to act on her own behalf and give the assailant a handy tool for discrediting and blaming her.

Some battered women are trapped in battering relationships because of sexism. Barbara Hart states: "The most likely predictor of whether a battered woman will permanently separate from her abuser is whether she has the economic resources to survive without him." Women do not have economic resources equal to or approaching those of men. Nearly half of all female-headed households with children live in poverty, as compared with only 8 percent of male-headed households. The majority of African-American and Latina female-headed households live at or below the poverty level. Many battered women cannot find a job, and an assailant can damage a woman's employment record by harassing her at work, causing excessive lateness and absenteeism.

Further, many battered women do leave. Almost all battered women try to leave at some point. For battered women who leave, the violence may just be beginning. Batterers escalate their violence when a woman tries to leave or show signs of independence. They may try to coerce her into reconciliation or retaliate for the battered woman's perceived rejection or abandonment of the batterer. Men who believe they "own" their female partner view her departure as an ultimate betrayal that justifies retaliation. Because leaving may be dangerous does not mean that battered women should stay. Cohabiting with the batterer is highly dangerous, because violence usually increases in frequency and severity over time and because a batterer may engage in preemptive strikes, fearing abandonment or anticipating separation. Although leaving may pose additional hazards, at least in the short run, the research data and the experience of advocates for battered women demonstrate that ultimately a battered woman can best achieve safety and freedom apart from the batterer. Leaving requires strate-

gic planning and legal intervention to avert separation violence and to safeguard survivors and their children.

Excerpted from an article of the same title by Susan G. S. McGee, available through
http://comnet.org/dvp/. Reprinted with Permission of Susan McGee, The Domestic
Violence Project/ SAFE House (Ann Arbor, Michigan). The original document contains many citations to support or elaborate on statements made in it. For additional
information, including safety plans to help a battered woman escape, explore the
domestic violence and sexual assault resources at *http://www.stopviolence.com*.

Perhaps the most serious criticism of the dominance approach (as
well as of other prominent feminist approaches) is that it is
"essentialist"; that is, it assumes a monolithic "women's experience"
that can be described independent of other characteristics such as
race, class, age, and sexual orientation. Essentialism occurs when a
voice—mostly a white, straight, and socioeconomically privileged
voice—claims to speak for everyone. In an essentialist world, for
example, "Black women's experience will always be forcibly frag-
mented before being subjected to analysis, as those who are 'only
interested in race' and those who are 'only interested in gender' take
their separate slice of our lives" (Harris 1990, p. 255). By contrast, critical race feminism attempts to address simultaneously the importance
of an intersectional and anti-essentialist approach to crime and criminal justice (see Chapter 5 for a fuller discussion).

Criminal Justice Processing

As discussed in earlier chapters, the law defines what behavior is
considered a crime. This definition is neither static nor value-free but
varies across space and time. Admittedly some values—such as the
value placed on human life—are generally held to be so important
that they warrant being backed up by the law. But laws also exist to
serve the interests of the ruling class. Thus, how lawmakers consider
and treat women is reflected in the legal system's consideration and
treatment of women. Because law makers are predominately men,
laws primarily reflect men's interests.

If gender (and the social locations attendant to gender) played no
role at all, we would expect to find 51.1 percent of those arrested,
convicted, and incarcerated to be women. We would expect 51.1 percent of victims and 51.1 percent of those working in the criminal jus-

tice system to be women. Instead, as is discussed below, in nearly every category of offense, victimization, and work, women are underrepresented.

Victimization

Historically, the law has been reluctant to define women as victims who have crimes committed against them in their homes or as part of a relationship. For centuries, men benefited from not being held accountable for their crimes against women. The failure to recognize domestic violence as criminal behavior reinforced the patriarchal idea that "a man's home is his castle." Since the 1970s, however, society has started to consider violence against women a crime. As a result, in the 1990s "private matters" such as acquaintance rape, marital rape, and stalking became increasingly likely to be recognized as crimes. Other changes, noted in Box 4.4, help provide for a more accurate counting of the incidents of victimization experienced by women in the form of domestic violence and sexual assault.

Box 4.4

Getting a More Accurate Picture of Domestic Violence

The National Crime Survey is a large-scale telephone poll asking a panel of households about victimization experiences. Survey takers read through "screening questions" about types of crimes such as assault or theft, then follow up with more detailed questions if the respondent answers yes to a question. People working on the survey try to improve the survey instrument, but they must be careful because significant changes mean that data for different years cannot be compared, nor can analysts draw inferences about trends. But sometimes substantial redesigns are necessary because the survey questions are leading to an underreporting of victimization. A complete accounting is important to get an accurate picture of crime and violence in the United States as a basis for informed public policy.

One area of substantial change has been the questions designed to screen or prompt for victimization related to domestic violence and sexual assault. Listed here are the old and new screening questions for violent crime:

Box 4.4 (continued)

Old (1972–1992)	New (beginning January 1992)
1. Did anyone take something directly from you by using force, such as by a stickup, mugging or threat?	1. Has anyone attacked or threatened you in any of these ways . . .
2. Did anyone TRY to rob you by using force or threatening to harm you?	a. With any weapon, for instance, a gun or knife . . .
3. Did anyone beat you up, attack you or hit you with something, such as a rock or bottle?	b. With anything like a baseball bat, frying pan, scissors, or stick . . .
4. Were you knifed, shot at, or attacked with some other weapon by anyone at all?	c. By something thrown, such as a rock or bottle . . .
5. Did anyone THREATEN to beat you up or THREATEN you with a knife, gun, or some other weapon, NOT including telephone threats?	d. Include any grabbing, punching, or choking . . .
6. Did anyone TRY to attack you in some other way?	e. Any rape, attempted rape or other type of sexual assault . . .

Old (continued):

New (continued):
- f. Any face to face threats . . . OR
- g. Any attack or threat or use of force by anyone at all?

Please mention it even if you were not certain it was a crime.

2. Incidents involving forced or unwanted sexual acts are often difficult to talk about. Have you been forced or coerced to engage in unwanted sexual activity by . . .
   a. someone you didn't know before
   b. a casual acquaintance . . . OR
   c. someone you know well?

The changes in the screening questions have been combined with the introduction of computer-aided interviewing. Before, interviewers would work from paper copies of the survey and skip to the follow-up questions where appropriate. However, even well-trained interviewers do not always want to venture into uncomfortable conversations about domestic violence and sexual assaults, including probes for details. With the paper surveys, they could simply skip questions and move on. However, the computer will not allow them to continue until the screen is completely filled in with all the required information.

As a result of both changes, the National Crime Survey now has better and more detailed information about domestic violence and sexual assault. The screening questions are better at explaining what types of activities are important to the interviewers, and the use of computers compels the collection of more complete information about each incident. The levels of victimization recorded under each method are listed in the accompanying table.

Box 4.4 (continued)

Average Annual Rate of Violent Victimization per 1,000 Persons

Old Survey Methodology, 1987–91			New NCVS Methodology, 1992–93		
	Female	Male		Female	Male
Intimate	5.4%	0.5%	Intimate	9.4%	1.4%
Other relative	1.1	0.7	Other relative	2.8	1.2
Acquaintance/friend	7.6	13.0	Acquaintance/friend	12.9	17.2
Stranger	5.4	12.2	Stranger	7.4	19.0

Source: Tables from *Violence Against Women: Estimates from the Redesigned National Crime Victimization Survey,* NCJ 154348 (1995): *http://www.ojp.usdoj.gov/bjs/abstract/femvied.htm,* see also *http://www.ojp.usdoj.gov/bjs/abstract/vi.htm.*

Except for rape/sexual assault and, to a small degree, personal theft, every violent crime victimization rate is higher for males than for females. In 1998, 8.4 million violent victimizations (i.e., murders, rapes, sexual assaults, robberies, aggravated and simple assaults) were recorded. The victimization rate for men was 44.3 per 1,000, compared with 31.9 per 1,000 for women (Sourcebook Online: Table 3.4). For both men and women, victimization rates were highest for people between 12 and 19 years of age, in the lowest household income brackets, living in urban areas, with only a high school education or less. Among women, victimization was more likely for blacks than for whites or other racial minorities. Among men, victimization rates were similar across racial categories (Craven 1997).

Men are harmed by their membership in the more crime-prone of the two sexes. In day-to-day life, men (particularly black men) are more likely to be stopped, more likely to have their intentions considered suspect by women, and more likely to be feared. Also, male victims face the disadvantage of having relatively little attention given to their victimization. Besides men's greater risk of most types of victimization, the most striking differences between men and women's victimization patterns emerge when we consider the victim-offender relationship (see Table 4.1). The majority (63 percent) of men's nonfatal violent victimizations are committed by a stranger, while the majority (62 percent) of women's nonfatal violent victimizations are committed by someone the woman knows (Craven 1997). The pattern holds for homicide. Men are four times more likely than women to be victims of homicide. However, one-third of women homicide victims are murdered by an intimate such as a spouse, ex-spouse, or boyfriend or girlfriend, compared to around 5 percent of men. Put another way, about 85 percent of the more than 960,000 incidents of violence against an intimate involve women victims.

Table 4.1

All Victims of Murder and Nonnegligent Manslaughter, 1976–1996

Victim-Offender Relationship	Male Victims (*n*=340,687)	Female Victims (*n*=105,175)
Spouse	3.7%	18.9%
Ex-spouse	0.2	1.4
Girlfriend/boyfriend or other intimate	2.0	9.4
Other relative, friend, or acquaintance, or stranger to victim	49.6	42.5
Unknown to police	34.4	27.8

Source: Bureau of Justice Statistics (1998b).

According to the National Victim Center, crime victims may suffer physical, financial, and emotional injuries. For instance, they may suffer cuts, bruises, or broken bones or experience insomnia or a change in appetite. Economic harms include not only the loss or damage of property but also expenses not covered by medical insurance. Emotionally, victims may respond with shock, numbness, denial, anger, heightened anxiety, or any number of other feelings. Most of what has been written about victimization trauma for both women and men addresses the reaction to domestic violence and rape and, to a lesser extent, child abuse. Not much is said about the impact of other forms of violent victimization, such as assault. Also, while much research has examined the trauma associated with the rape of women, less has considered male rape victims.

Statistics suggest that men are less likely to be sexually assaulted than women; an estimated 2 percent of all men will be raped in their lifetime, compared to 15 percent of all women (Sourcebook Online: table 3.33). A study of crimes in Alabama, North Dakota, and South Carolina found that nearly 9 percent of rapes involve male victims. Yet definition of forcible rape in the UCR program is limited to incidents involving female victims (Greenfeld 1997). Male victims of sexual assault may be even less likely than female victims to report their assault because of the greater risk of stigmatization. Research reveals both similarities and differences between men and women's responses to rape and their reasons for not reporting. A man may fear being criticized or not being believed if he does not fight back when confronted with an attacker. Also, even though male sexual assault has nothing to do with the sexual orientation of the attacker or the victim, male victims may fear being perceived as homosexual. Gay men who are raped may think that the assault occurred because they are gay, while straight men may be as disturbed by the sexual aspect of the assault as the violence involved. Further, society perpetuates the idea that men should be able to protect themselves and therefore are somehow at fault when they are raped (Brochman 1991).

Identification and Adjudication

In the 1970s, explanations of women's lower level of criminal involvement were often based on an assumption that women have benefited from police officers' and judges' paternalistic and chivalrous attitudes. As a result, the perspective goes, women are less likely to be arrested, convicted, or incarcerated. Although popular in the 1970s, paternalism-based models have been criticized on a number of grounds. First, most studies asserting paternalism have not empirically evaluated whether it is in fact responsible for the differences (Daly 1994). Inadequate data and statistical controls for legal and extralegal factors (such as prior record or employment status) may account for the difference. Second, there is ample reason to question whether all women have benefited equally from judicial paternalism—and, indeed, whether black women have *ever* benefited from it (see Raeder 1993; Young 1986). Klein (1995, 1973) notes that chivalry is "a racist and classist concept . . . reserved for the women who are least likely ever to come in contact with the criminal justice system: the ladies, or white middle-class women" (pp. 10, 13). Historical evidence of the lack of chivalry toward black women includes the fact that they were placed in chain gangs while white women offenders were placed in reformatories (Rafter 1990). Similarly, white women's rebellion against gender roles may lead to psychiatric treatment, while black women are more likely to wind up in prison (Hurtado 1989). Black women have been characterized by larger society as "welfare queens," "Mammys" and "Jezebels," tough, masculine "black Amazons," and castrating, dangerous "sinister Sapphires"—not the sorts of women upon which chivalry is generally bestowed (Mullings 1994; Young 1986).

According to the UCR, around 10.3 million arrests were made in 1998. Overall, men are overrepresented as arrestees, making up nearly 80 percent of all persons arrested, and 90 percent or more of those arrested for forcible rape, weapons offenses, sex offenses (not including forcible rape and prostitution), and robbery. Overall, women make up 22 percent of all arrests, but are over 30 percent of those arrested for prostitution and commercialized vice, embezzlement, fraud, forgery, counterfeiting, larceny-theft, and being runaways. Only for two categories of offense—prostitution and commercialized vice, and running away—do women account for more than 50 percent of all arrestees (Department of Justice 1998).

One problem with relying on UCR arrest data, however, is that the offense categories are broad and derived from a wide variety of criminal acts. For example, as Darrell Steffensmeier (1995) points out, "fraud" includes both passing bad checks for small amounts and engaging in stock frauds involving large sums of money. "Larceny-theft" includes shoplifting a $10 item, stealing a radio from a parked car, stealing merchandise from one's workplace, and cargo theft worth thousands of dollars. Even though larceny-theft is considered a "serious crime" according to UCR definitions, most of the crimes women commit tend to fall at the lower range of offense seriousness. Most arrests of women are for shoplifting, passing bad checks, credit card fraud, and welfare fraud—not serious white-collar or corporate crimes such as false advertising, product defects, or insider trading. The crimes women commit tend to be extensions of women's domestic and consumer role activities (i.e., paying family bills and obtaining family necessities) rather than evidence of women becoming more like men in committing violent crimes.

Gender shapes both the type of crime committed and the forms a given crime takes. For example, Jody Miller (1998) observes that women and men report similar motivations to commit robbery. Yet the ways in which they commit robbery are strikingly different and highlight the clear gender hierarchy that exists on the streets. Women robbers take into account the gendered nature of their environment by robbing other females, who are less likely than males to be armed and are perceived as weak and easily intimidated. When women rob men, they draw on perceptions of women as weak, sexually available, and easily manipulated. Women use these perceptions to manipulate men into situations in which they become vulnerable to robbery. By contrast, men tend to use physical violence or a gun to confront the victim and typically target other men. Women typically are not targeted for street robberies, in part because they are less likely to carry a lot of money on them. Also, they are perceived as peripheral players in the action on the streets. Miller concludes that "Male robbers . . . clearly view the act of robbery as a masculine accomplishment in which men compete with other men for money and status. . . . The routine use of guns, physical contact, and violence in male-on-male robberies is a reflection of the masculine ideologies shaping men's robberies" (1998, pp. 50–51).

In general, women are less likely than men to have a prior record. A study of jail inmates revealed that 42 percent of women but only 28 percent of men are first-time offenders. Although about 10 percent of both men and women jail inmates are first-time violent offenders, substantially larger percentages of women inmates are first-time drug, property, or public order offenders. Men are also more likely to have violent histories. Around one in four men but only one in eight women have been previously convicted of a violent offense (Harlow 1998).

Prosecutors have considerable discretion in determining whether someone will be charged with a crime. Some scholars have suggested that women (particularly white, middle-class women) are less likely than men to have charges pursued against them because women's crimes are typically less serious than men's and women do not present as great a threat to society as men do. In some cases, however, the reverse is true, and women may actually be subjected to more vigorous prosecution than men, such as with the criminal prosecution of pregnant, drug-using women.

Depending on which drug a pregnant woman is using, the fetus may suffer growth deficiency and central nervous system impairments. The fetus may face a higher risk of low birth weight, sudden infant death syndrome, spontaneous abortion, premature rupture of the membranes, abnormal placentation, increased blood pressure, and congenital urinary tract anomalies (Gustavsson and MacEachron 1997). These effects have been associated with alcohol and tobacco use.

Despite the harms associated with legal drugs, efforts to criminalize pregnant women's drug use has singled out cocaine users—particularly crack cocaine users—for prosecution. "Drug addicted pregnant woman" tends to conjure up an image—not of a suburban white, middle-class woman who smokes, drinks, and takes prescription medications but rather of a poor, urban-dwelling, crack-addicted black woman. Few images generate less compassion than the latter. Moreover, the response has been increased willingness to criminalize the woman's behavior rather than expand the availability of drug treatment and prenatal care, particularly for women who have small children or are infected with HIV.

Compared to what is known about the effects of tobacco and alcohol on fetal health, the consequences of illicit drug exposure are less well established. Although maternal cocaine use does add avoidable risk to pregnancy, it is difficult to trace many newborn symptoms directly to cocaine use. Studies of cocaine exposure disproportionately involve samples of poor minority women and often do not separate out the effects of other factors that may adversely affect fetal health: poor housing or homelessness; poor nutrition; a lack of prenatal care; working around toxins or chemicals; and using tobacco, alcohol, and prescription medication (Humphries 1999). Also, largely unexplored are the possible effects of men's behavior. Some evidence suggests that chemically abusing men face a heightened risk of chromosome damage, and legal drugs (including tobacco) may damage sperm. Men's physical abuse of the mother may also contribute to ill health of the infant (Gustavsson and MacEachron 1997).

According to a 1996 report prepared by the Center for Reproductive Law and Policy, at least 200 women in more than thirty states have been arrested for their alleged drug use or other actions during pregnancy. Most of the women prosecuted have been low-income women of color. In many cases, women have been pressured into pleading guilty or accepting plea bargains. Where women have challenged their charges, they have generally been successful. Nearly every appellate panel and most trial courts have found that prosecutions of women for their conduct during pregnancy are without legal basis, unconstitutional, or both. Most have ruled that statutes cover only children already born, not fetuses. However, in 1996, the South Carolina Supreme Court upheld Cornelia Whitner's criminal child neglect conviction and eight-year prison sentence for drug use during pregnancy. Whitner was convicted even though she had requested that the criminal court place her in drug treatment and she ultimately gave birth to a healthy child (*State v. Whitner* 1996).

Even if one accepts that drug use is a major correlate of fetal health (although scholars cite poverty and environment as greater influences on children's development than prenatal drug use), there are limits to what can be accomplished by prosecuting pregnant drug-using women. Jails and prisons generally lack high-quality prenatal care programs, nutrition programs, counseling, housing assistance, or income support programs, much less violence- and drug-free environments. Deterring women from using drugs while pregnant could be better accomplished by expanding drug treatment available for women in general—and pregnant women, women with small children, and women with HIV in particular. A 1993 study made simulated calls to 294 drug treatment programs in five major cities (Breitbart, Chavkin, and Wise 1994). The results showed that while most programs accepted pregnant women on an outpatient or residential basis, the method of payment accepted and the availability of childcare significantly limited access. Only 70 percent of outpatient programs and 55 percent of residential/detoxification programs accepted pregnant women on Medicaid or for free. Moreover, the lack of childcare provisions severely restricted access for women requiring childcare. Only one-fifth of all programs accepted pregnant women *and* provided child care, even though past research has found that lack of child care precludes addicted women's participation in treatment.

Further, criminalizing maternal conduct may discourage women from seeking prenatal care and drug treatment out of fear that they will be subjected to prosecution. One woman reports:

> I know a lot of mothers say that they don't get prenatal care 'cause they feel like as soon as they walk through the door, they will be judged, "Oh, you're a crack-head. Why the ____ did you get pregnant anyway?" So they don't get prenatal care . . . they have those commercials about addicts that don't get prenatal care because they just don't give a ____. They do give a ____, but they are thinking about how they gonna be looked at when they walk in the hospital door, like they not good enough to be pregnant. (quoted in Rosenbaum and Irwin 1998, pp. 315–316)

The criminalization of maternal drug use presents a slippery slope; the precedent it sets could potentially justify prosecuting pregnant women for driving recklessly, getting in cars with reckless drivers, ignoring a doctor's advice to stay in bed, drinking alcohol or smoking tobacco, being homeless, or being involved with a violent partner.

Punishment and Imprisonment

Prisons typically house individuals serving sentences of one year or more. Jails, by contrast, hold detainees awaiting trial, individuals serving sentences of less than one year, and convicted felons awaiting transfer to their assigned prisons. In addition, jails serve as drunk tanks, truant halls, and shelters for the homeless mentally ill. Because jails hold diverse populations and are designed for short-term confinement, little emphasis is placed on long-range routines and programs. This situation poses a barrier to treatment for women with a substance abuse problem. Although women represent a small minority of all inmates, they are disproportionately represented among those incarcerated for drug offenses. The small numbers of women jail inmates and the general scarcity of resources for all inmates, however, sometimes places them directly in competition for resources and programs with men inmates. Many of the problems encountered in jails—such as a lack of work programs, health services, or vocational programs; family concerns; sexual harassment and abuse; and variations in sentences—also hold true for prisons and vice versa.

At midyear 1999, the nation's jails held 605,943 persons. In 1983, women made up 7.1 percent of all jail inmates, but increased incarceration rates for women have resulted in women making up 11.2 percent of the jail population in 1999 (Levin, Langan, and Brown 2000). Many jail facilities are unable to cope with the increased number of female jail inmates. A 1992 study reported that while 60 percent of jails hold women, only 13 facilities were "female-only." Of these, nine held fewer than 250 inmates, three held between 250 and 1,000 inmates, and only one was designed to house more than 1,000 inmates (Beal 1993).

As shown in Table 4.2, men and women are equally likely to be jailed for a public order offense. However, men are nearly twice as likely as women to be jailed for a violent offense, while women are more likely to be in jail for a drug offense. Examining more specific crimes within each of these general categories of offense reveals that women are nearly twice as likely as men to be jailed for larceny/theft and fraud, which probably reflects the greater likelihood of women being arrested for shoplifting and writing bad checks.

Table 4.2

Most Serious Offense of Jail Inmates, by Sex (1996)

Most Serious Offense	Men (*n*=445,952)	Women (*n*=50,657)
Violent offenses	27.6%	14.9%
Property offenses	26.3	30.0
Drug offenses	21.4	27.4
Public-order offenses	24.3	24.7
Other offenses	.4	1.2

Source: Harlow (1998).

In part because men are more likely than women to be convicted of a violent felony and are more likely to have prior convictions, they are also more likely to be incarcerated and to serve longer sentences. Of all men convicted of felonies in 1996, about 40 percent were sentenced to prison, 33 percent to jail, and around 25 percent to probation. Among women felons, roughly 25 percent were sentenced to prison, 33 percent to jail, and around 40 percent to probation or some other nonincarcerative punishment. Men sentenced to jail had an average sentence of 6 months, compared to women's 5 months. Men sentenced to prison had an average sentence length of 5 years, three months, compared to women's average prison sentence of 4 years, 11 months (Levin, Langan, and Brown 2000).

As the result of mandatory sentencing minimums and other federal sentencing guidelines, the number of incarcerated persons boomed during the late eighties and early nineties. From 1990 to 1996 imprisonment rates increased by 43 percent among men and 65 percent among women (Gilliard and Beck 1998). On December 31, 1997, 1 in every 177 men and 1 in every 1,852 women were sentenced prisoners in state or federal correctional facilities. A recent Department of Justice study found that a man has a 1 in 11 chance in his lifetime of going to prison, while a woman's chances are 1 in 91 (Department of Justice 1998). (Chapter 5 explores how the disparities are even more striking when the intersections of race and gender are considered.)

A typical woman prisoner is black, 30–34 years of age, convicted of a drug offense, and held in California or Texas (Gilliard and Beck 1998). The woman prisoner probably lacks access to diverse educational, vocational, and other programs. She is likely to be incarcerated at a facility with a diverse population resulting from the lack of classification; because of the lack of women's facilities, serious and mentally ill offenders are more likely to be housed with less serious offenders in women's prisons, whereas in men's prisons these populations are segregated from each other (Belknap 1995). Mixing security classifications also makes it difficult to operate programs requiring less secure environments.

The typical woman prisoner is probably a mother of at least one child under the age of 18, with whom she lived before entering prison. Now that she is incarcerated, her child probably lives with grandparents. She does have contact with her child, usually in the form of a weekly letter or phone call. Distance, lack of transportation, and limited economic resources on the part of caregivers contribute to the only 50/50 chance her child will visit her (Bureau of Justice Statistics 1994a).

Women whose children are in foster care face several obstacles to maintaining their parental rights (Reed and Reed 1997). In addition to the woman prisoner's lack of programs and services, transportation, and economic resources noted above, her children may go through multiple foster home placements, making it difficult for her to keep track of their whereabouts. The courts may also consider incarceration to be an aspect of abandonment and thus a justification to terminate parental rights. Reed and Reed (1997) cite evidence suggesting that involuntary termination of parental rights occurs disproportionately among women prisoners.

The typical male prisoner is black, 25–29 years of age, convicted of a violent offense, and held in California or Texas (Gilliard and Beck 1998). Although more attention is given in the literature to women's experiences of victimization, evidence suggests that he probably was the victim of physical abuse or neglect as a child. A study of adult male felons in a New York prison found that 68 percent reported some form of victimization before age 12 (i.e., physical abuse, sexual abuse, or neglect) (Weeks and Widom 1998). Around one-third reported severe childhood physical abuse such as being kicked, bitten, burned or scalded, or threatened with a knife or gun. The male prisoner probably experienced some form of physical abuse, sexual abuse, or neglect before the age of 12, with physical abuse being most common (Weeks and Widom 1998).

Although more attention is given to women who are parents, the male prisoner is likely a parent of at least one child under the age of 18. He probably lived with this child before entering prison, although the child is now cared for by the mother. He also has contact with his child, primarily through a weekly or monthly letter or phone call. There is a 55 percent chance he will be visited by his child (Bureau of Justice Statistics 1994a).

Typically, programs, services, and facilities available to women are significantly lower in quality and number than those available to male inmates in the same facility or institutional system. If one subscribes to the view that "the squeaky wheel gets the grease," it is easy to understand why men's prisons command more attention than women's prisons do (Belknap 1996; Collins and Collins 1996). This difference is not the result of intentional discrimination but rather attributable to a number of other factors, including (Collins and Collins 1996):

- Women make up a comparatively small number of the incarcerated population (6 percent of prison population and 11 percent of jail population); the smaller number of women in prison and jail is used to justify fewer facilities and less money allocated to these facilities for programs.

- Traditional stereotypes based on men as economic providers and women as homemakers persist and lead to an attitude that vocational training is less important for women than it is for men.

- Women prisoners present fewer management and security problems than men prisoners.

- Facilities have limited budgets.

- "Jailhouse lawyers" are more of a fixture in male institutions than female institutions, making it more likely that legal attention will be given to the conditions inside male facilities.

In short, male facilities typically have more—and more diverse—programs than female facilities do (Belknap 1996), in part because of the occupational prevalence of stereotypical gender and sex roles. Stereotypical views of "appropriate" or "desirable" vocations for women are held not only by prison administrators but by the women prisoners themselves. Even if there were a large demand for less sex-stereotypical programs, most prisons lack the resources to introduce such programs as computer science and mechanics (Welch 1996a).

Although lawsuits on behalf of male inmates have drawn the most public and judicial attention, as of the end of 1994 at least 19 major class actions involving female inmates were decided, settled, or pending. Litigation for female inmates typically argues that the disparity in services, programs, or facilities has no justifiable basis and thus violates the Equal Protection Clause of the Fourteenth Amendment. The Equal Protection Clause does not require that every person or group be treated identically to every other. Instead, it requires that the government treat groups that are generally alike (or "similarly situated") the same *or* have a good justification for discriminating against one of the groups (Collins and Collins 1996).

While district courts have generally ruled in support of the women inmates, equal protection claims have not been as well received at the appeals level. The court of appeals tends to be more reluctant to consider women and men inmates to be "similarly situated" (or generally comparable) and thus more willing to assert that the concept of equal protection does not apply.[3] One of the key barriers to considering men and women inmates similarly situated is that the number of inmates is one of the factors taken into account. In other words, as long as the differing size of the two groups is relevant, it will be difficult to find male and female inmates comparably situated. In a 1996 National Institute of Corrections report, *Women in Jail: Legal Issues*, the authors observe that the effect of past appellate court rulings "may be to virtually end the use of equal protection arguments to improve conditions in female facilities" (Collins and Collins 1996, p. 13). A review of published research and litigation suggests disparity in a number of areas, including sexual harassment, medical care, physical conditions of confinement, and vocational, educational, and social programs and services.

The type of sexual harassment of woman inmates and misconduct toward them may range from inappropriate remarks made by correctional staff to invasions of privacy to sexual abuse and violent sexual assaults. The inmate's abuser may be a female correctional officer but is more likely a male. A woman inmate may be raped vaginally, anally, or orally. Guards have used mandatory pat-frisks or room searches to grope inmates' breasts, buttocks, and vaginal areas. Some officers may use actual force or the threat of it, while others use their authority to provide or deny goods and privileges in order to compel an inmate to have sex (or to reward her for having done so).

Although the Eighth Amendment does not mandate comfortable prisons, interpretation of that amendment suggests that people are sent to prison *as* a punishment; they are not sentenced to prison *for additional* punishments. Indeed, the report by the human rights group Amnesty International on the sexual abuse of female inmates in the U.S. is titled, "Not Part of My Sentence" (1999). The title originates from a comment by a female inmate that performing oral sex on officers was not part of the judge's sentence. Overall, Amnesty International noticed a "significant difference" between international standards on the treatment of female inmates and law in the United States:

> International standards provide that female prisoners should be supervised only by female guards. In contrast, under laws of the USA, a male guard may watch over a woman, even when she is dressing or showering or using the toilet. He may touch every part of her body when he searches for contraband.

The grievance procedure in many facilities requires a woman inmate to confront the implicated officer informally before filing a formal grievance or inform the officer that she is lodging a complaint. This requirement exposes her to retaliation by the officer and deters her from making a complaint. Even if she pursues a complaint, she may encounter internal investigative procedures that are biased against her. The problems are exacerbated in cases where the department of corrections does not provide adequate staff training, conducts cursory investigations, and administers weak punishments (Human Rights Watch 1996).

Under the Eighth Amendment protections against cruel and unusual punishment, all inmates have a right to adequate medical care. For poor medical care to be considered a violation of the Eighth Amendment, however, it must be proved that the level of medical care provided (or not provided) demonstrates "deliberate indifference to serious medical needs"—a difficult standard to meet (*Estelle v. Gamble* 429 U.S. 97, 1976). Women's medical care may be deficient, particularly in services specific to women, such as gynecological examinations and prenatal care and education. In 1993, 23 major cases dealing with female offenders were pending, and nearly half of these cases dealt with medical/mental health issues (Collins and Collins 1996).

Consider the conditions at facilities under the control of the nation's capital. In 1992, the District of Columbia opened an 800-bed

Correctional Treatment Facility (CTF) next to the old D.C. detention facility. The CTF was designed to be a model treatment center for addicted and mentally ill inmates. The dramatic increase in the number of women prisoners, city budget problems, and pressure from groups lobbying on behalf of the women prompted officials to redesignate 236 of the CTF beds for women that previously had been allocated for inmates with mental health problems. As the corrections budget continued to dwindle, the building, work programs, and medical services began to deteriorate. In 1993, a class action suit was filed on behalf of female inmates at CTF, as well as at the two other facilities that housed women inmates (*Women Prisoners of the District of Columbia Department of Corrections v. District of Columbia* 1995). Between 5 and 6 percent of women who enter a jail or prison are pregnant. Many of the issues raised in *Women Prisoners* relate to the provision of prenatal care, an issue that becomes increasingly more critical the longer a woman remains incarcerated.

Among other things, the district court ordered the District of Columbia Department of Corrections (DCDC) to hire additional medical staff; establish a prenatal clinic; add questions about women prisoners' reproductive, contraceptive, and sexual history at the intake interview; add a gynecological and breast examination to the health appraisal; develop written protocols for routine and follow-up care for common gynecological problems (e.g., syphilis, gonorrhea, chlamydia), PAP tests, pelvic examinations, and breast examinations; conduct follow-up on women who obtain an abnormal PAP test result; develop and implement a written prenatal protocol; and arrange for each pregnant woman prisoner to see an obstetrician at regular intervals. The court of appeals struck down every single one of these provisions with one exception: they upheld the order to cease using physical restraints when transporting pregnant women to the hospital.[4]

In general, women's facilities tend to be smaller, fewer in number, and qualitatively different from men's prisons. For example, women's prisons are more likely than men's to have a cottage-style design and less likely to have intimidating features such as gun towers, high concrete walls, and armed guards. The Connecticut State Farm and Prison for Women at Niantic is typical. The original buildings date back to the 1920s and 1930s, when cottages were used to house small groups of women so they could "live with a motherly matron in a family setting" (Rierden 1997, p. 7). The legacy of this era has meant that women's prisons still tend to infantilize and domesticize women while reinforcing gender stereotypes (Belknap 1996). Over time, however, there has been an increasing move toward the confinement model used in men's prisons. For example, in 1988 the Niantic complex added a dormitory. Designed to hold 104 inmates, it soon came to hold double that amount. It features poor fluorescent lighting, wall-to-wall women, and a deafening noise level.

In the aforementioned District of Columbia case, the district court found several structural flaws in CTF, including insufficient heating, a malfunctioning ventilation system, and defective toilets. At a second facility, women inmates were housed in converted military barracks that were not initially designed for continued residency. Renovations and preventive maintenance were either lax or nonexistent. Also, the dormitories were overcrowded, which in turn increased the risk of spreading infectious diseases, produced high noise levels, and created filthy living conditions. Fire hazards were also a problem. For example, water leaked into areas where electrical equipment was exposed, the fire alarm system was antiquated, and there were not enough exits to accommodate the number of people living at the facility.

Workers

The criminal justice system includes legal secretaries, court transcribers, and social workers, all of which are predominately women-dominated occupations. But the image of criminal justice professionals is more typically of police officers, prison guards, attorneys, and judges, the vast majority of whom are men. If gender (and the social locations attendant to gender) played no role at all, we would expect to find 51.1 percent of those working in the criminal justice system to be women. Instead, in nearly every category of work, women are underrepresented. For example, around 25 percent of all full-time law enforcement employees are women, most of whom are employed as civilians rather than police officers. Nationally, only 10.1 percent of police officers are women, although this figures goes up to 15.2 percent in the 65 cities with populations of 250,000 or more.

Women make up nearly a third of all staff employed in state and federal correctional facilities and around one-quarter of all custody/security staff. Women make up a greater percentage of employees in state facilities than they do in federal facilities, and there are a higher percentage of female employees in the South than in other regions. For example, women constitute 31.8 percent of all custody/security staff employed in the South, compared to only 10.3 percent of those employed in the Northeast (Department of Justice 1998). According to the 1990 Census, nearly one-quarter of all lawyers and around one-fifth of all judges are women. The predominance of men is most noticeable at the highest levels of the justice system. When examining characteristics of presidential appointees to U.S. District Court judgeships over years, we find that the overwhelming majority of appointees have been men, although the situation has slowly been improving. From 1963 to 1976, fewer than 2 percent of Johnson's, Nixon's, and Ford's appointees were women. By contrast, over 25 years later, around 20 percent of President Bush's appointees to District Court judgeships were women, as were nearly 30 percent of those appointed by President Clinton (Bureau of Justice Statistics 2000a).

There are two reasons why proportional representation of women (and other minority groups) is of concern. First, there is the issue of fairness. It is important to have "descriptive" representation for women and minority men so that the system at least appears to represent "we the people." Second, it is important to achieve not only symbolic representation, but also substantive representation. That is, a diverse group of women (and other minority group members) presumably brings experiences and insights to the field that a similarly diverse group of men may not (Williams 1991[1982]). For example, the recruitment of women trial court judges might result in less paternalistic treatment of women lawyers, victims, and defendants (Spohn 1990). The National Center for Women and Policing suggests women will have a positive impact on policing by helping to reduce police brutality, increase the efficacy in police response to domestic violence, and increase the emphasis on conflict resolution over force.

Scholars disagree on the extent to which a profession is changed by the increased presence of women. Some hold that it is the profession that forces women to adapt, and not the other way around. The job or occupational model focuses on the work people do and on the subculture that arises from it as an explanation for workers' behavior and attitudes. In the case of the police, Martin (1990) asserts that the occupational subculture is male dominated and that this domination places women in an inferior role within the occupation. Gender discrimination is not a function of the occupational subculture per se, but rather the manifestation of specific values contained within the subculture. If the subculture is male dominated, women's integration and their assimilation into the subculture is problematic. In a male-dominated occupation, women may feel compelled to choose a role identity that falls along a continuum ranging from identifying with the job to identifying with one's gender. Either role identity causes conflicts within a male-dominated occupation and is counterproductive to women's integration into the occupation. Problems may manifest themselves in women's decreased job satisfaction and promotion opportunities.

No doubt processes both internal and external to the occupation shape the experience of workers of both genders. Focusing exclusively on how a person's job shapes one's experience does not take into account the way in which women's work experiences and opportunities are limited by gendered roles (such as that of wife and mother) in the larger society. Focusing on how gender influences one's experience in an occupation may exaggerate gender differences and result in the failure to consider the ways in which women and men are similar in their attitudes and responses to their work environment.

As it currently stands, male dominance potentially presents several problems for women professionals entering criminal justice occupations. Although fewer gender differences in work assignments are found today than 20 years ago, women may still be "shielded" from work that is perceived as dangerous or stressful, such as patrolling the streets, guarding violent offenders, or handling challenging cases. Women may also face sex stereotyping in the type of work they perform. Women police officers may be disproportionately assigned to handle administrative and staff support functions (Martin 1990). Women attorneys tend to be concentrated in probate, tax, and family law, and in securities work, while litigation is a predominantly male specialty (Pierce 1995). Women correctional officers may be more likely to supervise in prisons for women and juveniles and to be assigned administrative or clerical support positions (Martin and Jurik 1996). Britton (1997) reported that 27 of the 36 correctional officers she interviewed perceived that sex differences in job assignments were based on perceptions of women's ability to deal with violence. She likens the situation to women in the military, who are seen as a beneficial presence in peace time but as a potential liability in the event of a war. Women may be considered capable to handle the job under ordinary circumstances but are presumed incapable of handling a violent crisis. Because there is always the possibility that a situation will become violent, women officers are seen as less capable than men officers.

In some cases, the line between sex stereotyping and acknowledging the sensitive nature of gendered crime is a blurry one. For example, research in England and Wales suggests that women police officers are disproportionately assigned to handle sex offenses and domestic disputes (Brown 1998; Holdaway and Parker 1998). It is not clear, however, the extent to which such assignment reflects an attempt to be more sensitive to the needs of women victims of these crimes, to a stereotyped idea of women's suitability for police work, or to some combination of the two.

A woman may feel pressured to perform better than her male colleagues, in part because she feels that a woman's individual performance will reflect positively or negatively on all women. For example, a female correctional officer reported, "They expect us to be better, every way you can think of . . . how clean is the shift, how you write up reports, how quickly you turn in your reports, etc. They can excuse or overlook a male officer making a mistake, but not the females" (Belknap 1995, p. 411). A female police officer explained, "It's a man's world, and we've got to try and fit in as females, and that's hard. . . . Where I lack in the physical, I make up in the mental. I have to outsmart them, and a lot of times I have to talk people into handcuffs if I don't have any backup. You have to use your head more" (quoted in Buhrke 1996, p. 57).

Women may also lack access to the "old boy" network, a situation that presents a Catch-22 situation. On the one hand, if women socialize with male colleagues, they may be perceived to be sexually available, which reflects negatively on women's professionalism. On the other hand, if women do not socialize (either by choice or by exclusion), they risk not learning information related to their job or promotion opportunities and may be labeled as "cold" or "lesbians" (Belknap 1995; Fletcher 1995; Martin and Jurik 1996).

In law enforcement, only 6.5 percent of top command positions (chiefs, deputy chiefs, commanders, and captains) and 9.2 percent of supervisory positions (lieutenants and sergeants) are held by women (National Center for Women and Policing 1998). One reason for the lack of women in senior positions in law enforcement, corrections, and the law is systemic discrimination. For example, women constitute around 13 percent of the total number of enlisted military personnel, as well as 13 percent of all officers (Department of Defense 1996). Many law enforcement and corrections agencies give veteran preference points to applicants who have been discharged from active military duty and who served during a period of conflict. Because women are less likely to have military experience, they are less likely to receive this advantage. Promotion decisions may be based partly on experience with high-profile cases or assignments that women are less likely to have. Also, women are more likely than men to be supervised by someone of the opposite sex, which may contribute to women receiving lower evaluations.

Women working in criminal justice occupations may also encounter sexual harassment in a variety of forms. Such harassment may contribute to a hostile working environment in which submission to unwelcome sexual advances and comments becomes a condition of employment. Women who complain may be ostracized by their colleagues. According to a Denver police dispatcher's lawsuit, some women who worked in the police department's radio room in the early 1990s had to put up with "name-calling, fondling, obscene e-mail messages, advice on 'better orgasm(s),' offers of oral sex, pornographic cartoons and requests for nude photos" (ACLU 1997, p. 1). After the dispatcher complained, the harassment became more hostile and focused on her, and she resigned. Women lawyers also report unwanted sexual invitations, attention, and behavior. One woman lawyer was harassed by a male partner who was notorious for such behavior. When he tried to grab her breasts at a firm cocktail party, she slapped him. She reports, "afterwards . . . the snide remarks, the knowing glances, the comments, 'How's your left hook?'" that she described as the "second public humiliation" (Pierce 1995, pp. 108–109).

Joanne Belknap (1995) distinguishes between *gender harassment* which includes nonsexual "putdowns" of women, and *sexual harassment,* which refers to offensive sexual comments or behaviors. The women correctional officers in her study reported the presence of sexual harassment but tried to ignore or minimize it. For example, one woman CO describes how she reacts to hearing male COs say, "There goes fat ass" after she passes them: "I turn around and smile because they want to upset you . . . I consider the source, and it isn't too much better than the inmates" (p. 414). For racial and ethnic minority women, it may not be possible to identify harassment as racial or sexual, because the two forms are not easily separable. Women of color may also fear their claims of harassment will not be taken as seriously as those of white women. Lesbian police officers may also face harassment on the basis of their sexual orientation (see Box 4.5).

Box 4.5

Gay and Lesbian Police Officers

The presence of women and gay men on the police force challenges the traditional heterosexually masculine definition of the occupation. Just as being a competent female officer challenges assumptions that policing is a masculine occupation suited only for masculine men, so too does being a competent gay male officer. Many straight male police officers are against anything feminine, be it a female police officer or a male police officer they perceive to be effeminate.

Homophobic attitudes in society at large and within law enforcement in particular create many problems for the gay or lesbian officer. As of June 1997, in most states an employer is perfectly within its rights to fire (or refuse to hire, or refuse to promote) an employee solely because of his or her sexual orientation. Thus, the gay or lesbian officer who is being mistreated on the job lacks legal protection to confront the problem.

Unlike race or sex, officers can choose to try to conceal their sexual orientation. Thus, some officers may experience the stress of staying closeted. Gay officers may try to present a heterosexual image by playing along with the macho sexual bravado. A lesbian officer may tolerate flirtations from male officers in order to protect her sexual identity or dispel rumors that she is a lesbian (Leinen 1993). Some lesbian officers report harassment on the basis of their gender or their sexual orientation or a combination of both. Male officers are expected to be masculine or risk being labeled a "faggot." Women officers are expected to be feminine—or at least not masculine—or risk being labeled a "bulldagger" or a "dyke."

Gay and lesbian officers may also have to endure the homophobic attitudes of colleagues. For example, in 1998 two male New York City police officers filed a sexual harassment lawsuit against the city and the NYPD. One of the officers, a 13-year member of the force, reported being subjected to offensive and harassing conduct by officers, including being assaulted, forced into his locker, handcuffed, and suspended from a coat rack, and having members of the command attempt to force him into simulating oral sex with another officer (King 1998). Some gay and lesbian officers fear for their safety. A lesbian officer observes, "If I were a gay man, I don't know if I'd be out . . . I can see where a gay man would really be in fear for his life every single day from his fellow officers" (quoted in Buhrke 1996,

p. 110). For some officers, the torment and ridicule may be severe enough to cause them to seek early retirement or psychiatric treatment.

Recognizing the need of gay and lesbian police officers and other criminal justice professionals to have an arena to discuss their concerns in an atmosphere free of job-related reprisals, the Gay Officers Action League (GOAL) was established in 1981. GOAL continues to provide a safe environment for people who have been, and continue to be, victims of harassment and discrimination in the workplace, while at the same time attempting to change homophobic attitudes in the workplace and in the community at large. Other organizations, such as Law Enforcement Gays and Lesbians (LEGAL), also offer support for gay, lesbian, bisexual, and transgender workers in the criminal justice system.

By treating women as sex objects, men can both heighten the boundaries between themselves and women and assert their authority as men in the workplace (Pierce 1995). Sexual harassment sends a message to women that they are valued for their appearance, not their professional performance. Harassment also reinforces the idea that women are outsiders and subordinates in an occupation and punishes them for entering men-only domains (Martin and Jurik 1996).

Media Representations

In recent years, scholars have begun to address the depiction of women criminal justice workers and victims in the news media, movies, and novels. Not surprisingly, the sexism existing in other social institutions is also found in the media. Benedict (1992) and Meyers (1997) are among those who have explored news coverage of violence against women. Both authors reach similar conclusions that women victims are depicted as "virgins or vamps"—as either "good girls" who are undeserving of violence or "bad girls" who are at least partially responsible for their own victimization. In the former category are those who are very young or very old, had been tortured or murdered in a particularly gruesome manner, or had been attacked by a serial murderer, serial rapist, or someone characterized as mentally ill (Meyers 1997, p. 57). The news coverage in these cases tends to stress both the heinous nature of the crime and the victim's fragility and vulnerability to reinforce the victim's "innocence."

This is not to say that the male offenders are necessarily blamed. In cases where the offender is portrayed as emotionally unbalanced, psychological problems appear to diffuse the offender's culpability (Benedict 1992; Meyers 1997). The stories tend to focus on the offender's psychological state at the time of the offense and on any events that may be seen as precipitating the violence. The "newsworthy" event was what happened to make the offender "snap." The victims are peripheral; the murders appear incidental.

By contrast, a "bad girl" is generally depicted as deserving of violence "because she was on drugs, drunk, not properly cautious, engaged in questionable activities, or involved in work or exhibiting behavior outside the traditional role of women" (Meyers 1997, p. 62). In terms of sex crimes, the "vamp" or "bad girl" is a woman who "by her looks, behavior or generally loose morality, drove the man to such extremes of lust that he was compelled to commit the crime" while the "virgin/good girl" is victimized by a man who is "a depraved and perverted monster, [who] sullied the innocent victim, who is now a martyr to the flaws of society" (Benedict 1992, p. 23). The news media's "good girl/bad girl" dichotomy is inherently contradictory in that it insinuates that only men can save women from being victimized by men (Meyers 1997).

Benedict (1992) suggests individual and systemic reforms that the press should undertake in its coverage of sex crimes. Among them, she recommends the compilation of a "Words to Watch For" list to draw reporters' attention to unintentional and unfair innuendos, including adjectives routinely used about female crime victims and not about men (e.g., curvaceous, bubbly, pert, naive, full-figured, hysterical). Reporters and editors should also strive to be balanced: if the victim's looks or sex life are described, then so too must be the suspect's. Examples of systemic reforms designed to improve coverage include journalists and editors choosing accuracy over speed and ceasing to justify sensationalist or irresponsible crime coverage by claiming that it is what the public wants. The press also should reconsider whether descriptions of victims and their behavior are necessary at all.

Benedict also argues that press biases of race, class, and gender are so rife that they can only be rectified if the newsroom is diversified, asserting that "as long as the press is predominantly white, male, and uninformed about rape, sex crimes will never be covered fairly" (1992, p. 265). According to the American Society of Newspaper Editors, women made up only slightly more than one-third of people in the newsroom in 1996. Racial and ethnic minorities make up over one-quarter of the population, but only around 12 percent of newsroom employees. Interestingly, though, more than half of the Asian Americans and blacks in newsrooms are women, compared to 37 percent in the overall workforce.

A few scholars have examined the portrayal of women criminal justice workers in popular culture. Images of women attorneys in popular films from the 1940s through the 1990s have accurately reflected the scarce representation of women in the law, the gender-based attitudes toward women as lawyers, and the "femininity-achievement conflict" faced by attorneys (Bailey, Pollock, and Schroeder 1998). But in other regards, films have offered a distorted image, emphasizing women's sexuality rather than their professionalism, exaggerating the dangerous and more sensational aspects of the profession, and overrepresenting young, glamorous, single, and childless women. A woman attorney is permitted a happy ending only when she gets her man and keeps her career.

Based on her study of policewomen in videos from 1972 to 1996, Hale (1998) observes that less than 10 percent of movies made between 1983 and 1996 showed women as minority-police officers. She also concludes that dated myths of femininity still exist. Policewomen are kept "in their place" by dying, being injured, or becoming romantically involved with their male counterparts. Women are only portrayed as effective police officers in those movies where they are the superior officer, FBI trainees, detectives, or inspectors.

Summary and Conclusions

This chapter has focused primarily on the influence of gender in the criminal justice system. This chapter has aimed to describe the distribution of women and men throughout the criminal justice system. We have also tried to present some idea of the factors contributing to and the consequences of women's underrepresentation as offenders, victims, and workers in the administration of criminal justice. Increasingly, scholars are challenging the treatment of gender in existing theory and research, moving away from treating women as anomalies toward locating women at the center of research. We are also seeing more attempts at exploring the way race, ethnicity, class, and other social characteristics interact with gender to shape one's experience.

To date, the criminal justice system's vision of gender has been less than 20/20. Early criminologists had tunnel vision and focused only on the male criminal. Eventually, this myopia was corrected and women began to appear on the periphery. Over time, women have moved more directly into the line of vision. As a result, the crimes committed against them are no longer invisible and there is increased recognition of the need to overcome gender inequality. Yet mainstream research still tends to be focused on men, and it remains blind to the fact that men have a gender, too. Only recently, for example, has serious attention been given to how masculinity operates to influence men's behavior and attitudes.

While great strides have been made in the last 30 years toward achieving gender equality and justice, there is much ground yet to be covered. Future study of gender and crime must continue to consider how social relations of gender, race, and class interact. James Messerschmidt's (1997) "structured action theory" proposes that gender, race, and class are not equally significant in every social setting involving crime but rather vary in their importance depending on the situation, on the context. Yet we are only beginning to understand the processes and factors that shape these situations.

Dorie Klein (1997) recommends that future treatments of gender and criminal justice move away from an approach that assumes a clear division between victims and offenders. This approach distorts the interpretation of women's and men's real experiences and has limited the theoretical advance of feminist criminology. She observes that it has also led to strange political bedfellows, such as alliances between activists for female crime victims and advocates of harsh policies for offenders. Instead, Klein and others recommend blurring victim-offender distinctions and recognizing the prominence of histories of victimization in the lives of many women and men offenders.

As long as victims of either gender do not report crimes against them for fear of being stigmatized, blamed, or ridiculed; as long as women and men are harmed by purportedly "gender neutral" policies; as long as workers are sexually harassed in the workplace; as long as women and minority men are treated as "problems" or "anomalies"; as long as the institutions governing the treatment of men and women in courts, government, and the media continue to be dominated by one sex, criminology has its work cut out for it.

Notes

1. Over 90 percent of black women who have children live with them, compared to only 51 percent of black men (Bureau of the Census 1993). Statistics suggest that among black offenders, the proportion living with their children is lower. A study of black women prisoners found that the majority of black women prisoners lived with their children before entering prison (Bureau of Justice Statistics 1994). However, around one quarter did not. The statistics on male inmates were not broken down by race. However, the same study found that only slightly more than half of the men lived with their children prior to incarceration. Given that black men are less likely to live with their children than white men (Hatchett et al. 1991), the number of black offenders who lived with their children prior to entering prison is probably less than 50 percent.

2. Many people use *homophobia* to describe the hatred and fear that underlie hate crimes against gays and lesbians. However, many of the perpetrators actively seek out gays to target (by "cruising" gay bars and neighborhoods), which is unlike people who experience other clinical phobias (for example, people who suffer from a clinical fear of spiders do not go into damp garages looking for spiders to step on).

3. Cf. *Klinger v. Department of Corrections*, 31 F. 3d 727 (8th Cir., 1994), cert. denied, 115 S. Ct. 1177 (1995); *Pargo v. Wlliot*, 69 F. 2d 280 (8th Cir., 1995), 894 F. Supp 1243 (D. Iowa, 1995); *Women Prisoners of the District of Columbia v. District of Columbia*, 877 F. Supp. 634 (D.D.C., 1995), modified 899 F. Supp. 658 (D.D.C., 1995).

4. In early 1997, the District of Columbia Correctional Treatment Facility (CTF) came under private-sector control of the Correctional Corporation of America (CCA). The medical standards continued to deteriorate. HIV-positive pregnant women were not getting medication that would protect unborn children from the virus. Another pregnant HIV-positive woman came down with shingles, a painful but highly treatable skin condition. The inmate went a week without treatment until the condition spread to her face, where it could have threatened her eyesight. Moreover, the condition was too advanced to respond to oral therapies and the woman was admitted to a hospital for intravenous drug therapy to get the shingles under control (Mencimer 1997). ✦

Chapter 5

Intersections

Spheres of Privilege and Inequality

Rosa Lopez is a Salvadoran woman with a fourth-grade education who came to the United States over 25 years ago. She became involved with the O. J. Simpson murder trial while working as a housekeeper for one of Simpson's neighbors. Rosa Lopez's testimony (which provided an alibi for Simpson) was given with the aid of an interpreter, and the attorney's questions to her were translated from English to Spanish. In her essay, "Rosa Lopez, Christopher Darden, and Me: Issues of Gender, Ethnicity, and Class in Evaluating Witness Credibility," associate professor of law Maria L. Ontiveros ([1995] 1997) counters the prevalent view that Lopez was a liar. She suggests that when one considers issues of culture, class, and gender, an alternative view is possible.

During direct examination, Rosa Lopez established that O. J. Simpson's Ford Bronco was parked in front of his house after the alleged time of the murder. She also testified that she planned to leave the United States and not return. Among the reasons she cited for leaving was her fear that she would be physically harmed if she stayed in the United States.

On cross-examination, prosecutor Christopher Darden attacked her credibility on several fronts. For example, he showed how Lopez had provided conflicting names, birthdates, and addresses on official documents that had been completed under the penalty of perjury. He argued that Lopez either manufactured the Bronco sighting or changed the time of the sighting at the suggestion of the defense. He argued that she had no reasonable fear for her physical safety.

Rosa Lopez's credibility was further undermined by her demeanor and her answers during cross-examination. On dozens of occasions she responded to questions by saying "no me recuerdo" ("I don't remember"). Other times, she responded to Darden's questions by answering "if you say so, sir." Ontiveros notes that at times Lopez "appeared to concede or change her answers. She appeared hesitant and unsure. Sometimes her answers were nonresponsive or did not seem to make sense" (p. 270)

A linguist sent a letter to the court pointing out that Rosa Lopez's tendency to answer people in authority by saying "if you say so, sir" is not altogether surprising given her humble background. Moreover, she is from a Spanish-speaking culture that is more subtle, more indirect, and less confrontational than that found in the United States. For example, while interpreters and court watchers alike agree that "No me recuerdo" translates to "I don't remember," the message Lopez sought to convey is less clear. Upon redirect examination, she confirmed that "no me recuerdo" meant "No," not "Possibly yes" and that her usage of the phrase was common in El Salvador.

Darden also implied that Lopez must not have seen anything, because if she had, surely she would have mentioned it to her employers, whom she saw every day. But even Court TV commentators recognized that this reasoning ignores the class differences between Lopez and her employers, which discourage intimate or even collegial conversations.

Darden cast doubt on whether Lopez feared for her personal safety if she stayed in the United States, pointing out that no one had threatened her with physical harm. But Ontiveros raises a number of realities that Darden ignored. First, thousands of people "disappeared" during the war in El Salvador, including Lopez's own 15-year-old daughter. Further, Rosa Lopez had heard of the arrest of another defense witness for forgery charges. The prosecution justified Lopez's fears of arrest when they considered prosecuting her for the discrepancies on official forms. Given that being "arrested" could be life-threatening in El Salvador, Rosa Lopez's fears become more understandable, even believable.

Rosa Lopez's credibility also appeared damaged because she used several different addresses. Yet among low-income people without a permanent address it is not uncommon to give one relative's address as a residence for mail even while living with another relative. Prosecutor Darden suggested Lopez was dishonest because she had used several last names including Lopez, Reyes, and Martinez. Darden was ignorant of Latino naming conventions whereby people use the last names of both their parents, with the father's name appearing first. Moreover, "Reyes" could easily be a religious name given because Rosa Lopez was born on the feast of the three kings.

Ontiveros concludes that she did not find Rosa Lopez to be totally believable, but neither did she find her to be the clear-cut liar depicted by the prosecution. The ordeal of Rosa Lopez serves, nonetheless, to underscore the importance of "viewing all witness credibility through the lens of culture, class, and gender" (p. 269).

Introduction

I magine standing in the middle of an intersection with a view down several streets that run in different directions. If a friend stands at the end of one of those streets, she can share some of the same view, but her perspective will also be different: the features that are closest will be different and she will have a view down different side-streets. Now, think of those streets as being social dimensions such as class, race, ethnicity, gender, age, and sexual orientation. The view of those streets represents a person's life experiences, worldview, and "social location." To follow through on this analogy, if we described a person's social location based solely on race (for example), it would be incomplete and possibly confusing. An accurate description requires other markers—such as gender and social class—to get a "fix" on the location. That's what this chapter is about: recognizing that every person is at the center of multiple intersections. No one fits into any one category; instead, everyone exists at the intersection of many categories that shape not only their view of the world and the actions they take but other people's view of them (Wildman [1996] 1997). As straightforward as this seems, scholars of crime and justice have been slow to embrace the idea of "intersectionalities" for a number of reasons.

Many people—criminologists among them—still assume that gender is relevant only when discussing women, race is relevant only when discussing blacks and other people of color, and class is a characteristic of only the very rich or the very poor. Similarly, many people assume sexual orientation applies only to gays and lesbians. Moreover, people tend to focus on one social dimension at a time, independent of others. Even the widely used phrase "women and minorities" does not take into account that approximately 15 percent of the population are *both* women *and* racial or ethnic minorities. Women of color cannot choose to be treated as a member of the oppressed sex one day and a member of an oppressed racial group the next. They simply—and complexly—are both, although race may be more important in some situations and gender in others.

The intersections of class, race, and gender describe a way of viewing social inequalities as interrelated and interacting. The point of this chapter is to provide an appreciation of why examining multiple inequalities is not just important, but vital to understanding the criminal justice system. This chapter discusses some challenges to considering intersectionality and introduces some of the issues raised by its consideration. In addition, we hope to illustrate some of the myriad ways in which intersections play out in understanding the administration of the criminal law and the experiences of victims, offenders, and workers.

Our ability to describe how intersectionality manifests itself in the criminal justice system is limited by a number of practical considerations. First, as noted in the Preface, it is simply not possible to discuss every permutation, even if we confine ourselves to examining the intersections of say, class, race, and gender. Lynch (1996) has observed that even restricting the discussion to a three-class, two-gender, two-race (white, nonwhite) model results in some 36 possible race, gender, and class victim-offender combinations. Describing them soon becomes too complex a process to be practical or meaningful. Further, the process of constructing adequate conceptual frameworks to help us grasp the multiple meanings and implications of intersectionality is still under way (Daly 1995). Theorists are slowly but steadily developing a vocabulary that permits discussion of the links and conflicts among multiple crosscutting social relations in a clear, comprehensible way.

Another barrier to understanding intersections is that most academic and government sources of criminal justice information reduce the social relations of class, race, and gender to static, categorical variables. With the widespread availability of computers and statistical software has come increased attempts to isolate specific effects of class, race, and gender on, say, a person's likelihood of being arrested or incarcerated. These (largely quantitative) attempts to disaggregate effects come at the expense of understanding how these structuring factors interact with one another. *Gendered racism*, for example, is not the effect of gender simply added to the effect of racism. Each separate effect is complicated and heavily dependent on context, so their combination is likely to occur in highly complex ways.

This emphasis on quantitative methods and statistical analysis has resulted in a tendency among academics to conduct research from the assumption that we can "hold all else constant" (e.g., "What is the likelihood that a woman will be sent to prison and how does that compare with the likelihood of a man being sent to prison, if we hold constant prior record and offense seriousness?"). But while "holding all else constant" and controlling for legal and extralegal characteristics makes sense in a regression equation, it bears little semblance to the lives of the people who are represented by the variables. More generally, Currie has observed that "where both historical and current forces have kept some minorities disproportionately trapped in the lowest reaches of the economy, the distinction between economic and racial inequality itself is in danger of being uselessly abstract" (1985, p. 149). Statistical attempts to examine the effects of race while controlling for class are thus likely to produce little in the way of meaningful results. Some of the limitations of quantitative analysis can be addressed by using interaction terms, including additional variables, and assuming nonlinear dynamics. But the root of the problem is conceptual, not statistical (see Box 5.1).

Box 5.1

Ask a Simple Question . . .

Fact: Men are more likely than women to be murdered in their lifetime. Blacks are more likely than whites to be murdered in their lifetime.

Question: Who is more likely to be murdered, a white man or a black woman?

Fact: Blacks constitute about 12 percent of the United States population and around half of those incarcerated in state or federal prisons. Women make up over half of the United States population and around 7 percent of those incarcerated in state or federal prisons (Beck and Mumola 1999).

Question: Are black women overrepresented or underrepresented in correctional facilities?

Having trouble answering these questions? To take the first example, logic probably made it relatively easy for you to figure out that black men face the highest likelihood of being murdered relative to black women and whites. The conclusion that white women face the lowest likelihood of being murdered relative to white men and blacks was probably also straightforward. But to answer the question posed with any degree of confidence, you need more information, not just on race and gender but also on race and gender combined—e.g., for black women, white men, and so on. Provided with this information, you would discover that black women actually face a higher likelihood of being murdered than white men. As discussed elsewhere in this chapter, young non-Hispanic black women experience death rates from homicide or legal intervention over twice as high as white men's.

The second question is probably best answered "Both." Black women are both overrepresented (as blacks) and underrepresented (as women) in prisons. Of course, if you are one of the 40,000 black women incarcerated in a state or federal prison, you have more at stake than simply a choice of words (Greenfeld and Snell 1999). While the disproportionate incarceration of blacks has received a great deal of attention, most of this attention has been focused on black *men*. Similarly, a typical discussion of "women's experiences" has all too often assumed that the experiences and needs of white women are shared by black women. It was this situation that the editors of a classic text on black women were addressing when they named their book *All the Women Are White, All the Blacks Are Men, But Some of Us Are Brave* (Hull, Scott, and Smith 1982).

The issues raised by these two questions go beyond mere semantics and wordplay. This exercise speaks in a small way to the importance of considering characteristics such as race and gender not as *separate* constructs but as *interlocking* ones.

Reports from government agencies reflect a preference for quantitative information. As noted in Chapter 3, official reports typically use panethnic/racial categories such as black, Hispanic, and white (and occasionally Asian and Native American) that mask great variations along generation, class, language, gender, and ethnicity lines within each of the groups. Also, government agencies tend to treat race and sex as separate variables rather than as overlapping social locations. Even reports published by the Bureau of the Census, the Department of Labor, and the Department of Justice seldom present breakdowns by race and gender simultaneously that would permit readers to compare, for instance, the offenses committed by white men to those committed by white women. As noted in Chapter 2, it is extremely difficult to find information about social class that permits even basic comparisons.

In sum, these barriers, as well as space and time constraints, render a comprehensive discussion of intersections impossible. Much of the scholarship that best helps us understand how intersections play out in the social world tends to be descriptive and narrative, emphasizing the contextual aspects of people's day-to-day existence. We believe that qualitative studies, in combination with quantitative data, are best suited for demonstrating the nuanced meanings of class, race, gender, and their intersections. Thus, this chapter relies not only on statistical information to illustrate the different ways that benefits and harms are distributed throughout the criminal justice system, but also on examples from qualitative studies. By drawing on the rapidly growing body of literature from a number of disciplines using a variety of methodological approaches, we hope to convey not only the challenges but the importance of considering intersectionality.

Class, Race, and Gender in Society

In 1999, the U.S. Bureau of the Census estimated the population of the United States at 273,645,000. Non-Hispanic white women represented nearly 37 percent of the population, followed by non-Hispanic white men (35.1 percent), non-Hispanic black women (6.4 percent), non-Hispanic black men, Hispanic women, Hispanic men (each composing 5.8 percent of the population), non-Hispanic Asian and Pacific Islander women (2 percent), Asian and Pacific Islander men (1.8 percent) and American Indian, Eskimo, and Aleut women and men (a total of .8 percent).

Economic Sphere

As discussed in the previous chapters, the United States is deeply stratified in terms of class, with women more likely to be poor than men, and blacks and Hispanics more likely to be poor than whites. White men still dominate the top managerial and executive positions in the corporate world. As recently as 1997, there were no black CEOs and only two white women CEOs of Fortune 500 companies (one in a cosmetics company and the other at Mattel, which makes Barbie).

As shown in Table 5.1, a much higher percentage of women of color than white men live below the poverty line. Roughly one in three black and Hispanic women and one in four black and Hispanic men live below poverty level compared to one in ten white women and white men. Households headed by single white women are much less likely than other women to live below the poverty level. Nearly half of all Hispanic and around 40 percent of all black single female-headed households live below poverty level, compared to one-third of Asian and Pacific Islanders and around one in five non-Hispanic white female-headed households (Bureau of the Census 1999b).

Table 5.1

Number (in thousands) and Percent of Women and Men Living Below Poverty Level, by Race and Hispanic Origin, March 1998

	Women Below Poverty Level		Men Below Poverty Level	
	Number (in 1000s)	% of Total Within Racial/Ethnic Category	Number (in 1000s)	% of Total Within Racial/Ethnic Category
All races	20,387	14.9%	15,187	11.6%
White	13,944	12.4	10,452	9.6
Black	5,317	28.9	3,799	23.6
Hispanic origin	4,463	29.8	3,845	24.5

Source: Bureau of the Census (1998a).

According to 1997 Census data, nearly half of all whites report a median annual income of $30,000 or more, compared to only around 28 percent of black men, 22 percent of white women, and 17 percent of black women. White workers of both sexes earn more than their black or Hispanic counterparts, and men earned more than women (Bureau of Labor Statistics 1999a). The differences among men, however, are much greater than those among women. White men's weekly earnings ($614) are 31.4 percent higher than the earnings of black men ($468) and 57.7 percent higher than those of Hispanic men ($390). By contrast, white women's earnings ($468) are 17.0 percent higher than black women's ($400) and 38.9 percent higher than those of Hispanic women ($337). In the past 20 years, black and white women's inflation-adjusted earnings have increased, while men's earnings have decreased. From 1979 to 1998, white women's earnings increased 15.6 percent, black women's real earnings increased only 7.5 percent, and Hispanic women's earnings *decreased* by 2.6 percent. During this same period, the inflation-adjusted earnings for men dropped around 6.5 percent for both white and black men, and 19.3 percent for Hispanic men.

Men and women's earnings are greatly affected by the amount of education they have completed and the types of jobs they hold. Still, earnings differences between men and women persist at all education levels and across racial and ethnic categories. As shown in Table 5.2, a white male with only a high school education makes almost as much as a black, white, or Hispanic woman with a four-year college degree. Also, as the information in Table 5.3 suggests, whites and men are overrepresented among employed persons 16 years of age or older, with whites and men overrepresented in executive, administrative, and managerial positions and men disproportionately employed in blue-collar positions (such as operator, fabricator, or laborer). Examining combinations of race and sex reveals that white men are overrepresented in executive, administrative, and managerial positions and in blue-collar occupations. Black men are also overrepresented as blue-collar workers. Unlike white men, however, black men are overrepresented in the service sector but not in managerial professions.

Table 5.2
Median Annual Income by Educational Attainment for Persons 25 to 34 Years of Age by Sex, Race, and Hispanic Origin, March 1998

	Total	Less Than High School Graduate	High School Graduate	Associate Degree	Bachelor's Degree
White males	$26,672	$15,750	$24,736	$29,962	$36,117
Black males	21,232	11,602	19,426	25,270	27,324
Hispanic males*	18,780	14,198	20,342	25,136	29,608
White females	17,876	7,730	13,810	20,166	26,748
Black females	16,400	6,959	14,020	21,522	26,640
Hispanic females*	12,363	7,805	12,690	20,727	25,605

*May be of any race.
Source: Bureau of the Census (1998b).

As discussed in Chapter 4, women are concentrated in clerical and service occupations. This general pattern holds for both black and white women, though white women are more likely than black women to hold clerical positions, while black women are more likely to be employed in service areas. Further, black women are underrepresented in managerial and administrative positions, but white women are not.

Table 5.3

Employed Persons by Occupation, Race, and Sex, 1998

(totals in thousands)

	Executive, Administrative, and Managerial (*n*=19,062)	Administrative Support, Inc. Clerical (*n*=18,405)	Service Occupations (*n*=17,879)	Operators, Fabricators, and Laborers (*n*=18,273)
Male	55.6%	21.5%	40.3%	75.4%
White	88.5	82.6	76.9	80.1
Race/Sex				
White men	50.2	17.1	31.2	61.4
Black men	3.1	3.0	6.8	11.3
White women	38.5	65.6	45.9	18.7
Black women	4.1	10.0	10.7	4.4

Source: Bureau of Labor Statistics (1999b).

Political Sphere

Overall, whites have the greatest political participation in terms of registering to vote and actually voting, followed by blacks, then Asian and Latino citizens. For example, slightly more than half of Asian and Latino citizens voted in the 1992 presidential elections, compared to 59 percent of blacks and 70 percent of whites. Most of the participation differences between whites and blacks or Latinos can be accounted for by sociodemographic differences in education, age, and class—although there is growing concern (to be discussed below) about the number of African Americans prohibited from voting because of their past criminal record. College-educated Asian American citizens still trail equally educated whites by about 20 percentage points in registration and voting (Lien 1998). The gender gap in voter registration and voting rates is much less distinct than the racial gap and varies across racial groups. In general, women register to vote and vote at slightly higher rates than men. This gender gap appears to be wider among blacks and Latinos than among whites. Again, however, Asians present a slightly different situation, as Asian women registered and voted in 1992 at virtually the same rates as Asian men. Pei-Te Lien concluded that

> Compared to the role of gender, race is more influential in shaping a respondent's party identification, presidential vote choice, and pol-

icy attitude toward affirmative action in a multiracial society. Gender may be as good a predictor as race when it comes to estimating voting participation and the holding of liberal ideology. However, when race intersects with gender, the political attitudes and behavior of Asians and other nonwhites appear to be better predicted by their racial identity than by the intersection of the two. (p. 887)

Men of color and women continue to be underrepresented as elected officials. In 1998, women made up around one-fifth of the 7,424 state legislators. Of the 1,656 women state legislators, 15 percent are women of color. Of the 535 seats in the 106th U.S. Congress in 1999, 65 were held by women. Of these women, 28 percent are women of color, including 12 African American women, 1 Asian American woman, and 5 Latinas. The 1992 elections yielded only the second African American senator of the century and the first African American woman: Carol Moseley Braun. Today, there are around 40 black members of Congress.

In an effort to raise their political profile, some women of color have formed their own political action groups. A tight-knit cadre of black female political operatives formed the self-proclaimed "Colored Girls Club" to bring women back to the Democratic party, to attract the large numbers of black voters who are registered but do not vote, and to reach people who are otherwise alienated from the political process. In Houston, a group of Hispanic women organized a similar political action committee to raise the profile of Latinas in public life.

Representation by women and minority men in public offices is important in helping call attention to problems that white male politicians may not be aware of or interested in addressing. One such problem is "DWB," or the practice of police stopping people for "Driving While Black/Brown" (see Chapter 3 for a more detailed discussion of this problem). Typically the targets of such practices are black men. In 1999, the *Los Angeles Times* survey found that 18 of the 39 black law makers and 3 of the 19 Latino House members in the 106th Congress reported that they or someone in their immediate family had been stopped by police for no reason other than the color of their skin (Fullwood 1999). One of the youngest members of Congress, Rep. Harold E. Ford from Tennessee, described how he was stopped by a police officer at Reagan National Airport in Washington, D.C. The officer "demanded to see identification, and when I showed it to him, he couldn't believe it was my car and that I was a member of Congress. . . . Finally, he let me go. No apology or nothing. It really hurt me. If I'm treated like this, I can imagine how folks who don't have access to the things I do as a member of Congress are treated." Evidence suggests these concerned voices are being heard. In June 1999, President Clinton directed federal law enforcement agencies—including those overseeing immigration and customs—to start collecting data on the race, gender, and ethnicity of any citizens in order to determine the scope of racial profiling. As of October 1999, law makers (many of whom themselves have been subjected to racial profiling) had introduced 18 bills in statehouses and the U.S. Congress requiring law enforcement officials to document how often such stops occur (Samborn 1999).

Social Sphere

Women have made real progress in narrowing the gender gap in higher education, though gaps across race and ethnicity remain. As shown in Table 5.4, over 80 percent of people in the United States have a high school education, and nearly one-quarter have at least a bachelor's degree (Bureau of the Census 1998b). But a breakdown by race and sex produces a somewhat different picture. Among whites, around 84 percent of men and women are high school graduates, and men are only slightly more likely than women to have earned a bachelor's degree. In terms of high school completion, only a small gap exists between blacks and whites (with no statistical difference between blacks and whites aged 25 to 29 years old). However, only around 15 percent of black women and men have earned a bachelor's degree, compared to 23 percent of white women and men. Hispanic men and women are much less likely than white or black men and women to have graduated from high school.

In 1997, 11 percent of persons 16 to 24 years of age were "status dropouts"; that is, individuals who were out of school and had not earned a high school credential (such as a diploma or a G.E.D.). Non-Hispanic white women were least likely to have dropped out (6.7 percent), followed by non-Hispanic white men (8.5 percent), non-Hispanic black men (13.3 percent), and non-Hispanic black women (13.5 percent). Around one-quarter of all Hispanic women and men were status dropouts (Bureau of the Census 1998c). The economic consequences of leaving high school without a diploma are severe, resulting in a greater likelihood of being unemployed, earning less money when a job is secured, having fewer opportunities for promotion, and being more likely to receive public assistance. Young women who drop out of school tend to have children at younger ages and are more likely to be single parents than women who graduate from high school. High school dropouts are also overrepresented among the nation's prison and jail population (see Chapter 2).

Table 5.4

Educational Attainment of Persons 25 and Over by Sex, Race, and Hispanic Origin, 1998

	Number (in thousands)	High School Graduate or More	Bachelor's Degree or More
All races			
Men	82,376	82.8%	26.5%
Women	89,835	82.9	22.4
White			
Men	70,062	83.6	27.3
Women	75,016	83.8	22.8
Black			
Men	8,578	75.2	13.9
Women	10,798	76.7	15.4
Hispanic (may be of any race)			
Men	8,055	55.7	11.1
Women	7,989	55.3	10.9

Source: Bureau of the Census (1998b).

In terms of physical well-being, much progress has been made in diagnosing, treating, and preventing disease in the past 30 years. Yet a disparity still exists between the minority and majority populations in terms of opportunities for lifelong health care. According to a 1999 National Vital Statistics Report, women tend to have a life expectancy six years longer than that for men. This statistic is misleading, however, given that within a category of gender, whites tend to have a longer life expectancy than blacks or Hispanics. Thus, the life expectancy for black women (74.7 years) is almost the same as for white men (74.3 years).

Part of the racial disparity in life expectancy and overall health reflects class differences; the higher a person's social class, the longer he or she can expect to live and the better his or her health. The impact of low socioeconomic status on health is disproportionately felt by blacks, Hispanics, and Native Americans relative to non-Hispanic whites because members of these groups are disproportionately likely to be poor. Because of lower incomes, people who are racial and ethnic minorities are more likely to lack health insurance; to use fewer preventive, diagnostic, and treatment-related health services; and to live near a hazardous waste facility. Also, although behavioral and biomedical research helps develop treatment and disease prevention programs, much of the behavioral and biomedical research, including clinical trials, historically has focused primarily on the health concerns and treatment of white males.

Comparing the three leading causes of death among men and women 15 to 24 years of age also reveals differences across race, ethnicity, and sex (Hoyert et al. 1999). Overall, women in this age group have a much lower rate of death per 100,000 population than men (46.3 versus 124.0 deaths) and non-Hispanic whites have a much lower death rate than non-Hispanic blacks or Hispanics of any race (77.5 versus 139.2 and 87.0, respectively). But perhaps most revealing are the differences that emerge in the death rates and leading causes of death when comparing men and women non-Hispanic blacks, non-Hispanic whites, and Hispanics of any race (see Table 5.5). In general, death is a rare occurrence among young people 15 to 24 years of age. But comparisons across race and gender combined for this age group reveal that young black men have a death rate twice that of white men and four times that for white women.

Focusing on women's greater life expectancy and generally better health than men has two misleading consequences. First, comparisons made strictly between men and women hide the fact that many women of color face a risk of death or illness higher than that faced by white men. For instance, while nearly two-thirds of all white men who had colon cancer in 1989 survived five years, only slightly more than half of black women did so. Second, it masks the differences in health and well-being *among* women across race and ethnic categories. For example, white women are more likely to get breast cancer than black women. Yet nearly 9 out of 10 of white women diagnosed with cancer in 1989 survived the next five years, compared to only 7 out of 10 black women, possibly because of differences in the availability of preventive care and access to treatment (Kramarow et al. 1999).

Table 5.5
*Death Rates per 100,000 for the Leading Causes of Death for 15 to 24
Year-Olds, by Sex, Hispanic Origin, and Race, 1997*

	Men			Women					
	Black (non-Hispanic)	White (non-Hispanic)	Hispanic (of any race)	Black (non-Hispanic)		White (non-Hispanic)		Hispanic (of any race)	
	Overall 215.8	Overall 109.0	Overall 129.1	Overall	62.0	Overall	43.8	Overall	38.3
1	Homicide 113.3	Accidents 54.0	Accidents 49.9	Accidents	14.4	Accidents 21.5		Accidents 14.9	
2	Accidents 46.2	Suicide 19.5	Homicide 42.7	Homicide	13.3	Suicide	3.7	Homicide	4.8
3	Suicide 16.0	Homicide 13.2	Suicide 14.4	Heart disease	4.9	Cancer	3.6	Cancer	3.5

Source: Hoyert et al. (1999).

Thus, while the distribution of social benefits across race or across gender is important, the distribution across race *and* gender combined also deserves attention. To do otherwise presents a distorted view by implying that all women are situated similarly to all men, or that all members of one racial or ethnic group are situated similarly to another. Examining race and gender separately masks the extent to which non-Hispanic white men are situated better politically and economically than any other group in the United States. It also contributes to women of color, located as they are in the middle of intersecting avenues of economic, political, and social oppression, having their concerns overlooked or marginalized.

Class, Race, and Gender in Criminology

Drawing from the work of Michael Lynch (1996) and others, we can broadly outline the process by which class, race, and gender have transformed critical criminological thought, beginning with an examination of the *jurisprudential model* of criminal justice. The jurisprudential model is an ideal, not a reality. It is based on "rationality, equality before the law, and treating of like cases alike" (Agozino 1997, p. 17). Social characteristics are not just overlooked in this model, they are deliberately excluded. To consider social characteristics of the actors is to violate the judicial process. Because social characteristics are not *supposed* to influence the handling of a case, the jurisprudential model assumes that they do not; it regards law as constant and universal with the same facts resulting in the same decisions. In this regard, jurisprudential theorists adopt the perspective of the participants, not the observers. Lawyers and judges presumably frame their arguments and decisions in terms of how the rules logically apply to the facts. If people are sentenced differently for the same offense, it is because they differ on key legally germane characteristics, such as prior record and offense seriousness. Rules—and rules alone—determine how a case is decided. Consequently, when class, race, or sex discrimination occurs, it is considered an exception, not the rule.

In contrast to the jurisprudential model of justice, a *sociological model* assumes that political, economic, and social characteristics influence the administration of justice. Far from being constant from one case to another, law is assumed to be variable, changing with the social relations of the parties (see, for example, the discussion of Black's *Behavior of Law* in Chapter 2). Whereas the jurisprudential model is concerned with how the system *should* work, the sociological model examines how it actually *does* work. Sociological models, then, have concerned themselves with a variety of extralegal characteristics, including class, race, and gender.

The treatment of class, race, and gender in criminological scholarship has varied. One approach has been to focus on one social relation to the near exclusion of others. For example, the *radical perspective* that emerged in the late 1960s and 1970s drew heavily from Karl Marx's ideas about capitalism and class relations. As discussed in Chapter 2, the basic reasoning is that those with economic power (i.e., wealthy people) have access to political power and thus have the greatest ability to determine what is considered a crime and how society responds to crime. Later variations to this approach incorporated race and gender, but basically reduced race and gender to economics and class (Reiman 1998a). Economic and political power is correlated with race and gender, with whites wielding more power than nonwhites, and men wielding more power than women. Combining the factors of class, race, and gender location, it follows that wealthy white men will be relatively most advantaged within the social structure (including the criminal justice system) while poor minority women will be most disadvantaged.

Over time, however, the almost exclusive focus on class broadened to give greater importance to race and gender. More criminologists recognize that gender and race are not just correlates of class but also are independent structuring forces that affect how people act, how others respond to and define a person's action, who has the power to define and label certain actions as "criminal" or "deviant," and how law and law enforcement are organized to control behavior (Lynch 1996).

Race and gender have now surpassed class in being viewed as key organizing concepts of society. Feminist perspectives have helped criminology address the deficiencies in existing approaches to gender in criminal justice. Critical race feminism emerged from critical race theory. *Critical race theory* developed in the late 1970s through the efforts of scholars such as Derrick Bell and Alan Freeman, who were discontent with the slow pace of achieving racial justice (Delgado 1995). Building on critical sociology, neo-Marxism, and postmodern approaches, critical race theorists assume that racism is an ordinary, ingrained aspect of American society that cannot be readily remedied by law. The racism that permeates society is part of a socially constructed reality that exists to promote the interests of elite groups. Critical race theorists, then, aim not only to expose the ways in which existing arrangements support racism but also to construct alternative social realities.

Also stemming from the critical race theory genre is an emerging body of scholarship that considers what it means to be white in the United States (see Chapter 3). Far from being a safe haven for white supremacists, critical white studies prompt whites and nonwhites alike to consider the legacy of whiteness and to ask such questions as: How do whites benefit from membership in the dominant race? What part does the law play in defining who is white? How has our culture constructed whiteness and blackness such that they are not neutral descriptors but laden with meaning, value, and status? (Delgado and Stefancic 1997).

Critical race feminism arose in part to address the essentialism that has pervaded feminist and critical race theories (Wing 1997). Specifically, critical race feminists have objected both to feminist approaches that presume white, middle-class women's experiences are representative of all women's experiences and to critical race scholarship that presumes minority women's experiences are the same as those of their minority male counterparts. The effect of essentialist perspectives has been to "reduce the lives of people who experience multiple forms of oppression to addition problems: 'racism + sexism = straight black women's experience'" (Harris 1997, p. 11). But racial and ethnic minority women victims, offenders, and workers are not simply subjected to "more" disadvantage than white women; their oppression is of a qualitatively different kind.

Critical legal scholarship in the form of narrative or storytelling is used as a means of analyzing, challenging, and destroying the dominant myths, presuppositions, and "truths" that make up the main-stream culture's views of race and gender. The scholarly accounts of dominant groups too often suppress, devalue, and marginalize the experiences and perspectives of women and minority men. Storytelling is used to break the silence and convey complex issues in a readily accessible form designed to promote understanding. For example, law professor and critical race theorist Richard Delgado (1995 [1993]) explains the debate surrounding essentialism with his fictional alter ego, "Rodrigo Crenshaw." In this chronicle, Rodrigo has gotten "caught in the crossfire" at a Women's Law Caucus meeting:

> The debate about essentialism has both a political and a theoretical component," Rodrigo began. . . "In its political guise . . . members of different out groups argue about the appropriate unit of analysis—about whether the Black community, for example, is one community or many, whether gays and lesbians have anything in common with straight activists, and so on. At the Law Women's Caucus, they were debating one aspect of this—namely, whether there is one, essential sisterhood, as opposed to many. The women of color were arguing that to think of the women's movement as singular and unitary disempowers them. They said that this view disenfranchises anyone—say, lesbian mothers, disabled women, or working-class women—whose experience and status differ from what they term 'the norm.'
>
> "And the others, of course, were saying the opposite?"
>
> "Not exactly," Rodrigo replied. "They were saying that vis-à-vis men, all women stood on a similar footing. All are oppressed by a common enemy, namely patriarchy, and ought to stand together to confront this evil . . . [Black feminists'] focus on their own unique experience contributes to a 'disunity' within the broader feminist movement . . . [it is troubling] because it weakens the group's voice, the sum total of power it wields. Emphasizing minor differences between young and old, gay and straight, and Black and white women is divisive, verging on self-indulgence. It contributes to the false idea that the individual is the unit of social change, not the group. It results in tokenism and plays into the hands of male power." (pp. 243–246)

In addition to paying increased attention to class, race, and gender and the ways in which they interact in an oppressive system, scholars such as Stephanie Wildman, Adrienne Davis, and Peggy McIntosh have suggested that the focus of attention should be not only racism, sexism, and classism, but the idea of *privilege* (see Box 5.2). Sexism, racism, classism, and other forms of systematic discrimination would not exist if some people did not benefit from them—that is, if some people did not possess a privileged position in our society's hierarchy. However, discussions of the "isms" are much more common than blunt discussions of privilege.

Box 5.2

You Know You're Privileged When . . . (Part III)

In keeping with this chapter's focus on intersectionality, we have expanded on the forms of white privilege discussed in Chapter 3 and male privilege discussed in Chapter 4. This list attempts to identify some of the specific characteristics of middle-class, white male privilege.

- People who meet me for the first time will assume that I have a regular job and no criminal record.
- I get praised from women friends and colleagues when I demonstrate that I can cook, clean, or care for small children.
- If someone needs help with a technical activity such as setting up a new computer with the necessary hardware or software, they assume I have the expertise and can be trusted with the responsibility.
- When I dine at a restaurant alone or with a woman, I will not be seated by the kitchen or near the entrance to the toilets.
- When making a major purchase, such as a car or a home, it will be assumed that I not only have the means to make such a purchase but that I understand the business aspects of it, such as mortgage points and amortization.
- When I wear expensive clothing or jewelry or drive an expensive car, I will be treated as though I obtained these goods through the fruits of my own legitimate labor rather than through illegal activity or my association with a sexual intimate.
- If I am a parent of small children who works long hours outside the home, people will perceive me as a good provider who only wants the best for his family, rather than as someone who puts career above family or is otherwise a faulty, absentee parent.
- In the event I am assaulted while walking home at two in the morning, no one will assume I was involved in an illicit business transaction that went bad or blame me for being out late at night.
- If I am an attorney scheduled to appear in court, I can be reasonably confident as I enter the courthouse that I will not be mistaken for a secretary, court reporter, or defendant.
- No one will imply that I got my job based on my race or sex.

Moreover, this focus on racism and sexism may contribute to the very problems they identify by obscuring the system of power that causes them to begin with. Calling someone a racist lays the blame on the individual rather than the cultural, social, and legal mechanisms that support racism (see Chapter 3's discussion of individual and institutional racism, along with the accompanying text). As a result, instead of being concerned about systemic racism, whites tend to focus on how to avoid the label. Also, the "isms" language suggests that patterns of domination and subordination are interchangeable; someone subordinated under one form of oppression would be similarly situated to someone else subordinated under another form. As a result, white women who define themselves as oppressed under sexism may not consider the ways in which they are privileged by racism or heterosexism.

According to Wildman and Davis (1997), one of the major features of privilege is that all members of society are evaluated against the characteristics held by the privileged. And there are other mechanisms by which members of a privileged group benefit. For example, in evaluating applications, law schools value mastery of English more than the ability to speak more than one language. Further, when Linda Wightman (1997) examined every application to U.S. law schools for the 1990–91 academic year, she found that twice the number of whites as blacks got into law schools on the basis of alumni preference, an elegant essay, or recommendations by powerful people. These students would not have been admitted on grades and test scores alone. "Legacy admissions" favor children of influential alumni or donors over other applicants. In 1995, twice as many students admitted to University of California schools were admitted through legacy admissions than through affirmative action programs (Padilla 1997, n. 2). Yet students admitted as "legacies" are perceived as deserving (rather than unfairly privileged), while students admitted under affirmative action are viewed by many as having received an undeserved advantage involving "reverse discrimination" against the privileged groups.

Privilege may also be exercised by members of the privileged group through silence, as illustrated by Stephanie Wildman's experience of being summoned to jury duty. During *voir dire*, prospective jurors were asked to introduce themselves. The defense attorney then proceeded to ask each Asian-looking male prospective juror whether he spoke English. No other jurors were asked this question, nor did the judge object to this questioning. Wildman reports that the Asian American man seated next to her flinched when he was asked, leading her to wonder how many times in his life he had been subjected to the question.

> I considered beginning my own questioning by saying, "I'm Stephanie Wildman, I'm a professor of law, and yes, I speak English." I wanted to focus attention on the subordinating conduct of the attorney, but I did not. I exercised my white privilege by my silence. I exercised my privilege to opt out of engagement, even though this choice may not always be consciously made by someone with privilege. (Wildman with Davis 1997, p. 316)

Structured action theory is another approach that attempts to acknowledge the power of a socially dominant class, race, and gender in defining social action. Structured action approaches are among those pointing out that masculinity or femininity cannot be fully understood in isolation from class or race or sexual orientation. In the United States, the dominant form of masculinity (or "hegemonic masculinity") is based on white, professional/managerial class, heterosexual males and emphasizes characteristics such as paid employment, subordination of women and girls, authority, control, and rationality (Connell 1987, 1995; Messerschmidt 1997; Pyke 1996). Crime provides one structurally permitted means of establishing a man's masculinity when other channels for doing so are blocked to his race, ethnicity, class, or age. For example, Jana Bufkin (1999) relies on structured action theory to illustrate how bias crimes are a means of "doing" gender. These overwhelmingly male bias crime offenders situationally achieve masculinity by attacking members of groups (i.e., women, homeless people, people with disabilities, religious minorities, racial and ethnic minorities, and homosexuals/bisexuals) who undermine the hegemonic masculine ideal.

The form of femininity most valued and supported in U.S. culture is also based on a white, middle-class, heterosexual norm. The "emphasized femininity" is that which complements hegemonic masculinity and is defined through it: marriage, housework, child care, fragility, sociability (Connell 1987; Martin and Jurik 1996). More generally, Hart's work on depictions of lesbianism and female killers suggests the category "woman" is reserved for white, upper-class, heterosexual females. This categorization serves a disciplinary function, patrolling the bounds of "normal" femininity by creating an "othered" (not woman) category onto which women's deviance can be displaced. Thus, "the ultimate violation of the social instinct, murder, and the perversion of the sexual instinct, same-sex desire, were linked as limits that marked the boundaries of femininity" (1994, p. 30). Lesbians and killers (and women of color) resided together in the "not woman" category. Indeed, Hart suggests that the killer in the movie *Single White Female* had to be white because her status as a killer would have been too obvious if she had been lesbian or black.

Increasingly, scholarship emphasizes that race, gender, and class are not only social constructs but also interactive processes involving creative human actors rather than static, categorical variables. The challenge remains to understand the complex ways in which class, race, and gender simultaneously structure people's actions and others' reactions to them—and to identify the forms of privilege that keep racist, sexist, and classist systems in place. Two noteworthy studies in the sociology of crime that have captured the various nuances in the interactions between class, race, and gender, are Madriz's (1997) examination of women's fear of crime (1997) and Totten's (2000) investigation into adolescent girlfriend abuse. In both of these ethnographies, the authors are able to capture the qualitative differences in the life experiences of men and women, boys and girls, majorities and minorities, in relation to socioeconomic status or class and crime and crime control. Both are able to demonstrate that there is no standardized "class" experience, "race" experience, or "gender" experience, but rather there is a repertoire of class, race, and gender experiences. These experiences have emerged in the context of social groupings or various combinations of two or more of these inseparable ingredients in the formation of personal and social identity.

In *Nothing Bad Happens to Good Girls*, Esther Madriz (1997) explores the fear of crime among young and old, African American, Latina, and white upper-, middle-, and working-class women. In the process, she is able to demonstrate how fear of crime perpetuates gender inequalities and contributes to the differential social control of women by class and race/ethnicity. In *Guys, Gangs, and Girlfriend Abuse*, Totten (2000) explores the relations between early childhood abuse, familial and gender ideologies, and the construction of masculinity on the one hand, and the marginal male socialization experiences of straight, gay, white, black, and Asian teenagers on the other hand. In this integrative study, Totten is not only able to make sense out of the patterned differences of girlfriend abuse with respect to the physical, sexual, and emotional violence meted out by boyfriends, but is also able to explain how the reproduction of violence and social control in these young people's lives is related to the abuse of gays and racial minorities. Totten is able to show how these adolescent males' feelings of powerlessness, despair, and humility regarding their economic future prospects and living up to the masculine ideal of "breadwinner" and their anxieties about and fears surrounding their heterosexuality both contribute to their bashing of girlfriends and gay people.

Intersectionality, Crime, and the Law

The law does not define crimes based on the class, race, and sex of the offender. Evidence suggests, however, that these social locations do play a role in shaping who is seen as a "criminal" and what punishments they deserve. Katheryn K. Russell (1998) proposes that because we are inundated with criminal images of black men, the picture that comes to mind when we think about crime is the *criminalblackman*, that "crime and young Black men have become synonymous in the American mind" (p. 71). Among the evidence she cites are racial hoax cases in which someone fabricates a crime and blames it on another person because of his race or in which an actual crime has been committed and the offender falsely blames someone because of his race. Using news articles available through LEXIS/NEXIS, Russell identified 67 such racial hoaxes between 1987 and 1996. In all of the cases, the hoax victim was a male. 47 of these cases involved whites who fabricated crimes against blacks; 7 of the cases involved charges fabricated by police or court officers.

The widespread perception that black men are engaged in criminal activity contributes to an uncritical acceptance of different punishments for similar crimes. One of the most widely publicized examples is the debate over the punishment for powder cocaine and crack cocaine (a derivative of powder cocaine) offenses. The federal Anti-Drug Abuse Act of 1986 stipulated that a person convicted of possession with intent to distribute 50 grams or more of crack cocaine or 5,000 grams of powder cocaine must be sentenced to at least ten years in prison. This 100:1 disparity was justified in part on the grounds that crack is a more addictive form of cocaine.

Belief in the greater addictive properties of crack was seriously undermined by a review of research studies that found the physiological and psychoactive effects of cocaine to be similar *regardless of the form* (Hatsukami and Fischman 1996). Further, critics charged that the sentencing provision represented a form of institutionalized or unconscious racism by punishing offenses for crack cocaine (which is disproportionately used by black men) 100 times more severely than those for powdered cocaine (disproportionately used by white men).

Recognizing the merits of these arguments, in 1995 the U.S. Sentencing Commission proposed reducing the disparity, but Congress rejected the proposal. A subsequent 1998 attempt to reduce the disparity to 10:1 (by reducing the amount of powder cocaine necessary to trigger the mandatory minimum sentence from 500 to 50 grams, ensuring that even more low-level offenders would be incarcerated) was also unsuccessful. The 100:1 disparity remains.

Cathy Shine and Marc Mauer (1993) of The Sentencing Project call attention to another example suggesting bias against poor minorities that has received much less publicity: the discrepancies in punishment between drug users and drunk drivers. According to the Uniform Crime Reports, there were 8.5 million arrests for criminal offenses nationwide in 1997. The most frequent category of arrest was drug abuse violations (1,101,302 arrests), followed by larceny-theft (1,032,467 arrests) and driving under the influence (DUI) (971,795 arrests). Drug abuse and DUI accounted for roughly one in five arrests.

Both alcohol and drug use have the potential to harm not only the user but also those around him or her. Shine and Mauer report that alcohol is associated with 94,000 deaths annually, with estimated societal costs of $85 billion. Drug use results in an estimated 21,000 deaths a year (through overdoses, diseases, and violence associated with the drug trade) at an estimated cost of $58 billion. Although the criminal uses of alcohol and illicit drugs both cause great harm to society, the responses to these crimes are strikingly different. In particular, the criminal justice system punishes the possession of illicit drugs much more severely than it punishes drunk driving. While drunk drivers are typically treated as misdemeanants and receive nonincarcerative sentences, persons convicted of drug possession are typically charged with felonies and are more likely to be incarcerated. In New York State, for instance, persons convicted of drug possession are 24 times as likely to be sentenced to prison as those convicted of drunk driving.

Shine and Mauer suggest that, in addition to reflecting the historic tolerance of alcohol, the differential societal response to the criminal use of alcohol and illicit drugs may stem from the different profiles of the perceived "typical" drunk driver and drug offender. For both drug abuse and DUI offenses, the overwhelming majority of arrestees are male (over 80 percent). However, nearly 90 percent of all those arrested for drunk driving are white, compared to less than two-thirds of those arrested for drug abuse violations. Blacks make up approximately one in ten of all those arrested for driving under the influence but over one in three of all persons arrested for drug abuse violations. Shine and Mauer (1993) note that DUI offenders are typically white, male blue-collar workers, while persons convicted of drug possession are disproportionately low-income or indigent African-American and Hispanic males. The authors conclude: "Although substantial numbers of deaths are caused by drunk drivers, our national approach has emphasized prevention, education, and treatment. . . . For drug abuse, particularly among low-income people, treatment initiatives have lagged behind the move to 'get tough'" (p. 35).

Criminal Justice Processing

Victimization

"Men are more likely to be victimized than women." Official statistics attest to the veracity of this statement. In particular, young black men are at a great risk for homicide victimization. Their risk of being murdered is 4–5 times greater than that of young black women, 5–8 times higher than that of young white men, and 16–22 times higher than that of young white women. Furthermore, a breakdown of official victimization rates by both race and sex reveals that "some groups of men are less likely to be victimized than some groups of women." As shown in Table 5.6, American Indian women experience higher rates of violent victimization than Asian males, black males, and white males (Bureau of Justice Statistics 1999a). Similarly, black women experience higher rates of violent victimization than Asian men and almost the same likelihood of violent victimization as white men.

Table 5.6
Annual Average Violent Victimization Rates (per 1,000) for Persons 12 or Older, by Sex and Race, 1992–96

	Women	Men	Men:Women Ratio
American Indian	98	153	1.6:1
Asian	21	37	1.8:1
Black	56	68	1.2:1
White	40	59	1.5:1
All races	42	60	1.4:1

Source: Bureau of Justice Statistics (1999a).

Among young black men, the leading cause of death is homicide and legal intervention, while for the other groups it is accidents and adverse effects. Moreover, black women die as the result of homicide or legal intervention at twice the rate of white men. Chapter 3 introduced research by Johnson and Leighton (1999) that examined the claim of racial genocide in the United States by analyzing observed death rates against what would be expected if whites had the death rates of African Americans and vice versa. These researchers report that in 1991, 80 percent of the African-American deaths in the "homicide and legal intervention" category were excess deaths (in excess of what would be expected with the white death rate). Rather than the 10,430 black men observed in that category, only 1,791 were expected, given the white male death rate. Rather than the 2,274 black women, only 570 were expected, given the white female death rate.

If, on the other hand, whites had the black homicide rate, the body count would be almost 80,000 instead of the 12,000 observed in the 1991 statistics. The 9,253 white men killed by homicide would become 67,592, and the 3,063 white women victims would become 13,600. The authors note that "if white lives were threatened by homicide on this scale, massive public health prevention efforts would be put in place to ameliorate this deadly problem." Instead, policy responses have been based "on punishment practices which we *know* as a matter of historical experience will not deter violence in any substantial way and which may even promote rather than retard violence" (Johnson and Leighton 1999; emphasis in original).

Further, perceptions of the victim and his or her "worthiness" vary depending upon class, race, or gender. For example, when a black man is assaulted, many people may be more inclined to assume he was doing something that precipitated the violence, perhaps by being involved in the drug trade. A study of homicides reported in the *Los Angeles Times* found that newspapers tend to accord white women victims who are very young or very old the most media coverage (Sorenson et al. 1998). A white, middle-class woman may be seen as the ultimate "victim," deserving of the most sympathy, especially when her behavior was consistent with the "pedestal values" described at the beginning of Chapter 4.

Intimate violence is a gendered victimization experience as 85 percent of all victims are women (Greenfeld et al. 1998; see also Box 5.3). In 1996, the per capita rate of intimate murder of black women was seven times higher than the rate for white females. A victim's ability to obtain help in escaping the abuse is strongly shaped by class, race, and ethnicity. While the physical experience of being battered is the same for all women, women who are racial and ethnic minorities face additional barriers to seeking help in the form of shelter or other economic support (Rasche 1995 [1988]; Rivera (1997 [1994]).

Box 5.3

Stalking

Is sending a person a birthday card or flowers a crime? How about calling a person on the phone? Paying a surprise visit to someone's workplace? Standing across the street from someone's house? Taken individually, these acts are perfectly legal. However, when considered as part of a pattern of behavior intended to make someone feel afraid, they may be defined as *stalking* (Leonard 1998). In 1990, California passed the first antistalking law, prompted by the 1989 murder of television actress Rebecca Schaeffer by an obsessed fan who stalked her for two years. Since then, all 50 states and the District of Columbia have passed similar legislation.

Most states define stalking as "the willful, malicious, and repeated following and harassing of another person" (Tjaden and Thoennes 1998). Legal definitions vary widely from state to state in the activities they consider harassing, in threat and fear requirements, and in how many acts must occur before the conduct can be considered stalking. One of the challenges to prosecuting stalkers is that most state antistalking statutes stipulate that to qualify as a stalker, the perpetrator must make a credible threat of violence against the victim. Thus, even if the perpetrator is acting in such a way that would cause a reasonable person to be very frightened or fear bodily harm (against themselves or someone close to them), the person cannot be prosecuted for stalking unless an explicit threat is made.

Both men and women can be victims and offenders of stalking, but data from the National Violence Against Women (NVAW) Survey indicate that nearly 80 percent of the victims are women and 87 percent of the perpetrators are men. One out of every 12 women and every 45 men have been stalked at some time in their lives. The average stalking situation lasts nearly 2 years. In general, no difference was found in stalking prevalence between white women and minority women, or among men of different racial and ethnic backgrounds. However, some evidence suggests that American Indian/Alaska Native women report proportionately more stalking victimization than women of other racial and ethnic backgrounds.

Nearly 95 percent of female victims and 60 percent of male victims identified their stalker as male. Most women are stalked by some type of intimate partner, while men tend to be stalked by strangers and acquaintances. Also, a strong link exists between stalking and other forms of violence in intimate relationships. Four out of five women who were stalked by a current or former husband or cohabiting partner were also physically assaulted by that partner, and nearly one-third were also sexually assaulted by that partner.

It is not clear why men are more likely to be stalked by strangers and acquaintances. Some men may be stalked in the context of inter- or intragroup gang rivalries. There is some evidence that gay men are at greater risk of being stalked than straight men, possibly because the perpetrator may be motivated by hatred toward gays or by sexual attraction. Police may not take men's reports of being stalked as seriously. In one case, the judge told a man who was being stalked by an ex-girlfriend that he should be "flattered by all the attention." The ex-girlfriend killed the man several weeks later (Brody 1998a).

Stalking victims reported that informal police interventions (such as police warnings) tended to be more effective than formal interventions (such as arrests or restraining orders) in getting the stalking to stop. One-quarter of women stalking victims and 10 percent of men stalking victims obtained restraining orders against their stalkers. However, about 70 percent of these restraining orders were violated. In about one-fifth of the cases, the victim attributed the cessation of the stalking to having moved away or to the stalker getting a new love interest.

The NVAW report makes several recommendations to address stalking, including eliminating credible threat requirements from antistalking statutes, training the mental health and criminal justice communities on the particular psychological and safety needs of stalking victims, and conducting research on the effectiveness of law enforcement interventions. More information about stalking is available through the domestic violence and sexual assault section of *http://www.stopviolence.com.*

Jenny Rivera ([1994] 1997]) focuses attention on the experiences of battered Latinas, though many of her points hold true for other racial and ethnic minority women. She observes that a shortage of bilingual and bicultural criminal justice workers creates a system ill prepared to address many battered Latinas' claims. Women who are racial and ethnic minorities must decide whether to seek assistance from an outsider who "may not look like her, sound like her, speak her language, or share any of her cultural values" (p. 261). The economically marginalized position of many women of color means they have limited resources to fill the gaps in available support services to assist them (e.g., by securing an attorney, seeking counseling, hiring a translator, telephoning family and friends who reside outside the United States). Minority women are frequently stereotyped. For example, Latinas are often seen as docile and domestic, or sensual and sexually available. Such racial and ethnic stereotypes devalue Latinas and may place even more social distance between the woman and those assigned to handle her complaint.

Similar problems exist within the Asian/Pacific Islander community. In addition, "the low status they hold in the traditional Asian/ Pacific family hierarchy as children and as females, compounded with a culturally based emphasis on maintaining harmony even if it is at the cost of the individual's well being, continues to discourage these teenagers from asserting their rights and needs" (Yoshihama et al. in Levy 1998, p. 192). Shame and guilt are still associated with aspects of abuse (especially sexual abuse), which further increases the barriers to reporting and to receiving help.

An immigrant woman may face additional challenges to seeking help. If she doesn't speak English, police officers may rely on the batterer to provide the translation. Immigrant women's families may be far away, contributing to the experience of isolation. Or, as Tina Shum, a family counselor at a social service agency, observed, many battered Asian immigrant women share a house with extended family members where there is no privacy on the telephone and no opportunity to leave the house (Crenshaw 1991). Based on her field study of Los Angeles battered women's shelters located in minority communities, Kimberlé Crenshaw (1991) found numerous instances in which immigrant women were basically held hostage by their boyfriends or husbands, who threatened the woman with deportation if she reported the abuse. Even if such threats are unfounded, women with no independent access to information may still be intimidated by them. Many women do not realize that even if they are not U.S. citizens, they are still entitled to police protection from abuse.

Some minority women are reluctant to seek help from the police. They may fear the police will do too little and not take their victimization seriously. Or they may fear the police will do too much and deal with the abuser too harshly. Many women of color have had experiences with the police—either in the United States or in their country of origin—that led them to distrust or place little confidence in the police. Interviews with operators of domestic violence shelters in Harlem revealed that police brutality was the dominant issue in minority communities, while violence against women was not even a close second. "Women of color fear that the protection they seek could result in their men being beaten or even killed by cops. And if the batterer, often the sole source of support for the victim and her children, is charged with a felony, he could spend his life behind bars under the 'three-strikes-and-you're-out' mandate" (Swift 1997: B7).

Responses to battered women need to acknowledge not only that women of color experience sexual and patriarchal oppression at the hands of their male partners, but that they "at the same time struggle alongside them against racial oppression" (Rice 1990, p. 63). For black women, the emphasis on racial solidarity and not "airing dirty laundry" has often meant placing the needs of a collectivity (family, church, neighborhood, or race) over their own needs. This emphasis often "promotes a paradigm of individual sacrifice that can border on exploitation" and that may have dire consequences in terms of their need for help escaping abuse (Collins 1998, p. 29).

Identification and Adjudication

As discussed in earlier chapters, crime is disproportionately committed by men, with black men and women overrepresented in many offense categories. Discussions of crime and offender characteristics have focused to such an extent on black men that, as noted earlier, "criminal" has almost become a synonym for black men. While official crime statistics that fail to combine race and gender make the task of identification awkward, certain crimes seem to qualify as "white men's crimes" on the basis of whites' overrepresentation (and women's underrepresentation) in these offense categories. The *1998 Sourcebook of Federal Sentencing Statistics* (U.S. Sentencing Commission

1999) reports the percent of offenders in each primary offense category by gender and by race separately.

For arson, tax, gambling/lottery, pornography/prostitution, civil rights, environmental/wildlife, antitrust, and food and drug offenses, 70 percent or more of the offenders are white (which we would expect, given the proportion of whites in the U.S. population) and 70 percent of the offenders are male (which is not surprising, given that women and minority men are seriously underrepresented as CEOs and in other executive positions of large corporations, effectively blocking them from the access necessary to engage in large-scale white-collar crimes). It is, for example, not surprising that all 46 of the individuals convicted in Operation Ill-Wind, a large-scale defense procurement fraud investigation, were white males (Pasztor 1995).

Thus, the intersections of class, race, and gender shape not only perceptions of crime but the nature of criminal behavior itself. Opportunities to commit other types of crimes are also shaped by class, race, and gender. Drawing on interviews with women cocaine users, Sheigla B. Murphy and Marsha Rosenbaum (1997) identified ways in which race and class interact to profoundly influence the type of cocaine available (cocaine powder or crack rocks), patterns of use, and the consequences of drug use. Murphy and Rosenbaum consider the lives of two young women "who used cocaine too much": Monique, a poor underclass black woman living in an impoverished inner-city neighborhood, and Becky, a white, middle-class woman. Although there were similarities between the two women's experiences (e.g., both first snorted cocaine in a mixed-gender group with friends, both continued to use cocaine not because of the high but to be part of a social scene), several factors differentiated Monique's and Becky's experiences with cocaine.

Monique, growing up in housing projects, was exposed to powder cocaine in early 1985 and was shown how to smoke crack within a year. The availability of crack in her neighborhood (with less risky drugs being harder to find) and the prevalence of crack use or dealing among her friends contributed to the escalation of Monique's crack use. By contrast, Becky lived in a white, middle-class neighborhood. Her first cocaine source was someone at an upscale rock and roll club. During the first two years, Becky's cocaine use was limited to the one night a week she worked at the club, though her cocaine snorting increased once she began to work more steadily at the club and as more of her friends used powder cocaine.

Becky, with her own private room at work and at home, was able to conceal her drug use, whereas Monique's crack use kept her outside her house and on the streets. While Becky's avoidance of detection helped her avoid the label of "deviant" despite her rising drug use, Monique was arrested, was stigmatized both formally and by her family, and suffered a loss of self-esteem.

As the example of Becky and Monique illustrates, being poor means having few possessions, limited legitimate means to acquire them, and little reason to hope the situation will improve. Being black and poor places a person in closer geographical proximity to opportunities to buy crack cocaine and in closer psychological proximity to actually smoking it. By contrast, class and race protect someone who is a white, middle-class person with a stake in conformity from serious consequences of drug use and, as in Becky's case, can make a "period of heavy cocaine use a mere detour on the road to a solid future" (Murphy and Rosenbaum 1997, p. 109).

Punishment and Imprisonment

Approximately 1.9 million sentenced prisoners were under state or federal jurisdiction at midyear 1999 (Bureau of Justice Statistics 2000a). Around 41 percent of these prisoners were black males, 33 percent were white males, and 16 percent were Hispanic males; almost 4 percent were black females, 3 percent were white females, and 2 percent were Hispanic females. (These figures do not include people held by the Immigration and Naturalization Service.) Between 1990 and 1997, the number of prisoners sentenced to more than one year increased by 62 percent. The increase was greatest for black and white women (80 percent increase for each group), followed by black males (61 percent) and white males (54 percent). Among Hispanics, who may be of any race, the number of females incarcerated increased 97 percent, while the number of male inmates rose 62 percent. Table 5.7 shows that while men are incarcerated at much higher rates than women, within a category of sex, the incarceration rates vary widely by race and ethnicity. For instance, the incarceration rate for black women is eight times that for white women.

Table 5.7

Number of Sentenced Prisoners Under State or Federal Jurisdiction per 100,000 Residents, by Sex, Race, and Hispanic Origin, 1997

	Female	Male	Female:Male Ratio
American Indian	80	905	1:11.3
Black (non-Hispanic)	200	3,209	1:16.0
White (non-Hispanic)	25	386	1:15.4
Hispanic (may be of any race)	87	1,273	1:14.6
Total	53	841	1:15.9

Source: Bureau of Justice Statistics (1999c).

According to a 1997 Bureau of Justice Statistics report, men are more than eight times as likely as women to be incarcerated in prison at least once during their lifetime, and blacks are nearly twice as likely as Hispanics and six times more likely than whites to be admitted to prison at some point in their lives (Bureau of Justice Statistics 1997b). But these statistics tell only part of the story. The same study shows that among men, more than one in four blacks and one in six Hispanics, compared to one in twenty-three whites, are expected to serve a state or federal prison sentence if current first-incarceration rates do not change. And while women overall appear to have lower lifetime chances of incarceration than men, black women (3.6 percent) have nearly the same chance as white men (4.4 percent) of serving time in prison. Compared to Hispanic women and white women, black women are more than two and seven times, respectively, as likely to be admitted to prison during their lifetime.

The reality of these statistics for individuals includes how the experience of being incarcerated breeds feelings of despair and hopelessness, frustration and rage. These feelings, combined with the stigma of having been incarcerated, can make it difficult to get a job upon release, prompting some scholars to call incarceration "the 'Scarlet Letter' of unemployability." Thus, high rates of black male incarceration undermine the economic viability of the black community (Johnson, Farrell, and Stoloff 1998). Further, the high rate of incarceration for black men can undermine the seriousness with which batterers participate in court-mandated intervention programs. Rather than being seen as something they need to take seriously, minority men sometimes see the arrest and the sentence as another example of racism in the criminal justice system and yet another effort to keep black men down.

Another unintended consequence of the war on crime has been the limiting of people's ability to use political participation as a means of changing the system. According to a report by The Sentencing Project, in all except four states, inmates lose their right to vote while they are incarcerated. Further, thirty-one states prohibit offenders from voting (a process called "political disenfranchisement") while they are on probation or parole, and of these, thirteen states disenfranchise most felons for life. Marc Mauer, director of The Sentencing Project, estimates that 4.2 million Americans are either currently or permanently disenfranchised from voting, including one in seven black males of voting age. Mauer concludes that "the cumulative impact of such large numbers of persons being disenfranchised from the electoral process clearly dilutes the political power of the African American community" (1997, p. 12).

Moreover, the criminal justice policies and practices that disproportionately affect men of color have an impact on women as well (Danner 1998). As corrections budgets have been increased, state funds to support low-income women and their children have been slashed along with social service jobs that are disproportionately staffed by women. The economic consequences are exacerbated by some of the current welfare reforms (Phillips and Bloom 1998). The Personal Responsibility and Work Opportunity Reconciliation Act of 1996 replaced the Aid to Families with Dependent Children (AFDC) program with the Temporary Assistance to Needy Families (TANF) program. In an effort to promote "personal responsibility," the Act prohibits individuals who violate parole or probation orders from receiving TANF or food stamps. The Act does not distinguish between minor technical violations (such as missing an appointment) and more serious transgressions (such as committing a new crime). Another provision bans persons convicted of drug felonies from receiving TANF or food stamps for the rest of their lives.

Critics of the Act express concern that children will feel the repercussions of provisions intended to punish their mothers. Given the increasing numbers of women arrested for drug offenses, combined with the greater likelihood of a woman being poor and having primary responsibility for children, the Act has a disproportionately large negative impact on poor, drug-using mothers, who are more likely than a man to rely on public assistance and to have responsibilities for children. Thus a poor woman who is also a mother suffers consequences for her behavior in a way that a middle-class man with no responsibilities for children does not.

Further, the Act affects relatives caring for the children of incarcerated parents. An estimated quarter million minor children have mothers incarcerated in prison or jail, and around 1.7 million minor children have incarcerated fathers (Greenfeld and Snell 1999). Ninety percent of the children of incarcerated fathers live with their mothers. But for women, a grandparent caregiver is the most common arrangement across racial and ethnic lines, with 57 percent of black mothers, 55 percent of Hispanic mothers, and 41 percent of white mothers leaving their children in the care of a grandparent (Snell and Morton 1994).

TANF requires that relative caregivers meet the same work requirements as parents living with their children, even though many caregivers report that assuming responsibility for another's children causes major disruptions in their lives. Consider the account of Island, a 60-year-old woman in New York City. Her son is a crack dealer. Her siblings are alcohol users. Her siblings' offspring and her own children are drug users. Drug use has rendered her family "transient and undependable" (Dunlap 1992, p. 198). Island explains that "I raised my children. I raised my sister's nine. I raised my brother's two. And I raised all of my nieces and nephew, I done raised 89 kids. . . ." (p. 199). Current legislation mandates that a person may not receive assistance for more than 60 months in a lifetime. Thus, today a relative caregiver like Island who has exhausted this limit while raising her own (or a relative's) children would be ineligible for assistance if she later cared for other related children.

One possible solution is to formally place the children of incarcerated parents in foster care with a relative. On the face, this seems like an attractive alternative. The Act already directs states to place children with relatives rather than strangers where possible, and the average foster care payment is typically greater than the average monthly AFDC child-only grant. However, as Phillips and Bloom (1998) point out, to receive foster care assistance the children must be in state custody. Thus, a relative needing financial assistance and supportive services to care for the children may have to allege abuse or neglect against the child's parent, which in turn may later result in the termination of the incarcerated person's parental rights.

Conventional discussions of punishment tend to treat corrections as if it were a discrete and independent social institution. But the direct and indirect results of trends toward increasingly severe punishment point out the flaws in such an approach. These indirect effects should not be compared to the "ripple effect" that results when you toss a pebble into a pond. Rather, the impact of having one in three black men under the control of the criminal justice system and the secondary impact of incarceration on poor women and children is more like the 40-foot tidal waves that follow an earthquake. Far from being an entity separate unto itself, the criminal justice system has become inextricably intertwined with the welfare system, the political system, and—with the increasing privatization of corrections—the economic system.

Workers

As discussed in Chapter 4, proportional representation of all women and minority men in criminal justice occupations is important not only to lend the appearance of a system that represents "we the people" but also to increase the opportunity for diverse experiences, insights, and reactions to be recognized. Yet, as Table 5.8 illustrates, many criminal justice occupations are overwhelmingly white and male.

Police work appears to be the most male occupation, while lawyering has the greatest percentage of women and whites. Correctional officers encompass the greatest proportion of nonwhite workers. The justice occupations that employ whites and men in the greatest proportions typically pay better than those employing greater percentages of minorities and women. For instance, the average annual salaries in 1998 of lawyers, judges, and police patrol officers were $75,890, $62,080, and $39,060. By contrast, the salaries of legal secretaries, court reporters, and correction officers were $30,990, $27,240, and $30,550, respectively (Bureau of Labor Statistics 1999c).

Table 5.8 also shows that non-Hispanic white men are overrepresented in all the major criminal justice occupations except stenographer. Although white men make up only slightly more than one-third of the United States population, they constitute two-thirds or more of all judges, all lawyers, and all police officers and detectives, and nearly 60 percent of all correctional officers. Black and Hispanic men are underrepresented as judges, lawyers, and stenographers, and men of "other" races are underrepresented in all occupations. Black and Hispanic men are employed as police officers and correctional officers in proportions approaching or greater than their proportion in the U.S. population.

White women constitute over one-third of the U.S. population but nearly 80 percent of all stenographers. Black women's employment as correctional officers and stenographers approximates their representation in the larger population. Overall, though, women are markedly underrepresented as judges, lawyers, and police officers. White women tend to fare the best in these categories, with approximately 20 percent of all judges and attorneys being white women.

Table 5.8

Major Criminal Justice Occupations by Race, Hispanic Origin, and Sex, 1990

	U.S. Population	Judges (*n*=750,077)	Lawyers (*n*=519,184)	Police Officers (*n*=184,667)	Correctional Officers (*n*=32,394)	Stenographers (*n*=79,880)
Male	48.8%	77.2%	75.2%	88.0%	81.1%	9.5%
White (non-Hispanic)	70.4	88.1	92.2	80.2	68.3	86.6
Non-Hispanic origin						
White men	35.1	69.4	70.7	72.1	57.7	8.5
Black men	5.8	4.3	1.9	8.7	16.6	.4
"Other" men	2.4	1.0	1.0	1.6	1.5	.2
White women	36.6	18.6	21.5	8.1	10.6	78.2
Black women	6.4	2.7	1.5	2.7	6.9	6.5
"Other" women	2.4	.6	.6	.2	.3	2.1
Hispanic origin (of any race)						
Men	5.8	2.5	1.6	5.6	5.3	.3
Women	5.8	.9	.8	.9	1.1	3.7

Source: Bureau of the Census (1990).

All women and racial minorities interested in working in most areas of criminal justice share the challenge of entering overwhelmingly white, male work environments, with women of color being multiply disadvantaged. Based on her interviews with 35 white and 31 black women police officers, Susan E. Martin (1992) concluded that white patrolmen tended to be protective of white women but not black women. Moreover, black men could not be counted on to support and assist black women because black male officers were fewer in number, they were under pressure by white men not to support the black women, and some (as with some white men) were opposed to women on patrol. Further, white female officers tended to view gaining acceptance by male officers as more important and valuable than being accepted by other women, leading one black female supervisor to conclude that "getting unity is like pulling teeth." Several studies suggest similarly negative experiences are encountered among women attorneys and law students of color (see Padilla 1997).

Racial and sexual harassment also act to preserve many criminal justice professions as disproportionately white male domains. "Racialized sexual harassment" may keep some women of color from entering or remaining in a predominately white male criminal justice occupation, although this phenomenon remains largely unexplored in criminal justice research and is not specifically included in professional codes of ethics (see Box 5.4). Sumi K. Cho (1997) describes racialized sexual harassment as resulting from the unique configuration of power relations facing women of color in the workplace. Cho observes that Asian Pacific American women are particularly at risk of being racially and sexually harassed. The "model minority" stereotype falsely portrays Asian Pacific Americans as super-successful in the economic, educational, and professional spheres. Further, the model minority traits of passivity and submissiveness are gendered by repeated cultural portrayals of Asian Pacific women as obedient and servile, as well as exotic, hypereroticized, masochistic, and desirous of sexual domination. Similarly, Maria L. Ontiveros ([1993] 1997) and Patricia Hill Collins (1990) note that Latinas and African American women are also stereotyped as naturally sexual or sexually denigrated. These scholars recommend reconstructing our perceptions of "sexual harassment" to acknowledge the issue of harassment of women of color. Treating cases strictly as "sexual harassment" may misstate the dynamic and permit the structures that give rise to such harms to remain unchallenged.

Box 5.4

What Codes of Ethics Have to Say About Harassment

Overall, professional codes of ethics for police and corrections officers tend to be short and rarely include specific language about sexual or racial harassment. A review of ethical codes by Leighton and Killingbeck (in Leighton and Reiman 2001) revealed that the most specific and detailed language could be found in codes developed by organizations such as the American Sociological Association (ASA), the American Psychological Association (APA), and the National Association of Social Workers (NASW). Of these codes, only the ASA specifically mentions racial harassment, although the NASW code has strong statements about requiring social workers to develop knowledge of diverse cultures and be sensitive to cultural diversity.

Printed below is the wording from several codes of ethics. The wording from the American Society of Criminology code is proposed but had not yet been approved by the membership of that organization at the time this book went to publication.

American Sociological Association

Sociologists do not engage in harassment of any person, including students, supervisees, employees, or research participants. Harassment consists of a single intense and severe act or of multiple persistent or pervasive acts which are demeaning, abusive, offensive, or create a hostile professional or workplace environment. Sexual harassment may include sexual solicitation, physical advance, or verbal or non-verbal conduct that is sexual in nature. Racial harassment may include unnecessary, exaggerated, or unwarranted attention or attack, whether verbal or non-verbal, because of a person's race or ethnicity.

American Society of Criminology

Sexual harassment includes advances, solicitation, or requests for sexual favors from those over whom an individual exercises professional authority or with whom one attends classes or works. Harassment may consist of a single intense act or multiple persistent acts that are unwelcome, offensive, and/or that create a hostile work, school, or professional environment. Harassment can include written or electronic communications and nonverbal conduct such as touching, staring, or physically following an individual. It can also include verbal behavior that reflects excessive attention to physical appearance, especially after notice has been given that such attention is unwelcome.

American Psychological Association

(a) Psychologists do not engage in sexual harassment. Sexual harassment is sexual solicitation, physical advances, or verbal or nonverbal conduct that is sexual in nature, that occurs in connection with the psychologist's activities or roles as a psychologist, and that either: (1) is unwelcome, is offensive, or creates a hostile workplace environment, and the psychologist knows or is told this; or (2) is sufficiently severe or intense to be abusive to a reasonable person in the context. Sexual harassment can consist of a single intense or severe act or of multiple persistent or pervasive acts. (b) Psychologists accord sexual-harassment complainants and respondents dignity and respect. Psychologists do not participate in denying a person academic admittance or advancement, employment, tenure, or promotion, based solely upon their having made, or their being the subject of, sexual harassment charges. This does not preclude taking action based upon the outcome of such proceedings or consideration of other appropriate information.

National Association of Social Workers

The NASW code is notable for its explicit and strong language regarding individual dignity, social justice, and cultural diversity. Unlike many other codes, it contains a provision encouraging social workers to engage in social and political action to promote social justice. Although workers in the criminal justice system are not bound by this language, we sincerely believe they should adopt the spirit of the following section:

Social workers should engage in social and political action that seeks to ensure that all people have equal access to the resources, employment, services, and opportunities they require to meet their basic human needs and to develop fully. Social workers should be aware of the impact of the political arena on practice and should advocate for changes in policy and legislation to improve social conditions in order to meet basic human needs and promote social justice. Social workers should act to expand choice and opportunity for all people, with special regard for vulnerable, disadvantaged, oppressed, and exploited people and groups. Social workers should promote conditions that encourage respect for cultural and social diversity within the United States and globally. Social workers should promote policies and practices that demonstrate respect for difference, support the expansion of cultural knowledge and resources, advocate for programs and institutions that demonstrate cultural competence, and promote policies that safeguard the rights of and confirm equity and social justice for all people. Social workers should act to prevent and eliminate domination of, exploitation of, and discrimination against any person, group, or class on the basis of race, ethnicity, national origin, color, sex, sexual orientation, age, marital status, political belief, religion, or mental or physical disability.

The full text of Leighton and Killingbeck, including active links to the professional codes of ethics mentioned in it, is available through *http://www.paulsjusticepage.com*.

Some signs do suggest that the perception of racism and sexism in the workplace as solely the concern of the women and minority men who must endure it is changing. In *Childress v. City of Richmond, Va.* (F3d, 1998 WL 12558, 4th Cir., 1997) seven white male police complained within the police department and later to the Equal Employment Opportunity Commission (EEOC) that a supervising officer's disparaging remarks (i.e., "pussy posse," "vaginal vigilantes," "a most useless nigger") and discriminatory conduct toward women and black male officers created a sexually and racially hostile work environment. (These seven officers were among over a dozen others who signed a letter asking for a psychiatric evaluation of the supervisor.)

Affirmative action programs have been undertaken in an effort to remedy the effects of past discrimination on the basis of race, gender, ethnicity, religion, and age. Resistance to affirmative action may be stronger among some white men in law enforcement positions (Morris, Shinn, and Dumont 1999).[1] Some people who oppose affirmative action subscribe to the myth that it amounts to "reverse discrimination." The reality is that affirmative action does not cause white men to lose their right to study law or be hired for good jobs in criminal justice; rather, it helps women and minority men gain these rights (Kangas 1996).

Consider that when Supreme Court Justice Sandra Day O'Connor graduated third in her class at Stanford Law School in 1953, the only position she was offered was as a legal secretary. And until the late 1970s, the requirements for women wanting to become police officers were *higher* than that for men. Yes, acknowledging the rights of women and men of color to become lawyers and police officers has meant that some white men no longer have an unfair advantage. But, as Steve Kangas (1996) observes, "The loss of undue privilege is not the same thing as the loss of rights."

Another affirmative action myth suggests that police departments and law firms must meet "quotas" in hiring women and minority men, regardless of whether they are qualified (Kangas 1996). In reality, affirmative action programs are designed to determine the percentage of qualified women and minorities available to an organization and to set flexible goals to be reached in good faith. The courts impose quotas only in the case of blatant discrimination against clearly qualified minorities. For example, in 1979 the San Francisco Police Department (SFPD) was 85 percent white and 95 percent male. To settle a federal discrimination suit filed by black officers (and later joined by women and other minority police officers), the court required the SFPD to set goals for hiring and promoting women and minority men. Nearly twenty years later, the SFPD was 62 percent white and 85 percent male. Court supervision was ended in 1998, even though the goal of a force made up of 45 percent minorities and 20 percent women had not been met, because all interested parties felt SFPD had demonstrated good faith efforts to integrate the department. As a result, the police department looks more like San Francisco.

As Table 5.8 suggests, even with affirmative action, women of color continue to experience barriers to their full participation in most criminal justice-related occupations. Nonetheless, some people fear that women of color receive a double affirmative action benefit because of the underrepresentation of both women and people of color in higher education and positions of power. Instead, history has shown that racism and sexism may be manipulated to the detriment of black women, as Susan E. Martin (1992) noted when citing the 1973 case of *United States vs. City of Chicago*. In this case involving the Chicago Police Department, the judge imposed quotas for promotions to encourage the hiring of more racial and ethnic minority officers and women. Initially, black women were called from the promotion list as blacks. When the white women officers realized the black women officers were being promoted ahead of them, the white women filed a claim asserting that all women should be treated as one single minority group. The judge ruled that black women could not be given double benefits, with the approval of the lawyer from the Afro-American League (which was representing all black officers), who failed to consult the women. Thus, the black women had to compete with the white women, whose test scores were better than theirs, rather than with the black men, whose test scores were not. When the black women filed a lawsuit protesting that decision, the judge agreed that they had a valid complaint but deemed their concerns "not timely."

Affirmative action has its limits. While affirmative action can help women of color gain access to historically white male domains such as police departments and law firms, it cannot guarantee they will be accepted by their white and male peers. Minority men and women can still expect to experience isolation, heightened scrutiny of their performance and personal lives, reduced likelihood of promotion and advancement, insufficient mentoring, isolation, and perceptions that they do not merit their jobs or have taken entitlements away from white men and women who are more deserving (Padilla 1997). But we should consider the example set by the seven white male officers who protested the sexist and racist conduct of a supervisor in the *Childress v. City of Richmond* case. Although the officers' suit was dismissed on the grounds that the seven officers did not have standing, given that the comments and actions were not aimed at them, the officers are to be applauded for not invoking their privilege to remain silent in the face of discrimination. All criminal justice workers are harmed by having to work in an environment where racism and sexism create tension and interfere with people's ability to do their jobs. Another reason for being concerned about the white male dominance of criminal justice occupations is that it undermines public confidence that our current system indeed provides "justice for all." (See Box 5.5).

Box 5.5

Supreme Hypocrisy? The Lack of Diversity Among Law Clerks

The Supreme Court is not covered by federal laws barring workplace discrimination, and many feel that it shows. Since becoming a member of the Supreme Court in 1972, Chief Justice William Rehnquist has had 82 law clerks. During that time, he has had only 1 Hispanic clerk and only 11 women clerks. Not once has he hired a black law clerk. Overall, only 1.2 percent of his clerks have been members of minority groups. The track record of his colleagues is not much better. Of the 428 law clerks hired during the respective terms of the current justices, only 7 were black, 5 were Hispanic African-American, 18 were Asian-American, and not a single one was Native American. Despite the fact that over 40 percent of law school graduates are women, women make up only one quarter of all clerks hired by current justices. Of the 34 law clerks hired in 1998, only 1 was a minority: a Hispanic woman.

These figures prompted Rep. Gregory Meeks (D-NY) to conclude "[I]f the court were a Fortune 500 company, the statistics alone would demonstrate illegal discrimination" (Meeks 1999). In a January 25, 1999 article in *Insight on the News,* Meeks defends his criticism of the Supreme Court's hiring practices. Becoming a clerk is a stepping stone to other positions, including Supreme Court justice. Yet the hiring practices create a structural barrier to achieving those positions. Moreover, Supreme Court law clerks wield considerable power, playing an extremely influential role in the Court's functioning.

"Clerks have the ear of the justices they serve. They have input on which cases the justices choose to consider. They write the initial drafts of most decisions. The Supreme Court's decisions are the law of the land and thus affect lives, determine how government resources are allocated, force legislatures to reformulate public policy choices, turn winners into losers, and make losers victors."

The influence clerks have on both the cases heard and the opinions the court renders should not be underestimated. Recent court decisions have narrowed opportunities for people of color as a result of limiting or ruling unconstitutional critical affirmative action programs or by diluting the application of the Voting Rights Act. Clerks preview and review these cases, which means they have had an impact on rulings involving civil rights, access to education, workplace discrimination, religious freedom, voting rights, the 2000 Census, welfare reform, immigrant rights, school desegregation, sexual harassment, and police brutality. Clerks also are at the intersection of death penalty appeals.

Many of these cases have a disproportionate impact on minorities or women. The diversity of the background and experience of clerks can help sensitize the justices. The views of clerks can help give the justices a broader, more rounded and varied perspective on such critical issues. In sum, by not setting a proactive example of inclusion, the highest court in the land undermines the ideal of justice that it purports to protect.

Meeks, Gregory W. 1999. "Does the Supreme Court Need Affirmative Action for Its Own Staff?" From *Insight on the News* (Jan. 25) 15 (3): 24, 26-27.

Media Representations

Research consistently demonstrates that the media not only represent but construct public understanding and perceptions of class, race, gender and crime. It is also well established that media representations, including "objective" news reports, do not mirror real life but are typically skewed in the interest of covering newsworthy cases—that is, cases that deviate from the statistical norm. But a study of homicides reported in the *Los Angeles Times* suggests a slightly different interpretation. Media coverage tended to focus on victims who were white, very young or very old, females, of high socioeconomic status, killed by strangers (Sorenson et al. 1998). The researchers went on to note that in addition this bias may influence public opinion of what constitutes "worthy victims," which in turn may influence violence prevention and control strategies.

Media representations of crime have also contributed to criminals being equated with young black men. "Evening news broadcasts, television crime dramas, and the 'real' crime stories of programs like *Cops* and *L.A.P.D.* bombard the American public with images of 'young black male' offenders under authoritative police control. The message is that the police are the thin blue line protecting law-abiding citizens from dark and dangerous street criminals" (Barlow 1998, p. 155).

Based on her analysis of *Time* and *Newsweek* cover stories from 1945 to 1995, Melissa Barlow (1998) concludes that crime began to be racialized in the current form in the 1960s, when criminals began to be equated with "young black males."

The nearly synonymous association with crime has not been confined to black men or limited to the news media. In the last 30 years, images of Latin men as drug-dealing, gun-packing criminals have proliferated in feature films such as *Code of Silence, 8 Million Ways to Die, Above the Law,* and *Crocodile Dundee II* (Rodriguez 1997). Television shows in the 1980s such as *Miami Vice, Hill Street Blues,* and *Hunter* featured Hispanics as wealthy drug lords, small-time hoods, drug addicts, and pimps (Lichter and Amundson 1997). Using content analysis to compare prime time television portrayals, Lichter and Amundson (1997) did find some improvement from the 1992 to 1994–95 seasons. Although Latinos remained "ghettoized" in a handful of series and rarely portrayed prosperous, well-educated characters, there was a dramatic decline in the criminal portrayals of Hispanic characters, from 16 percent of all Hispanic characters in 1992 to 6 percent in 1994. This level of criminality was higher than that for whites (4 percent) and blacks (2 percent). Another promising sign is that "reality" shows such as *Cops* and *America's Most Wanted* dramatically reduced their depiction of blacks and Hispanics as criminals. In 1992, 50 percent of all blacks and 45 percent of all Latinos in these shows committed crime; in 1994–95, these figures dropped to 20 percent and 16 percent, respectively.

Media accounts may also contribute to a distorted view of a particular culture's gender roles. For example, in Mexican culture, *machismo* can describe the nature of a man who provides his wife, children, and possibly other relatives with food, shelter and protection. But the U.S. media frequently distort this concept to mean something pathological and assign the term "macho" to a man who is controlling, temperamental, and overly aggressive. For example, when Ramon Salcido, a Mexican vineyard worker in California, murdered his daughters, his wife, two of his in-laws, and an employer, media accounts portrayed him as a "hot-blooded Latin who gloried in machismo," implying that his actions were not only culturally based, but typical of the way Latino men treat their wives (Ogawa and Belle 1999).

While women are less likely to be portrayed as criminals than men, their images have tended to be dualistic—either virgins or whores. At the same time, the image is different for women of color because they are so rarely portrayed; when they are, they are consistently negative and lower class. "[W]here are the everyday [Latina] women," Clara Rodriguez asks, "the non-crack-addicted mothers who also populate all levels of the Latino communities and who are, in fact, more prevalent in Latino communities than prostitutes, junkies, transvestites, and welfare and child abusers? Where are the women who are neither madonnas nor spitfires? They are absent" (Rodriguez 1997, p. 76).

Rodriguez's book, *Latin Looks: Images of Latinas and Latinos in the U.S. Media* (1997), offers several concrete suggestions to help viewers become more critical in their consumption of popular culture via television and movie viewing. Although Rodriguez focuses on the depiction of Latins in the media, most of her insights can be applied to the depiction of men and women of all races and ethnicities. For example, to identify how a character's class, race, color, and gender are used to convey a particular image in a television show or movie, it is helpful to ask questions such as: Is the character victimized? Who victimizes the character? How is the character victimized? Does the character attempt or commit a crime? What type of crime? How serious is the crime? Does the character use controlled substances? What are the character's goal(s)? How are these goals attained—through legal or illegal means? Through sex, money, personal charm, embarrassment, other people, intelligence? What is the character's level of professional prestige? What is his or her socioeconomic status? How major or minor of a role does the character have in relation to the plot? Does the character ultimately succeed or fail in the film?

Rodriguez also cites guidelines concerning the portrayal of racial, ethnic, and gender groups developed by Gordon Berry (1993) and recommends that these guidelines be voluntarily adopted by all sectors of the media industry. The guidelines compel the media industry (and us, as consumers) to ask whether content

- shows a diversity of professional and vocational roles and careers for men and women of racial and ethnic minorities;

- portrays racial and ethnic minority men and women throughout the range of socioeconomic conditions and lifestyle situations;

- defines or limits occupational aspirations in terms of race, ethnicity and/or gender;

- portrays both traditional and nontraditional activities being performed by characters, regardless of race, ethnicity, and gender; and

- portrays emotional reactions such as fear, anger, aggression, excitement, love, and concern regardless of race, ethnicity, and/or gender.

Summary and Conclusions

Understanding the crosscutting social relations of class, race, and gender poses a challenge, given that our theoretical frameworks remain, by and large, works in progress. Such attempts are further impeded by the shortage of official information that describes the distribution of social benefits and harms along class, race, and gender combined, not separately. Even with the limited information available, though, indicators of political, economic, and physical well-being indicate that social goods are not evenly distributed but rather are concentrated among upper-class white men while poor racial and ethnic minority women incur the greatest social costs.

While criminology has had a longstanding interest in class, only in the past 30–40 years has this interest been extended to include race and gender. The attention to the intersections of these social dimensions is an even more recent development. Since the late eighties, an increasing number of scholars have recognized the problems inherent in assuming that all women or all members of a particular race, for example, stand on a similar footing.

Among the most promising of developments has been a focus on the ways in which class, race, and gender are not only social constructs, but processes involving creative human actors. Structured action theory highlights the ways in which our dominant cultural conceptions of masculinity and femininity are based on the characteristics of white, middle-class heterosexuals. This scholarship also points to the ways in which class, race, and gender relations are institutionalized and reflected in the practices of the criminal justice system.

Constitutive criminology is likewise a promising development because it redefines crimes to be more inclusive of harms and domination that destroy the potential of human beings. It looks at the totality of cultural and structural contexts within which crime is produced and acknowledges the role of individuals in recreating social structures through their language and actions. Because human agents and social structures are mutually constitutive, this type of social theory highlights the potential for social change that lies within everyday speech, and actions, and the ongoing process of identity construction (Henry and Milovanovic 1999).

Another promising development is scholarship that shifts the emphasis on identifying systems of privilege that support existing systems of oppression but are rarely acknowledged by those who reap the benefits. Failure to recognize class, race, and gendered privilege serves to define discrimination as problems of the poor, people of color, and women while masking the responsibility members of the nonpoor classes, whites, and men have in addressing the problem.

This chapter points out that, far from "equal justice in the eyes of the law," one's experience of criminal and social justice varies across class, race, and gender. We find, for example, that offenses associated with black men, such as the possession and distribution of crack cocaine, are subjected to more scrutiny and harsher punishments than offenses more closely identified with middle-class white men, such as white-collar crimes, the use of powdered cocaine, and drunk driving. We also cited examples suggesting the role that class plays in sheltering people from the harshest consequences of the criminal justice system.

Whether addressing the needs of victims, offenders, or workers, we must be careful not to assume that "same treatment" is "fair treatment," because too often equal treatment is defined by a male norm or reflects white, middle-class biases and ignorance of the challenges faced by poor men and women of color. In evaluating proposed policies and legislation, we should take care to consider their impact on people occupying a range of social locations rather than, for instance, assuming all women face the same challenges in leaving an abusive partner. We should ask: What is this program, policy, or law supposed to accomplish? How will it actually be implemented? What are the ramifications for historically marginalized groups? Upon what assumptions is it based? Who is left out? What can we do to improve on this effort? (S. Miller 1998; Renzetti 1998). Similar questions should also be posed in our evaluations of the media. As we have seen, news accounts and other forms of popular culture manipulate class, race, and gender in a way that shapes public perceptions that some victims are more "sympathetic" than others, some offenders are more "dangerous," and some workers more "capable."

Given the challenges that remain, how will we gauge progress? Ideally, of course, we hope not only for a future that holds a more equitable distribution of wealth but also for one of political, economic, and physical well-being. We will see increasing numbers of people who benefit from class, race, or gender privilege or a combination thereof assuming responsibility for ending discrimination. Condemning the classist, racist, and sexist practices that exist inside and outside the criminal justice system will cease to be perceived as the near-exclusive domain of those who are directly harmed by them.

As stated at the beginning of this chapter, each person is standing at the center of an intersection. But we need not stand alone and we need not stand quietly. We can form alliances across varying social locations to challenge the existing power structure and expose the dysfunctional and debilitating effects of the current criminal justice system.

Such progress will come about only when we make visible what is currently invisible and taken for granted. When we recognize the ways in which our idealized views of masculinity/femininity, good/bad, irresponsible/responsible, deserving/undeserving, criminal/law abiding, trustworthy/suspect are based on "norms" that are not normal at all but characteristic of the intersectional identities of a few. When class, race, and gender are widely viewed as being as relevant to Bill Gates' life-chances as they are to those of individuals such as Jimmy Santiago Baca, Julian Bond, Angela Davis, Dolores Huerta, Leonard Peltier, Dith Pran, Janet Reno, and Young Shin.[2] When men are aware of their gender, whites are aware they have a race, and the masses realize that class is not just a characteristic of the very rich or the very poor.

Notes

1. As Lien (1998) points out, the relationship of race/gender to attitudes toward affirmative action is complex. On the whole, gender is unrelated to attitude toward affirmative action, whereas membership in any nonwhite group is associated with greater support. Yet when the influence of race is partialed out by gender and characteristics such as family income, citizenship, political orientation, and age are controlled for, Lien found that Asian and black women tended to be less likely to support affirmative action than their male counterparts, while the opposite held true for white women. Latinas did not differ from Latinos in the support for affirmative action.

2. These individuals are, respectively, Bill Gates, founder of Microsoft and the wealthiest person in the United States; Jimmy Santiago Baca, who served seven years in prison, where he taught himself to read and write, is the author of four books, and is co-writer/co-producer of the movie *Blood In, Blood Out;* Julian Bond, founder of the Student Nonviolent Coordinating Committee (SNCC) and chairman of the National Association for the Advancement of Colored People; Angela Davis, activist and formerly on the FBI's Most Wanted list, charged with kidnapping, conspiracy, and murder in a California courthouse shootout, and acquitted in a trial that commanded international attention; Dolores Huerta, co-founder (with Cesar Chavez) of the United Farm Workers; Leonard Peltier, American Indian Movement activist convicted of murdering two FBI agents in 1975, considered by some to be a political prisoner; Dith Pran, Cambodian newsman during the Khmer Rouge reign of terror in the 1970s, human rights activist, and current *New York Times* photographer; Janet Reno, U.S. Attorney General; and Young Shin, co-founder and executive director of Asian Immigrant Women Advocates and a longtime grassroots leader of efforts to improve working conditions for garment workers. ✦

Chapter 6

Crime, Justice, and Policy

W e have considered a variety of ways in which class, race, and gender have helped to shape the crime control experiences of various social groups in society. By integrating legalistic analyses of crime and justice with sociological analyses of inequality and privilege, we have conceptually tried to broaden the traditional framework for evaluating justice in America. That is, we have tried to connect the worlds of criminal justice with the worlds of social justice in order to expand visions of justice and responses to crime. We believe that each is inescapably tied to the other and, therefore, that if we are ever to significantly alter the patterns of crime and justice in the U.S., both worlds must be consciously tackled together (see also Leighton and Reiman 2001).

At the macro level, we have made the case that the social constructions of crime and the social realities of justice have developed within the backdrop of the changing institutional relations of the struggle for due process and equal protection on the one hand, and of the struggle for social justice and human rights on the other. At the micro level, we have made the case that the class, race, and gender backgrounds and positions of people differentially affect their interactions with the various practices and systems of law and justice. In short, the patterns of unequal definitions and applications of law enforcement, adjudication, and punishment are a product of the social and power relations of class, race, and gender.

At the macro-micro level, our analyses of class, race, and gender have confirmed that both legal and extra-legal mechanisms of control are used differentially on those marginal groups perceived as threatening to dominant groups in society. In part, this has been (and is) accomplished through the fact that the social construction of crime and crime control has been homogenized to the point that rich and poor, majority and minority, men and women, young and old tend to have similar beliefs about who constitutes the "dangerous class." In terms of what should be done with, to, or about the dangerous underclass, the prevailing consensus has primarily revolved around the philosophy and practice of containment, isolation, and retribution—"getting tough."

The larger name given to this philosophy is "law and order," which appropriately conveys its goal of securing the present social and economic order. The unanswered question relates to many aspects of social justice discussed in this book: Whose law, and what order? When the present order is marked by inequalities in class, race, and gender, "law and order" policies will have a disproportionate impact on socially marginal populations. For example, although the public construction of the criminal has been male, primarily dark and young, "The hidden victims of many of the get-tough policies have been women, particularly women of color" (Chesney-Lind 1998: xi). The recent implementation of "gender-neutral" sentencing policies designed with the goal of treating women and men the same has resulted in "equality with a vengeance."

At the same time, the criminal justice system has also been an obvious failure at lowering crime rates, even though criminal justice expenditures have far surpassed inflation for any extended period. Crime control policies have usually focused on strategies that are least likely to work, so Reiman (1998a) suggests that the failure to actually reduce crime has ideological benefits. The failure is not due to an intentional conspiracy, but "historical inertia" based on how the failure benefits those with the power to change the system. More specifically, the failure to actually reduce street crime keeps society's attention focused on street crimes rather than white-collar crimes (or crimes of domination) that are more likely to actually harm people. The culturally familiar *criminal blackman* sends the message that the biggest threat to our well-being comes from below us on the economic scale, not above.

Solutions to class, race, and gender inequities are not confined to the internal systems of crime control; they reside both inside and outside the criminal justice system. Equal justice will not be realized by incarcerating more white or female drug offenders, as most users and abusers never come to the attention of the authorities in the first place. It makes more sense to face up to the different social realities of justice, to acknowledge biases where they exist, to reduce the use of prisons for drug offenders and increase the availability of substance abuse intervention in the community. Hence, systems of retribution, including drug profiling and mandatory minimum sentencing, for example, need to be transformed away from their law enforcement and penal justice mandates and toward medical and community-based models of justice, where emphasis is placed on healing and recovering.

There are other examples, less well known, of how "gendered equality" often "ignores not only the gendered power dynamics within intimate relationships but also the structural limits to women's efficacy in disentangling themselves from such relationships that are present in these situations" (Massey, Miller, and Wilhelmi 1998: 29). For instance, in civil forfeiture cases involving the confiscation of assets from suspected drug offenders, judges have falsely assumed that social and economic power are equally distributed in a marriage or intimate relationship. Moreover, judges have blamed wives for their failure or inability to control their husbands (Massey et al. 1998). Finally, external to the systems of criminal and civil justice are systems of social justice that typically concern themselves with the inequities in the distribution of goods and services in society, or in the rewards and punishments more generally, as these are shaped by class, race, and gender relations. The various systems of social justice need to be explored, supported, and developed as well.

Traditionally, the study of crime control and the administration of criminal justice have been overly consumed with analyzing "equal protection under the law" and with viewing inequity and discrimination from a legalistic perspective (Barak 1980). Over the past thirty years, studies of the criminal justice system have broadened the legalistic analyses to include the more sociologically oriented analyses that at first examined class and crime control and, subsequently, race and crime control or gender and crime control. With a few notable exceptions, however, students of crime and justice have not attempted to examine the intersections of class, race, and gender (Madriz 1997; Messerschmidt 1997; Schwartz and Milovanovic 1996; Totten 2000). With our own limited data, theory, and methodology, we have tried to initiate an inquiry into the "intersections" as these factors converge across the criminal justice system. It is our hope that others will follow up on this kind of investigation.

Even if we have only started to disclose the parallels in class, race, and gender relations as they intersect with the worlds of crime and crime control, we believe that we have underscored the past and present social realities of justice in America. Our objective in this final chapter is to juxtapose the distinguishing features of some earlier and contemporary systems of justice to help identify alternative visions of justice practice for the future. We believe that such visions, and the practices of justice associated with them, allow for an accounting of the class, race, and gender relations of power and status as they have been (and are) invested in crime control and prevention.

Specifically, we believe that those practices of crime control that fall under the broader models such as "restorative justice" and "social justice," in contrast to those that fall under the narrower models such as "equal justice," hold out a much greater potential for moving in the direction of justice for all. They do so precisely because practices of restorative and social justice seek to develop social capital and community well-being in the future. These systems of justice facilitate approaches to crime control that are capable not only of dealing with marginality and conflict but of addressing the differential impact of class, race, and gender on crime and social justice. Conversely, practices of equal justice pretend that differences of class, race, and gender are immaterial or beside the point. These systems of justice rely on retributive and penal models of crime control that facilitate the reproduction of the deterioration of the marginal groups and persons in conflict.

Systems of Justice: Equal, Restorative, and Social

In terms of social policy, U.S. society needs to move beyond the application of individual justice as equal protection under the law. We need to move to models of justice that appreciate injustice and victimization as an expression of the wider political, social, and economic inequalities. Doing so would not abandon individualistic models of due process per se, but rather would integrate social justice issues so that differences of class, race, and gender are not reproduced throughout the systems of crime and justice. To appreciate these material relations and to act on them is to move to a higher level in the "evolution of justice" (Crawford 1988). To put it simply, persons who come before the various tribunals of justice have never been, nor are they now, equal. To the extent that folks ignore these relations and fixate instead on the niceties of legalistic fairness, they fall victim to the twin myths of equal justice. That is to say, on the one hand, people falsely consider unequal persons as equal by claiming a formal or legal equality among all persons, and on the other hand, people incorrectly deny the concrete social inequalities of class, race, and gender as these cut across crime, justice, and society.

The limits of criminal justice in America are attributable not only to the overemphasis on notions of individual or equal justice but to an overreliance on the claims of criminal justice impartiality. Consequently, discussions of injustice revolve around the procedural irregularities in the application of due process rather than the substantial irregularities in the definition of harm and injury in the first place or in the selective use or enforcement of those acts (see Chapter 2). The point is that there is a long list of harms that could be legally prohibited but have not been. These social pains or injuries emanate mostly from the invested structures of the political economy; they have not constituted "crimes worth pursuing" because they benefit powerful interests that may or may not trickle down to others in society. Even when such acts as price-fixing, consumer deception, antitrust violations, environmental pollution, racial discrimination, sexual harassment, and the like have been authorized as worth pursuing, for a variety of reasons they seldom are.

The conventional system of crime control primarily enforces its laws and justice by dealing mainly with direct and obvious forms of naked power in which one party forcibly denies another party his or her property, person, or ability to make a difference. Street crimes of robbery, rape, and homicide are obvious examples. Criminal justice is far less able to deal with the indirect forms of denial, such as psychological manipulation, domestic abuse, economic persuasion, and so on. Of course, it is usually argued that the functions of a criminal justice system do not include confronting the hidden and subtle forms of coercive control that exist in the institutional corridors of modern societies.

Equal Justice

The three models (or systems) of crime control and their respective practices, arrangements, and scenarios of justice assume different things about crime and criminals and thus respond accordingly. In the

United States, the ideals and realities of equal justice are older than the ideals and realities of restorative or social justice. Equal justice takes as a given or as unproblematic the rationality of the prevailing political, economic, and legal arrangements in general and of the administration of justice in particular. In these scenarios, crimes are the exceptional violations of the criminal laws by criminals acting rationally and immorally or irrationally and amorally.

In either way, criminal others are socially and culturally constructed as either "bad" or "mad" without any appreciable concern for the ways in which marginality by class, race, or gender contributes to this labeling process. In turn, these dangerously bad and mad members of the criminal classes are viewed as threatening outcasts who are deeply marked by moral deprivation and a profound lack of empathy and impulse control. Their crimes are seen as the result of individual pathology that has nothing to do with the larger social structure within which they operate. As they are demonized as different, popular fears and hostilities are aroused, and justifications are established for the practices of repressive justice (Barak 2000; Garland 1999; Reiman 1998a). Repressive justice, for example, emphasizes policies of zero tolerance, target hardening, proactive policing, judicial restraint, mandatory sentencing, penal warehousing, and treating youthful offenders as adults.

The repressive systems of justice primarily view crimes as legal offenses committed against the state by the bad and the mad, not by the marginalized. Punishment—especially within this scheme of crime control and justice, whether it deters, rehabilitates, incapacitates, or simply denounces—is grounded in the age-old rationales of an "eye for an eye" and the even older emotional reactions of revenge. Equal justice translates into "just deserts," which becomes punishment for the sake of punishment. These repressive policies of justice are preoccupied with maintaining security or public order, assuming first that a significant relationship exists between present forms of punishment and the stability of the social order. Second, they assume that a reasonable fairness of due process, or balancing of the rights of the individual and the rights of the state, exists.

Equal justice models, in other words, do not generally consider the interests of the injured parties, nor do they typically engage in practices of restitution, compensation, and healing, which work better in the context of flexible sentencing and community-based alternatives to prison. Such policies, however, like the curtailing of parole in many jurisdictions and the elimination of "time off for good behavior" clauses over the past twenty-years or more, have contributed to more repressive systems of justice. These models of equal justice in the United States have their roots in the mid-18th century, when the Age of Enlightenment in Europe was busy reforming the more arbitrary and barbaric justice practices of the medieval period.

Repressive models of justice today are indicative of policies of crime control that ignore their differential impact on marginal groups. In framing crime as exceptional and unordinary, these models reinforce policies of exclusion and isolation. They are divisive along class, racial, and gendered lines as they reinforce policies of separation that serve to further estrange and alienate their marginalized targets. As these policies of containment are applied to the business of imposing "law and order" and distributing punishment with fairness, they pay virtually no attention to the social structures, environments, and ecologies of crime that, for example, provide viable survival alternatives (e.g., crime) for marginal people whose legitimate opportunities for redistributing wealth, power, and status are limited (Hagan 1994; Sullivan 1989).

Proactive policing and prosecuting, associated with the periodic wars on illicit drugs during the 20th century, and more recently with the highly visible "zero tolerance" policies in New York City and elsewhere, have a long and distinguished tradition of differential law enforcement and selective punishment. These "get tough" strategies, in other words, have consistently worked against the collective long-term interests or solidarity of minority communities. As these efforts in concentrated law enforcement have been organized around initiatives identified as threatening the social order from the margins, they serve to reinforce the ever-increasing and fixed penalty sanctions for a relatively few crimes, which are disproportionately enforced against minorities, especially young and poor people of color. Similarly, coupled with the judicial restraint and reduction in sentencing options has been the New Penology, with its emphasis away from reform and rehabilitation and toward retribution and incapacitation. Targeted once again are those subgroups of marginal offenders (e.g., "career" or "habitual" criminals) who are subjected to even more extensive forms and lengths of punishment. In sum, these policies of equal justice have served to reproduce a repressive system that has helped institutionalize a permanent underclass of dangerous offenders.

Restorative Justice

Since the 1980s, restorative justice has been represented both inside and outside the United States by a wide diversity of programs that may or may not contain the "essential" elements or practices as ideally conceived. The idea of restorative justice has come to have many different meanings:

> The concept may refer to an alternative process for resolving disputes, to alternative sanctioning options, or to a distinctively different, "new" mode of criminal justice organized around principles of restoration to victims, offenders, and the communities in which they live. It may refer to diversion from formal court process, to actions taken in parallel with court decisions, and to meetings between offenders and victims at any stage of the criminal process (from arrest, presentencing, and prison release). It is a process used in juvenile justice, criminal justice, and family welfare/child protection cases. (Daly and Immarigeon 1998: 21–22)

Moreover, today, the term "restorative justice" has been associated with innovations in community corrections, informal justice, community service, alternative sentencing, community mediation, and victim-offender reconciliation. Given the overlapping usage of restorative justice concepts and practices by some of the retributive forms of justice, hard and fast distinctions between these models may be difficult to make.

Ideally, restorative justice views crime and criminals as more than illegally defined acts and deviant others. Criminality also refers to the needs of offenders and to the harms of victims, and to the mutual obligations and liabilities between offenders and victims. Significantly, offenders are not viewed as fundamentally different from nonoffenders. Rather, both are viewed as responding more or less rationally to their perceived needs, interests, and options. Restorative justice views crime control as less about the individual perpetrators versus the state and more about the interpersonal relationships of the offenders, victims, family members, and larger community from which they come. Restorative justice emphasizes the recovery of both the victim, through redress, vindication, and healing, and the offender, through recompense of the victim, fair treatment, and habilitation.

Whereas equal justice models are law and punishment oriented and highly legalistic, restorative justice models are holistic and harm centered. The former models revolve around how much pain and suffering has been inflicted on the wrongdoer; the latter models revolve around how much harm has been repaired or prevented. Zehr and Mika (1998) have suggested that restorative justice is being pursued when folks:

- focus on the harms of wrongdoing more than the rules that have been broken;

- show equal concern and commitment to victims and offenders, involving both in the process of justice;

- work toward the restoration of victims, empowering them and responding to their needs as they see them;

- support offenders while encouraging them to understand, accept and carry out their obligations;

- recognize that while obligations may be difficult for offenders, they should not be intended as harms and they must be achievable;

- provide opportunities for dialogue, direct or indirect, between victims and offenders as appropriate;

- involve and empower the affected community through the justice process, and increase its capacity to recognize and respond to community bases of crime;

- encourage collaboration and reintegration rather than coercion and isolation;

- give attention to the unintended consequences of [their] actions and programs; and

- show respect to all parties, including victims, offenders and justice colleagues. (pp. 54–55)

Policies of restorative justice have their legal roots in the ancient patterns of such diverse cultures as the Sumerian Code of UrNammu (2050 B.C.), the Hebrew Scriptures and the Code of Hammurabi (1700 B.C.), the Roman Law of the Twelve Tables (449 B.C.), and the earliest collection of the Germanic tribal laws, the Lex Salica (496 A.D.). Each of these legal systems required that offenders and their families settle accounts with victims and their families, not simply to ensure that injured persons received restitution or compensation but also to restore or establish community peace.

Restorative justice is not merely a relic of the distant past. Sanctions, in many precolonial African and Native American societies, for example, were compensatory rather than punitive, intended to restore victims to their previous positions. The contemporary Japanese system, emphasizing as it does "confession, repentance and absolution," is also about compensation to the victim and restoration of community peace (Haley 1989). Today, "indigenous populations in North America, New Zealand, Australia and elsewhere are experimenting with ways in which their traditional approaches to crime, which are restorative in intent, may exist in the context of the dominant Western legal system" (Van Ness and Heetderks Strong 1997: 9).

In practical terms, restorative justice is about victim-offender encounters, offenders compensating victims, victims taking an active or participatory role in the criminal justice system, and the reintegration of victims and offenders and the community. For example, victim-offender reconciliation programs offer a context in which the two parties to the crime have an opportunity to face each other. An encounter offers victims and offenders the chance to decide "what *they* consider relevant to a discussion of the crime, tends to humanize each of them to one another and permits them substantial creativity in constructing a response that deals not only with the injustice that occurred but with the futures of both parties as well" (Van Ness and Heetderks Strong 1997: 89).

Reparation, restitution, and compensation programs are more concerned with healing injuries than they are with inflicting punishment. Although not oblivious to the potential risks to public safety, their primary concerns are not with the diversion of nondangerous offenders from the confines of prison cells per se but with seeing that victims are made whole and that their offenders are involved in that process. Restorative justice, in other words, desires that both offenders and victims be allowed to actively participate in the formal criminal justice process. Reintegration of both victims and offenders recognizes their common needs to find wholeness and to establish themselves in the community as participating members. It is especially important for offenders from the marginal classes to be able to "self-actualize" into community participants. Whereas equal justice models separate formal and informal aspects of social control, polarize the offenders and victims and limit their contact, and reduce conflicts between offenders, victims, and the state to only legally relevant material, restorative justice models are about resolving interpersonal conflicts and helping establish peace in communities through the empowerment of victims and offenders.

In sum, restorative justice is built on three fundamental propositions: *(1) Justice requires that we work to restore victims, offenders, and communities who have been injured by crime. (2) Victims, offenders and communities should have opportunities for active involvement in the restorative justice process as early and as fully as possible. (3) In promoting justice, government is responsible for preserving order and the community for establishing peace* (Van Ness and Heetderks Strong 1997). More information about this topic is available through the restorative justice section of *http://www.stopviolence.com.*

Social Justice

The visions of social justice are broader than the visions of equal justice and restorative justice. Social justice takes a critical stance toward both the present American order, inclusive of the criminal justice system, and the prevailing practices of crime control in society. Even though social justice shares some assumptions and practices with restorative justice, the former sees crime as something more than a violation of people and relationships and crime control as something more than the promotion of repairing, reconciling, and reassuring offenders and victims.

Social justice also views crimes as politically, economically, and socially structured phenomena; criminals are rational and emotional actors engaged in the structural relations of class, race, and gender. For example, rich folks, regardless of race and gender, do not hold up fast-food markets or gas stations, and poor folks, regardless of race and gender, do not price-fix or monopolize the sale, distribution, and production of goods and services. To address both of these forms of crime, social justice stresses the importance of public policies on education, health care, social capital, and corporate regulation. These practices in crime control are well beyond the confines and tangential corridors of criminal justice administration.

One problem with the ideal realities of restorative justice is that the social realities of repairing harm and of involving victims, offenders, and their communities in these healing processes have rarely ventured beyond the immediate conflicts of the offenders and victims (McCormick 1999). That is, these restorative practices have typically been confined to specific incidents and particular individuals. Less attention has been "paid to the patterns of social inequality or disadvantage which make both victims and offenders, and indeed their communities, more prone to the experiences of criminal harm and to the processes of criminalization" (White 1998: 17). Social justice, in other words, places greater emphasis in crime control on building community and on repairing the larger social conflicts that predispose offenders and victims to criminal conflict in the first place.

Proponents of social justice have included members from various religious communities, organized labor, and the feminist movement. Its roots go back to the Quakers and the development of the first penitentiary, the Walnut Street Jail, in Philadelphia in the early 1800s. More recently, social justice has been an outgrowth of the prisoner movement in the 1960s and 1970s in the U.S. and of later movements in the 1980s and 1990s for universal and environmental human rights. Social Justice parts company with retributive (equal) justice, (and even with restorative justice) to the extent that the former argues that an equitable criminal justice system cannot be achieved in a society that unjustly treats, exploits, or oppresses persons based on the social trajectories of class, race, and gender.

Like restorative justice, social justice views crime as social harm and social injury, but it goes further in recognizing that there are "crimes against humanity" or crimes as violations of fundamental human rights, such as the right to life, liberty, happiness, and self-determination—what the Schwendingers (1970) defined some time ago as the right to be free from exploitation, oppression, hatred, racism, sexism, and imperialism. Accordingly, human rights violations encompass both the harms/injuries that have not necessarily been prohibited by criminal, regulatory, or civil law and the abilities of states and their agents to abuse, evade, or pervert the applications of law, domestic or international, for the purposes of securing order as well as preserving the social relations of the dominant political economy.

Scenarios of social justice refuse to accommodate or to ignore the production of inequalities in society and law's role in that construction. Rather than accept the limited views of justice contained in procedural and substantive criminal justice, social justice calls for a broader perspective that views crime, criminals, and criminalization as being connected, in part, to the interrelationships between how people are defined by whole systems and how the parts of this system attempt to correct the larger institutional harms, for example, through the auspices and programs of "affirmative action." This does not mean, however, that laws should necessarily compensate for inequalities or that standards of equal treatment should be replaced with arbitrary standards of substantive justice. As one consequence, these practices of compensation might simply lead to new or other injustices, especially against those groups of marginal people who have been the most left out of these healing processes. What social justice does mean is that:

> (1) the source and processes of injustice resulting from the production of society's inequalities need to be confronted, and (2) the principles of fair and equal treatment embodied in procedural law must be extended into the social body as part of the process whereby inequalities and their injustices are prevented. An ample theory of social justice, therefore, depends on a conception about the generation of substantive inequality and a related theory about the prevention of injustice through law. (Barak and Henry 1999: 160)

Hence, as a radical alternative to the limitations of equal justice protecting individual rights and to the remedial efforts of bureaucratic-administrative law favoring some groups but not others, proponents of social justice have been talking up the merits of "visionary gradualism" and "free-market socialism" (Harrington 1989). Grounded in the global principles of feminist, antiracist, and ecologist communitarianism, this view of social justice agrees to the capitalist structure of accumulation and economic growth, but it advocates that the buildup be redirected toward qualitative living for all and away from quantitative consuming for a much smaller minority of the world's population.

In a eulogy, West (1990) wrote of the late social activist Michael Harrington that his hope for human freedom and justice rested "upon the capacity of people to choose and implement democratic forms of socialization in the face of 'irresponsible,' 'unthinking' and 'unsocial' versions of corporate socialization"(p. 59). Democratic socialism does not do away with all privileges and inequality, yet it does believe in the eradication of the social subjugation, oppression, and exploitation of people and in the establishment of social justice for all people without regard to class, race, and gender. For example, homelessness and the crimes by and against the homeless have their roots in the violence of poverty and in the creation of dependent classes of people.

The structural relations of accumulation, inequality, and marginality deprive some people of a humane (minimum) share of the created wealth. Stated differently, social justice assumes that because we live in a world without physical and technological shortages, we can live in a world without social shortages. It also assumes that poverty and the dependent classes should be eliminated as much as possible, like smallpox or hunger. Finally, social justice believes that the accumulation of wealth should be limited in a free-market social economy only to the extent that it deprives others of the basic necessities of life. In the case of homelessness, the United States has enough social capital that our society can well afford to provide low-cost, low-income housing for those who need it without adversely affecting the for profit housing market of supply and demand (Barak 1991b).

In sum, systems of equal justice are concerned with the impartial enforcement of law and punishment; systems of restorative justice are concerned with victim-offender reconciliation; and systems of social justice are concerned with the ecologies of crime in a market society. We believe that fully informed analyses of the social realities of justice in America should be concerned with all three systems of justice. We also believe that a "correct" balancing of the three systems would move us closer to a reality of justice for all. We cannot claim to know what the exact balance should be, but we will identify some of the changes in current policy and practice that would make better use of justice resources. Such policy changes would be more effective in the reduction of criminality, particularly marginal criminality—and more humane toward victims, offenders, and consumers of crime and crime control.

The Struggle for Justice

Even though the formal struggles for equal justice are younger than the informal struggles for restorative or social justice, the U.S. has come closer to approximating the ideals and social realities of the former than of the latter. Given the unequal realities that still prevail in our society, that is not saying a whole lot for the quality of justice practiced here. However, in the larger scheme of things, "justice" for all has been a long time coming. Each of the struggles for justice is rooted in different historical periods. In premodern times the struggles for justice were informal, private affairs concerned with what could be called early systems of restorative and social justice. In modern times, we can ground the emergence and development of these three ongoing struggles for justice in very different epochs: preindustrial, industrial, and postindustrial.

Former UNESCO legal advisor Karen Vasak has referred to the struggles for specific rights in terms of three generations of rights. The first generation of rights represented the struggle for equal justice, or the struggle for "negative rights" in that they called for restraint from the state. These rights were derived from the American and French revolutions and the struggle to gain liberty or freedom from arbitrary state action. These rights are articulated in the Civil and Political Rights of the International Bill of Rights. Collectively, these rights have helped shape what we usually refer to as governmental control by "rule of law" rather than by "rule of man."

The second generation of rights represented the struggle for restorative justice, or the struggle for "positive rights" in that they called for "affirmative action" on the part of the state. These rights were derived from the experiences of the Soviet Union and they have also resonated in the welfare state policies of the West. These rights are articulated in the Economic, Social, and Cultural Rights of the International Bill of Rights. Collectively, these rights have helped shape what we usually refer to as the minimal duties or social obligations of the state to facilitate the "self-realization" of the individual.

The third generation of rights is represented by the contemporary struggle for social justice, or for universal "human rights" in that these rights call for international cooperation between all nation-states. These rights are currently evolving out of the emerging condition of global interdependence; they take shape and have meaning in forums such as the United Nations, and they include such developments as the establishment of the first international criminal court in 1999. Collectively, the third generation of rights recognizes that human rights obligations can no longer (if they ever could) be satisfied within the body of individual states acting alone (Barak 1991a).

Each generation of these structurally evolved rights has been the product of different historical struggles waged by peoples without rights to obtain these rights. With each new historical period, new notions have been expressed with respect to fundamental rights and to whom those rights pertain. It is our contention that these rights need to apply first and foremost to those groups of socially marginalized people who are most likely to commit the crimes that we have deemed worthy of pursuing. For example, Reiman (1990) has used John Rawls's "principle of difference," a requirement that inequalities work to the greater benefit of the worst off. Whether looking globally at social, political, and economic inequalities or locally at the distribution schemes for supplying shelter to the homeless or food to the hungry in the United States, he argues that these relations of inequality are justifiable only if the shares of goods and services to the "worst off" cannot be improved by decreasing those inequalities.

Implications for Policies of Crime Control and Criminal Reduction

U.S. policies of crime control have not relied evenly on theories and practices stemming from the three systems of justice. Crime control for the past quarter of a century has been most dependent on models of equal justice that have in practice been highly selective, retributive, and repressive toward America's most marginalized citizens. At the same time, the policies that flow from models of equal (and often repressive) justice and crime control have not only been emotionally charged and racially divisive in their relative enforcement and differential application of the law but have helped culturally construct the common criminal silhouette as a young black male. Equal justice practices have also been a means of separating out the dangerous classes and constructing exclusive groups of offenders for punishment. These practices have often represented unproductive or counterproductive efforts in the name of crime control. As many other studies have concluded, the "law and order" policies that have been in place have, rather than reducing crime and harms, contributed to the problems entailed in reducing crime and enhancing justice (Beckett and Sasson 2000; Cole 1999; Currie 1998; Lynch and Patterson 1991; Miller 1997; Reiman 1998a).

For example, the War on Drugs and its "double standards" of enforcement have had unintended consequences that extend well beyond the confines of the criminal justice system and into the community and beyond. As particular drugs and criminals were targeted as being the most dangerous, marginal peoples, especially minority communities of African, Latin, and Native Americans, were unequally repressed compared to majorities. The large-scale removal of young black males from their communities has depleted the supply of potential marriage partners for young black females. Some commentators have argued that these social relations of punishment have encouraged or legitimated young female-headed households, creating precisely the types of family formations that have been linked with higher rates of crime and abuse (Currie 1985; Messner and Rosenfeld 1994). More accurately, these trends in racial punishment have reinforced and exacerbated the impoverishment in which many of these households have found themselves entrenched.

Similarly, the increased processing of less serious marginal offenders throughout the criminal justice system has undermined the capacity of crime control to deliver on its full promise of due process and equal protection. Assembly-line, plea-bargained justice pertains not only to the accused but to the convicted as well, as each of these groups has become subject to the practices of "actuarial justice," or the forecasting of the costs and risks associated with managing dangerous populations (Feeley and Simon 1992; 1994). As a result, the centrifugal social forces of the profiles of dangerous offenders circulate throughout the administration of justice and the larger society, helping reinforce particular images of crime and criminals.

To break with these images and constructions of crime and criminals, we contend that the United States needs to scale back as much as possible its practices and policies of retributive and repressive justice. In their place, the policies and practices of restorative justice associated with the reintegration of offenders, victims, and their communities need to be expanded. In this way, crime control can move its emphasis away from pain and punishment and toward healing and developing. In the process, images and cultural constructions of "recovering" criminals and victims help transform the "dangerous" or "under" classes into the marginal and vulnerable classes, who are in need of social assistance. Moreover, the softening of criminal images, for example, through the marketing of reconciliation and compensation, needs to be connected to an assault on the more fundamental inequalities and relations of social injustice that are ultimately responsible for the levels and intensities of our existing crime problems.

In sum, policies of equal justice have been ineffective in reducing crime because they have failed to address the "root" or "systemic" causes of crime and delinquency for numerous reasons, most of those of a political and economic nature. In particular, over the past three decades, the distances between the poor and the middle and the rich have grown considerably. As the economic or class inequality has increased generally, so too has the marginalization of the poorest and least skilled or educated in American society, and in the course of this

254 Class, Race, Gender, and Crime: *Social Realities of Justice in America*

development, the antagonistic, conflictive relations of class, race, and gender have intensified.

As for the alternative scenarios of restorative and social justice, we look at these models as offering substantial ways to improve the quality of justice inside and outside the criminal justice system and to reduce interpersonal crime and violence in society. To begin with, these systems of justice engage in more human and inclusive models of crime control than do the models of equal justice. These "self" and "social" models of justice offer more holistic or integrative approaches to crime and justice than the equal models of justice do. Again, models of equal justice are subject to the legalistic confines of the rule of law. By contrast, models of restorative and social justice are subject to the broader horizons of the cultural ecologies of crime and crime control.

Restorative and social justice models encourage and actively support the participation of offenders, victims, and communities of interest in the processes of managing crime and justice. From these reinforcing perspectives, and from their shared point of view on the larger relations of crime and punishment, a crime control system or a system of criminal justice emanates, based on social healing, community peace, and the struggle for equality and inclusiveness in society. This approach does not abandon the legalistic models of due process and equal protection, but rather plays down the struggle for law and order and the need to inflict more pain and plays up the struggle for peace and justice and the need to incorporate practices of restorative and social justice, at least so these three overlapping systems of crime and justice may be evaluated, compared, and experimented with.

In conjunction with the crime control institutions of law making, law enforcement, and sentencing and punishment, we have the larger social and cultural constructions of crime and justice that are mass mediated daily. Before we tackle the legal institutions of crime control with our specific policy recommendations, we want to briefly reiterate our thoughts on the "crime problem" as it has been popularly portrayed and as it needs to be demystified. The representations of crime, criminals, and the administration of justice found in the news, in films, on television, and in literature, are fairly skewed or one-dimensional.

Criminals are typically "low life" predators who murder, rob, assault, and kidnap; crimes are typically acts carried out by the poor and racial minorities; and crime control is typically what the police,

courts, and prisons do. In lockstep with the social realities of equal justice, these portrayals are essentially legalistic narratives that reinforce
stereotypes of the dangerous classes and that rarely provide background or context for the behavior. If we take the case of sexual
harassment, sexual assault, and other sexual offenses, women are
clearly seen as the victims. However, their sexual victimization is
rarely discussed or interpreted in terms of masculinity or sexual
inequality but rather is typically confined to questions of security and
surveillance.

Thus, the images of these behaviors and the associated culprits, as
well as the responses to these crimes, not only serve to inflame public
fears and anxieties surrounding crime and its reduction but also help
reproduce scenarios of retributive and repressive justice that reinforce class, racial, and gendered patterns of exclusion and separation.
At the same time, many criminal justice practices reflect a masculine
bias or approach to crime-fighting. Feminists and others, for example,
have been critical of correctional officer and police training programs
for their overemphasis on physical strength, intimidation, and aggres-
siveness as a means of resolving disputes while devaluing interpersonal skills, group cooperation, and empathy. Similarly, feminist
criminologists are among those critical of boot camps for being
unnecessarily demeaning and abusive to inmates as well as for engendering elements of militarism, hard labor, and fear, all of which are
conducive to the abuse of authority and to the use of violence
(Morash and Rucker 1998).

There is a need not only to demystify the images of crime and
crime-fighting and of the administration of justice but to reconstruct
these images so that they include a fuller range of both the incidents
of harm and injury in society as well as the propagation of alternative
systems of crime reduction and justice enhancement. Finally, such
alternative practices as restorative and social justice need to become
mass-mediated popular constructions.

Based on our previous analyses of the relations of class, race, and
gender, and in the context of the cultural reconstruction of crime and
justice, we now present several policy options or recommendations
that we believe are capable of enhancing justice and reducing crime,
especially among those marginal groups who are traditionally processed through the various systems of juvenile and criminal justice in
America.

Law Making

In the area of *law making* at least two basic policy changes are called for. These changes are aimed at curbing the escalation of the war on crime in general and the war on drugs in particular. These policies are also supportive of the reintegration of offenders, especially nonviolent and less serious offenders, within their communities as legally productive members. The types of crime legislation that are specifically needed include social capital bills and harm reduction bills.

Investing in Social Capital. Domestic and cross-cultural studies alike reveal that relative deprivation, frustration, aggression, and violence are associated in the production of marginal criminality. To reduce these sources of criminality, we need to enact domestic policies of social control designed for reducing poverty and inequality. Relative and declining wages at the marginal ends of the employment market, for example, should be "subsidized" at living wages, even if that means those at the margins pay no taxes or even receive stipends of some kind.

In addition, the reduced social spending on children and families should be redeployed into those marginal communities and invested there as social capital for human development. Currie (1998) identifies four priorities that are a good start: preventing child abuse and neglect, enhancing children's intellectual and social development, providing support and guidance to vulnerable adolescents, and working intensively with juvenile offenders. While none of these suggestions is a cure-all, he notes that sometimes modest levels of assistance can make a great difference. Similarly, legislation is called for that increases economic support and social services, inclusive of jobs programs, education and technical training, and universal health and mental care. Finally, domestic policies of inclusion need to be developed, such as greater availability of drug treatment programs for all who need them and better delivery of mental health services.

Investing in Harm Reduction. Harm reduction can be accomplished in one of two ways: criminalization or decriminalization. For example, society needs stricter laws and more appropriate penalties for white-collar and corporate crime, pertaining especially to those harms that inflict the most pain and suffering on marginal communities, such as toxic pollution and waste elimination. Of course, to enforce these laws, funds must be allocated to augment old and to set up new investigating and prosecuting organizations for these types of "nonpersonal" crimes. In terms of reduction through decriminalization, legalization, or regulation, we have the situation of unequal drug enforcement, both in terms of those persons prosecuted and of the estimated 40 million consumers of illicit drugs not processed.

Our recommendation is for the wholesale shifting of the drug problem away from law enforcement and into the medical arena. In other words, the use and abuse of drugs should be treated as health problems and not as police problems. And, assuming that our society is not prepared to take this radical step politically, we call for less moralistic and more realistic laws that distinguish between high-risk and low-risk drug-related dangers. In other words, blanket policies of "zero tolerance" need to remove from their dangerous substance lexicons those drugs that provide no real threat to their users or to others, such as marijuana, while keeping in place stiff punishments for date rape drugs. With such scaling back on the war on drugs, not only would the rates of incarceration decline but scarce criminal justice dollars would be saved and could be made available for treatment and other programs of crime prevention. With such a domestic policy in place, we would be in a position to transfer resources away from punishment and the warehousing of nondangerous offenders and toward the healing and recovering of those in need, whether they are drug users or drug-free (see Trebach in Leighton and Reiman 2001).

Law Enforcement

In the area of law enforcement at least three policy-related changes are called for. These changes are aimed at curbing aggressive policing and strengthening the rule of law. These policies are also supportive of enhanced police-community involvement, especially in marginalized neighborhoods. The types of policies that are needed include de-escalation, reaffirmation, and enrichment.

De-escalating the War on Crime. We suggest two policy measures for de-escalating the war on crime. First, there should be a reduction in the paramilitary (i.e., SWAT teams) trends in law enforcement. Whether addressing local police "drug sweeps" in the early hours of the morning in public housing projects or the actions by the FBI or the Bureau of Alcohol, Fire, and Tobacco in such places as Ruby Ridge, Idaho, and Waco, Texas, law enforcement must distinguish between combating murderers or terrorists and confronting petty criminals or social deviants. The actions of the military and the police, in other words, need to maintain their separate and unique roles or functions in American society and elsewhere in the world. They should not become one and the same, and we should resist the convergences between the two organizations.

Second, proactive policing policies such as "zero tolerance" should be scaled back in selected communities. Once again, distinctions must be made between nonviolent and unthreatening behavior and behavior that poses serious risks of injury and harm. Petty offenses, especially those that involve physically and socially deteriorated communities, including the activities of the homeless, the addicted, and the mentally ill, should be filtered out of the criminal justice system. Instead, these problems associated with social stability, infrastructure decay, and issues of health should be referred to human service and voluntary agencies residing outside the jurisdictions of law enforcement.

Reaffirming Due Process and Equal Protection. The erosion of due process and equal protection rights over the past several decades has not been confined to the activities of the police; it also includes the representation of accused indigent offenders as well as those who have been convicted and incarcerated. With respect to law enforcement, there is a need to reinforce the rule of law. This approach calls for a reinstatement of those various legal safeguards that have been watered down, such as the "good faith" exemptions in having probable cause when obtaining reasonable search warrants. It also calls for the suppression of super-surveillance activities that invade people's right to privacy. With respect to the rights of the marginally accused and convicted, there is the need for more competent and better-paid legal counsel, especially in those cases involving capital crimes and the death penalty. Where appropriate, due process rights should also be expanded to include the latest technological developments. For example, all persons accused or convicted of a crime where DNA tests would be relevant to proving or disproving guilt or innocence should become law and made available to all accused defendants.

Enriching Community Control. The history of police-community relations is, at best, a "mixed bag," as the variety of activities that fall under this umbrella have been viewed both favorably and unfavorably by citizens. With respect to marginal communities in particular, there has been skepticism and mistrust from many residents, who often perceive or view these efforts as little more than public relations. In other words, there is a need to engage in proactive police-community relations that move beyond increased interactions and that result in ways to protect oneself, or in more information against criminal wrongdoers.

For example, the creation of citizen review boards with reasonable authority and power guards against overzealous policing and builds trust between the police and the community. Similarly, the inclusion of representative groups (e.g., minorities, women, gays) in neighborhood patrols is useful in sensitizing citizens and police to each other's needs. These types of crime control policies aim to increase the ability of individual citizens and neighborhood groups to come together with the police to "co-produce" or construct neighborhood improvement activities within larger plans of harm reduction and conflict resolution.

Sentencing and Punishment

In the areas of sentencing and punishment a number of related policies are called for. These changes are aimed at curbing excessive punishments and in reversing the trends of increasing lengths of penal incarceration. These policies are also supportive of diversifying and expanding the alternatives to imprisonment and in developing programs for personal self-actualization and social integration, both inside and outside of prison. The types of policies that are needed include a moratorium on prison construction and private prisons, abandonment of mandatory sentences, community-based initiatives, and human service delivery.

A Moratorium on Prison Construction and Private Prisons. The U.S. already has the largest per capita prison population of any Western Democracy and one of the highest in the entire world. Put simply, we do not need any more prisons. Prisons are a way to punish crime after it happens, so policies of prevention are preferable. Currently, many states are cutting budgets for education and social services—including crime prevention—to pay for prison expansion. Such public policy is not healthy or sustainable; it is much like mopping the floor while the tub overflows (Currie 1985; Leighton 1999).

Private prisons undermine public accountability and give segments of the population a vested interest in expanding the prison population. As corporations, private prisons are exempt from many disclosure requirements because the Freedom of Information Act does not apply. Private prisons do not provide a list of the racial break-down of prisoners, and other information may be protected by 'corporate policy' or 'trade secrets.' They form the most obvious part of a Criminal Justice-Industrial Complex that has arisen now that the end of the Cold War has reduced the Military-Industrial Complex (see Dyer 2000; the "Crime Pays" resources at *http://www.paulsjustice page.com*).

Abandonment of Mandatory Sentences. Because we have con-cluded that those who end up in prison are disproportionately repre-sentative of marginal classes, and because the current mandatory minimum sentences, even if uniformly applied, have adverse affects on African and Latino male Americans, we recommend maximum-time-served, but not minimum-time-served, sentencing. Ideally, we recommend abolishing the death penalty, for its use is too selective and generally excludes whole groups of people, to the detriment of some marginal groups. Short of abolition, we recommend the suspen-sion of the death penalty until such time as the states can guarantee the competencies of the defense attorneys that try their capital pun-ishment cases. We also recommend that judges be granted some dis-cretionary freedom to reduce the maximum time served by prisoners. Finally, we recommend abolishing the practice of treating juvenile and youthful offenders as if they were adult offenders.

Community-Based Initiatives. We strongly recommend the development and diversification of community-based models of pun-ishment. Such initiatives could have incarcerated inmates engaging in restorative forms of justice involving their victims and communities, or in work-release type programs in which the person is allowed out for hours, days, or weeks at a time. Community-based models of pun-ishment also include community service and restitution, compensa-tion to injured parties, halfway houses, probation, suspended sentencing, and more. Reducing sentence lengths and time served in penal institutions and expanding alternatives to imprisonment could establish a moratorium on new prison construction. At the same time, community-based alternatives would reduce the existing majority of penal institutions that have been found to be in violation of "cruel and unusual punishment," because of their conditions of severe over-crowding, often involving the doubling and tripling up of the number of inmates living in a space constitutionally defined for one.

Human Service Delivery. In the spirit of restorative and social jus-tice, and in the context of reintegration, we need to expand and develop a range of human services both inside and outside of prisons. With the billions of dollars saved from expensive new prison construction and from the lowered operating costs of serving hundreds of thousands fewer inmates each year, programs in transition, counseling, education and training, community justice, and so on could be established. Other related programs involving employment opportunities, "criminal anonymous" groups, and incentives for employers to cooperate and for others to initiate still other human services could also be supported in this fashion. Finally, related policy measures designed to promote "personal responsibility" by limiting or denying welfare benefits or public assistance to persons convicted of crimes need to be seriously reconsidered. For the most part, such policies tend to worsen situations of deprivation and to stoke the incentives for more, not less, criminality.

Summary and Conclusions

In *Class, Race, Gender, and Crime: Social Realities of Justice in America,* we have tried to capture the similar and dissimilar ways that crime and crime control are related to the social constructions of class, race, and gender. We have also sought to represent the overlapping or intersecting identities of class, race, and gender as they have involved both struggling human beings and structured social interactions. Moreover, we have focused on the ways in which systems of privilege and inequality, reflective of class, race, and gender, have informed the philosophies and practices of social control, inside and outside the systems of criminal and juvenile justice.

More specifically, we have demonstrated that four sets of relations still prevail in the social realities of crime and justice in America today:

- Class/race/gender inequalities produce a construction of crime categories under law that criminalize the conduct of those with the wrong class/race/gender, while leaving harms available to and produced by those with the right class/race/gender composition either as legal actions or as minor crimes or administrative violations.

- Class/race/gender inequalities produce ways of administering justice that visit harsher punishments and more violations of rights on those with the wrong class/race/gender makeup compared to those with the right class/race/gender composition.

- Class/race/gender inequalities produce different lived experiences depending on where people are situated in the world of privilege and inequality.

- Mass-mediated constructions of the class/race/gender character of crime and the composition of the "criminal" population play a significant role in reinforcing and reproducing the forms of oppression associated with crime and justice.

Accordingly, because of the above relationships and because of the failure and counterproductive efforts of the prevailing policies of a punitive justice in the United States, we have concluded that alternative ways of responding to deviant and criminal behavior are called for. What is required are less divisive, repressive, and punitive forms of justice that reinforce or reproduce the disadvantages of class, race, and gender relations. In their place must be substituted more integrative, restorative, and social forms of justice that address the unequal realities of class, race, and gender. The latter forms of justice not only recognize the disadvantages of class, race, and gender but acknowledge the vulnerability, alienation, powerlessness, isolation, banishment, and other debilitating aspects associated with membership in the marginally dispossessed classes of American society.

Integrative, reintegrative, and primary preventive models of social control and crime reduction focus on the development of all human beings, from conception forward, as they are caught up in various realities of institutional, structural, and cultural life (Barak 1998; Braithwaite 1989; Currie 1985; Henry and Milovanovic 1996; Messner and Rosenfeld 1994; Pepinsky and Quinney 1991). The assumption that all these approaches to crime control share is that there is much more to crime control than the processes of criminal justice administration. Each of these related strategies, whether referred to as "integrative," "reintegrative," "constitutive," or "peacemaking" criminology, takes seriously the conditions of crime production. In turn, each attempts to buffer the impact of these conditions by challenging some of our culture's fundamental values and beliefs about crime, criminals, control, and justice. Finally, each of these alternative models to repressive crime control strives toward developing domestic policies that support interactive systems of individual and community development, within the wider contexts of globalization.

Hence, policies that emphasize restoration and social justice revolve around notions of crime control whose objectives are to reconstruct mutual support, collective obligations, and co-responsibility for crime transcending the individualized acts of criminal behavior and addressing the fact that all members of marginal classes are at risk and in need of programs that further the actualization of their full potential and full employment at livable wages. For example, in the spirit of reintegrating the corporation (or corporate offenders) and enhancing the well-being of marginal communities, policies of capital investment in social and human development at the local level could be substituted as compensatory forms of punishment for these affluent offenders. Similarly, policies for reintegrating ex-convicts are called for that reconstruct images and stereotypes of "criminals" as vulnerable and recovering people, rather than as evil and menacing subjects of society. All and all, such approaches to social control view the problems of preventing crime and enhancing justice as part and parcel of the constructive efforts in social change aimed at transforming the structural relations of privilege and inequality. ✦

References

Agozino, Biko. 1997. *Black Women and the Criminal Justice System*. Aldershot, England: Ashgate Publishing Limited.

Alvesalo, Anne. 1998. "They Are Not Honest Criminals: The Construction of Legal Practices Around the Policing, Litigation and Counterlitigation Surrounding White Collar Crime and Entrepreneurship in Contemporary Finland." Paper presented at the annual meetings of the American Society of Criminology, Washington, D.C.

American Association of University Women. 1997. "Affirmative Action." (Position Paper) Washington, DC: AAUW.

American Civil Liberties Union. 1997. "Denver Police Sexual Harassment Case Begins." The ACLU Freedom Network website: http://www.aclu.org/news/w111097.d.html.

American Correctional Association. 1999. *1999 Directory: Juvenile and Adult Correctional Departments, Institutions, Agencies and Paroling Authorities*. Lanham, MD: American Correctional Association.

Amnesty International. 1999. "Not Part of My Sentence" - Violations of the Human Rights of Women in Custody. Available at http://www.amnesty.org/ailib/aipub/1999/AMR/25100199.htm

Andersen, Margaret. 1988. "Moving Our Minds: Studying Women and Reconstructing Sociology." *Teaching Sociology* 16:123–132.

Andersen, Margaret L. and Patricia Hill Collins. 1998. *Race, Class and Gender: An Anthology, 3rd ed*. Belmont, CA: Wadsworth Publishing.

Anderson, Charles H. 1974. *The Political Economy of Social Class*. Englewood Cliffs, NJ: Prentice Hall.

Anderson, S. E. 1995. *The Black Holocaust: For Beginners*. New York: Writers and Readers, Inc.

Aronowitz, Stanley and William DiFazio. 1994. *The Jobless Future: Sci-Tech and the Dogma of Work*. Minneapolis: University of Minnesota Press.

Auerbach, Jerold S. 1976. *Unequal Justice: Lawyers and Social Change in Modern America.* New York: Oxford University Press.

Austin, Regina and Michael Schill. 1991. "Black, Brown, Poor & Poisoned: Minority Grassroots Environmentalism and the Quest for Eco-Justice." *The Kansas Journal of Law and Public Policy* Summer:69.

Bailey, Frankie Y., Joycelyn M. Pollock, and Sherry Schroeder. 1998. "The Best Defense: Images of Female Attorneys in Popular Films." Pp. 180–196 in *Popular Culture, Crime and Justice,* Frankie Bailey and Donna Hale (eds.). Belmont, CA: West/Wadsworth.

Balos, Beverly and Mary Louise Fellows. 1999. "A Matter of Prostitution: Becoming Respectable." *New York University Law Review* 74:1220.

Barak, Gregg. 2000. "Repressive Versus Restorative and Social Justice: A Case for Integrative Praxis." *Contemporary Justice Review* 3(1):39–44.

——. 1998. *Integrating Criminologies.* Boston: Allyn and Bacon.

——. (ed.). 1996. *Representing O. J.: Murder, Criminal Justice and Mass Culture.* Albany, NY: Harrow and Heston.

——. (ed.). 1994. *Media, Process, and the Social Construction of Crime: Studies in Newsmaking Criminology.*

——. (ed.). 1991a. *Crimes by the Capitalist State: An Introduction to State Criminality.* Albany: SUNY Press.

——. 1991b. *Gimme Shelter: A Social History of Homelessness in Contemporary America.* New York: Praeger.

——. 1980. *In Defense of Whom? A Critique of Criminal Justice Reform.* Cincinnati, OH: Anderson Publishing.

Barak, Gregg and Stuart Henry. 1999. "An Integrative-Constitutive Theory of Crime, Law, and Social Justice." *Social Justice/Criminal Justice: The Maturation of Critical Theory in Law, Crime, and Deviance.* Belmont, CA: West/Wadsworth.

Barlow, Melissa. 1998. "Race and the Problem of Crime in *Time* and *Newsweek* Cover Stories, 1946–1995." *Social Justice* 25(2):149–183.

Beal, Glenda J. (ed.). 1993. *ACA National Jail and Adult Detention Directory.* Laurel, MD: American Correctional Association.

Beck, Allen J. and Christopher J. Mumola. 1999. *Prisoners in 1998.* Washington, DC: Bureau of Justice Statistics.

Beckett, Katherine and Theodore Sasson. 2000. *The Politics of Injustice: Crime and Punishment in America.* Thousand Oaks, CA: Pine Forge Press.

Beirne, Piers, and James Messerschmidt. 2000. *Criminology,* 3rd ed. Boulder, CO: Westview.

Belknap, Joanne. 1996. *The Invisible Woman: Gender, Crime, and Justice.* Belmont. CA: Wadsworth.

——. 1995. "Women in Conflict: An Analysis of Women Correctional Officers." Pp. 404–420 in *The Criminal Justice System and Women*. Barbara Raffel Price and Natalie J. Sokoloff, (eds.). New York: McGraw-Hill.

Bell, Derrick. 1990. "Chronicle of the Space Traders." *Rutgers Law Review* 42:1; revised and expanded version in *St. Louis Law Review* 34 (1990):3.

Benedict, Helen. 1992. *Virgin or Vamp: How the Press Covers Sex Crimes*. New York: Oxford University Press.

Berry, Gordon L. 1993. "Multicultural Portrayals on Television as a Social Psychological Issue." In *Children and Television Images*, Gordon L. Berry and Joy Keiko Asamen (eds.). Newbury Park, CA: Sage Publications.

Best, Joel. 1990. *Threatened Children: Rhetoric and Concern About Child Victims*. Chicago: University of Chicago Press.

Binstein, Michael and Charles Bowden. 1993. *Trust Me: Charles Keating and the Missing Billions*. NewYork: Random House.

Black, Donald. 1976. *The Behavior of Law*. New York: Academic Press.

Blast, Carol. 1997. "Driving While Black: Stopping Motorists on a Subterfuge." *Criminal Law Bulletin* 33:457.

Blau, Francine and John Graham. 1990. "Black-White Differences in Wealth and Asset Composition." *Quarterly Journal of Economics* May:321.

Blumstein, Alfred. 1995. "Interview with Professor Alfred Blumstein of Carnegie Mellon University." *Law Enforcement News*, 422:10.

Bonilla-Silva, Eduardo. 1997. "Rethinking Racism: Toward a Structural Interpretation." *American Sociological Review* 62:465–480.

Braithwaite, John. 1992. "Poverty, Power and White Collar Crime." In *White Collar Crime Reconsidered*. Kip, Schlegel and David Weisbord (eds.). Boston: Northeastern.

——. 1989. *Crime, Shame, and Reintegration*. Cambridge: Cambridge University Press.

Breitbart, Vicki, Wendy Chavkin, and Paul H. Wise. 1994. "The Accessibility of Drug Treatment for Pregnant Women: A Survey of Programs in Five Cities." *American Journal of Public Health* 84(10):1658–1661.

Britton, Dana M. 1997. "Gendered Organizational Logic: Policy and Practice in Men's and Women's Prisons." *Gender and Society* 11(6):796–818.

Brochman, Sue. 1991. "Silent Victims: Bringing Male Rape out of the Closet." *The Advocate*. 582:38–43.

Brody, Jane E. 1998a. "Researchers Unravel the Motives of Stalkers." *New York Times*. August 25:F1.

——. 1998b. "Some Ailments Found Guilty of Sex Bias." *New York Times*. November 10:F12.

Brouwer, Steve. 1998. *Sharing the Pie: A Citizen's Guide to Wealth and Power in America.* New York: Henry Holt and Company.

Brown, Jennifer. 1998. "Aspects of Discriminatory Treatment of Women Police Officers Serving in Forces in England and Wales." *British Journal of Criminology* 38:265–282.

Brown, Jodi M. and Patrick A. Langan. 1998. *State Court Sentencing of Convicted Felons, 1994.* Washington, DC: U.S. Department of Justice.

Brown, Robert McAfee. 1987. *Religion and Violence,* 2nd ed. Philadelphia: The Westminster Press.

Brune, Tom. 1999. "Census Will for First Time Count Those of Mixed Race." *Seattle Times* August 17: Online edition.

Bufkin, Jana L. 1999. "Bias Crime as Gendered Behavior." *Social Justice* 26(1):155–176.

Buhrke, Robin A. 1996. *A Matter of Justice: Lesbians and Gay Men in Law Enforcement.* New York: Routledge.

Bullard, Robert. 1994. *Unequal Protection: Environmental Justice and Communities of Color.* San Francisco: Sierra Club Books.

——. 1990. *Dumping in Dixie: Race, Class and Environmental Quality.* Boulder: Westview.

Bureau of Justice Statistics. 2000a. *Sourcebook of Criminal Justice Statistics, 1998.* Washington, DC: U.S. Department of Justice.

——. 2000b. *Local Police Departments 1997.* Washington, DC: U.S. Department of Justice.

——. 1999a. *American Indians and Crime.* Washington, DC: U.S. Department of Justice. NCJ 173386.

——. 1999b. *Probation and Parole in the United States, 1998.* Washington DC: U.S. Department of Justice. NCJ 178234.

——. 1999c. *Prisoners in 1998.* Washington DC: U.S. Department of Justice. NCJ 175687.

——. 1998a. *Changes in Criminal Victimization, 1994–95.* Washington, DC: U.S. Department of Justice.

——. 1998b. *Violence by Intimates.* Washington, DC: U.S. Department of Justice.

——. 1997a. *HIV in Prisons and Jails, 1995.* Washington, DC: U.S. Department of Justice.

——. 1997b. *Lifetime Likelihood of Going to State or Federal Prison.* Washington DC: U.S. Department of Justice. NCJ 160092.

——. 1994a. *Women in Prison.* Washington, DC: U.S. Department of Justice.

——. 1994b. *Young Black Male Victims.* Washington, DC: U.S. Department of Justice. NCJ 147004.

———. 1992. *Drugs, Crime and the Justice System.* Washington, DC: U.S. Department of Justice. NCJ 133652.

Bureau of Labor Statistics. 1999a. *Highlights of Women's Earnings in 1998, Report 928.* Washington, DC: U.S. Department of Labor.

———. 1999b. *Employment and Earnings* (monthly). January: Table 10ftp:// ftp.bls.gov/pub/special.requests/lf/aat10.txt

———. 1999c. "National Employment and Wage Data from the Occupational Employment Statistics Survey by Occupation, 1998." *Occupational Employment Statistics* December:Table 1, Table A-1.

Bureau of the Census. 1999a. *Population Estimates Program, Population Division. Resident Population Estimates of the United States by Sex, Race, and Hispanic Origin,* October 1.

———. 1999b. *Current Population Report, P60-207. Poverty in the U.S., 1998* Washington, DC: U.S. Government Printing Office. Table B-1. http:// www.census.gov/hhes/www/povty98.html.

———. 1999c. *Statistical Abstract of the United States, 1999.* Washington, DC: U.S. Government Printing Office.

———. 1998a. *Annual Demographic Survey,* March Supplement: Table 1. Washington, DC:U.S. Government Printing Office. http://www.census.gov.

———. 1998b. *Current Population Report, P20-513. Educational Attainment in the United States* March 1998 (Update). Washington, DC: U.S. Government Printing Office. http://www.census.gov:80/population/www/socdemo/ educ-attn.html.

———. 1998c. "Dropout Rates in the United States." *Current Population Survey.* (unpublished tabulations).

———. 1998d. *Current Population Survey: Educational Attainment in the United States, March, 1997.* pp.20–505. Washington, DC: U.S. Government Printing Office.

———. 1994. *Current Population Survey 1948–1994 Annual Averages.* Washington DC: U.S. Government Printing Office.

———. 1990. *Detailed Occupation by Race, Hispanic Origin and Sex.* Washington, DC: CenStats. http://tier2.census.gov/eeo/eeo.htm.

Burnley, Jane, Christine Edmunds, Mario T. Gaboury, and Anne Seymour. 1998. *1998 National Victim Assistance Academy.* Washington, DC: Office of Justice Programs, U.S. Department of Justice.

Butler, Anne. 1997. *Gendered Justice in the American West: Women Prisoners in Men's Penitentiaries.* Urbana: University of Illinois Press.

Calavita, Kitty, Henry Pontell, and Robert Tillman. 1997. *Big Money Crime.* Berkeley: University of California Press.

Cantor, Nathaniel E. 1932. *Crime: Criminals and Criminal Justice.* New York: Henry Holt and Company.

Carmichael, Stokely and Charles Hamilton. 1967. *Black Power: The Politics of Liberation in America.* New York: Vintage.

Carmona, Ralph C. 2000. "Standing Between Community and Chaos." *Los Angeles Times* June 26: B9.

Catalyst. 1998. *1998 Catalyst Census of Female Board Directors of the Fortune 500.* New York: Catalyst.

Center for Research on Criminal Justice. 1975. *The Iron Fist and Velvet Glove.* Berkeley, CA: CRCJ.

Center for the American Woman and Politics (CAWP). 1998a. "Sex Differences in Voter Turnout." National Information Bank on Women in Public Office. New Brunswick, NJ: Eagleton Institute of Politics, Rutgers University.

——. 1998b. "Women in Elective Office 1998." National Information Bank on Women in Public Office. New Brunswick, NJ: Eagleton Institute of Politics, Rutgers University.

Chalk, Frank and Kurt Jonassohn. 1990. *The History and Sociology of Genocide.* New Haven, CT: Yale University Press.

Chambliss, William. 1988. *Exploring Criminology.* New York: Macmillan.

Chambliss, William and R. B. Seidman. 1982. *Law, Order and Power, 2nd ed.* Reading, MA: Addison Wesley.

Chesney-Lind, Meda. 1998. "Foreword." In *Crime Control and Women.* Susan L. Miller (ed.). Thousand Oaks, CA: Sage.

——. 1996. "Sentencing Women to Prison: Equality Without Justice." In *Race, Gender, and Class in Criminology: The Intersection,* Martin D. Schwartz and Dragan Milovanovic (eds.). New York: Garland Publishing.

Chesney-Lind, Meda and Jocelyn M. Pollock. 1995. "Women's Prisons: Equality with a Vengence." Pp. 155–175 in *Women, Law, and Social Control.* Alida V. Merlo and Joycelyn M. Pollack (eds.). Needham Heights, MA: Allyn and Bacon.

Cho, Sumi K. 1997. "Converging Stereotypes in Racialized Sexual Harassment: Where the Model Minority Meets Suzie Wong." Pp. 203–220 in *Critical Race Feminism,* Adrien K. Wing (ed.). New York: New York University Press.

Christie, Nils. 1993. *Crime Control as Industry: Toward Gulags, Western Style?* London: Routledge.

Churchill, Ward. 1997. *A Little Matter of Genocide.* San Francisco: City Lights Books.

Churchill, Ward and Jim Vander Wall. 1990a. *Agents of Repression: The FBI's Secret Wars Against the Black Panther Party and the American Indian Movement.* Boston: South End Press.

————. 1990b. *The COINTELPRO Papers: Documents From the FBI's Secret Wars Against Domestic Dissent.* Boston: South End Press.

Clinard, Marshall. 1990. *Corporate Corruption: The Abuse of Power.* New York: Praeger.

Cole, David. 1999. *No Equal Justice: Race and Class in the American Criminal Justice System.* New York: New Press.

Coleman, James. 1985. "Law and Power: The Sherman Antitrust Act and Its Enforcement in the Petroleum Industry." *Social Problems* 32.

Collins, Patricia Hill. 1998. *Fighting Words: Black Women and the Search for Justice.* Minneapolis: University of Minnesota Press.

————. 1990. *Black Feminist Thought: Knowledge, Consciousness, and the Politics of Empowerment.* New York: Routledge.

Collins, William C., and Andrew W. Collins. 1996. *Women in Jail: Legal Issues.* Washington, DC: National Institute of Corrections.

Conley, John. (ed.). 1994. *The 1967 President's Crime Commission Report: Its Impact 25 Years Later.* Cincinnati: Anderson Publishing.

Connell, Robert W. 1995. *Masculinities.* Los Angeles: University of California Press.

————. 1987. *Gender and Power: Society, The Person, and Sexual Politics.* Stanford CA: Stanford University Press.

Costello, Cynthia and Barbara Kivimae Krimgold. (eds.). 1996. *The American Woman 1996–97: Where We Stand.* New York: W.W. Norton.

Council of Economic Advisers for the President's Initiative on Race. 1998. *Changing America: Indicators of Social and Economic Well-Being by Race and Hispanic Origin.* Washington, DC: U.S. Government Printing Office. http://w3.access.gpo.gov/eop/ca/index.html.

Craven, Diane. 1997. *Sex Differences in Violent Victimization, 1994.* Washington, DC: U.S. Department of Justice.

Crawford, James. 1988. *The Rights of Peoples.* Oxford: Oxford University Press.

Crenshaw, Kimberlé. 1991. "Mapping the Margins: Intersectionality, Identity Politics, and Violence Against Women of Color." *Stanford Law Review* 43:1258–1299.

Currie, Elliott. 1998. *Crime and Punishment in America.* New York: Henry Holt.

————. 1985. *Confronting Crime: An American Challenge.* New York: Pantheon.

Dahrendorf, Ralf. 1959. *Class and Class Conflict in Industrial Society.* Stanford, CA: Stanford University Press.

Daly, Kathleen. 1995 "Looking Back, Looking Forward: The Promise of Feminist Transformation." Pp. 443–457 in *The Criminal Justice System and*

Women, 2nd ed. Barbara Raffel Price and Natalie J. Sokoloff (eds.). New York: McGraw-Hill.

——. 1994. *Gender, Crime, and Punishment.* New Haven, CT: Yale University Press.

Daly, Kathleen and Meda Chesney-Lind. 1988. "Feminism and Criminology." *Justice Quarterly* 5:497–538.

Daly, Kathleen and Russ Immarigeon. 1998. "The Past, Present, and Future of Restorative Justice: Some Critical Reflections." *Contemporary Justice Review* 1(1):21–45.

Danner, Mona J.E. 1998. "Three Strikes and It's Women Who Are Out: The Hidden Consequences for Women of Criminal Justice Police Reforms." Pp. 1–14 in *Crime Control and Women.* Susan L. Miller (ed.). Thousand Oaks, CA: Sage Publications.

Davis, L. 1990. "Chronicle of a Debacle Foretold." *Harper's,* September: 50–65.

Day, Kathleen. 1993. *S & L Hell: The People and the Politics Behind the $1 Trillion Savings and Loan Scandal.* New York: Norton.

DeKeseredy, Walter S. and Martin D. Schwartz. 1996. *Contemporary Criminology.* Belmont, CA: Wadsworth.

Delgado, Richard (ed.). 1995a. *Critical Race Theory: The Cutting Edge.* Philadelphia: Temple University Press.

——. 1995b(1993). "Rodrigo's Sixth Chronicle: Intersections, Essences, and the Dilemma of Social Reform." Pp. 242–252 in *Critical Race Theory.* Richard Delgado (ed.). Philadelphia: Temple University Press.

Delgado, Richard and Jean Stefancic. 1997. *Critical White Studies: Looking Behind the Mirror.* Philadelphia: Temple University Press.

——. 1991. "Derrick Bell's Chronicle of the Space Traders: Would the U.S. Sacrifice People of Color If the Price Were Right?" *University of Colorado Law Review* 62:321.

Department of Defense. 1996. *Defense 96.* Washington, DC: U.S. Government Printing Office.

Department of Justice. 1998. *The Challenge of Crime in a Free Society: Looking Back, Looking Forward.* Washington, DC: U.S. Department of Justice. NCJ 170029.

Department of Justice, Federal Bureau of Investigation. 1997. *Crime in the United States, 1996.* Washington, DC: U.S. Department of Justice.

——. 1996. *Crime in the United States, 1995.* Washington, DC: U.S. Department of Justice.

Department of Labor. 1998. *Equal Pay: A Thirty-Five Year Perspective.* Washington, DC: Women's Bureau.

Domhoff, G. William. 1998. *Who Rules America?* 3rd edition. Mountain View, CA: Mayfield Publishing.

Douglas, William O. 1954. *An Almanac of Liberty.* Garden City, NY: Doubleday.

Doyle, James. 1992 " 'It's the Third World Down There!': The Colonialist Vocation and American Criminal Justice." *Harvard Civil Rights–Civil Liberties Law Review* 27:71.

Dunlap, Eloise. 1992. "Impact of Drugs on Family Life and Kin Networks in the Inner-City African-American Single-Parent Household." In *Drugs, Crime, and Social Isolation.* Adele V. Harrell and George E. Peterson (eds.). Washington, DC: Urban Institute Press.

Dyer, Joel. 2000. *The Perpetual Prisoner Machine: How America Profits From Crime.* Boulder, CO: Westview.

Edelstein, Charles D. and Robert J. Wicks. 1977. *An Introduction to Criminal Justice.* New York: McGraw-Hill.

Eichstaedt, Peter. 1994. *If You Poison Us: Uranium and Native Americans.* Red Crane Books.

Essed, P. 1991. *Understanding Everyday Racism: An Interdisciplinary Theory.* Newbury, CA: Sage.

———. 1990. *Everyday Racism: Reports From Women in Two Cultures.* Claremont, CA: Hunter House.

Etzioni, Amitai. 1990. "Going Soft on Corporate Crime." *Washington Post* April 1.

Ezekiel, Raphael. 1995. *The Racist Mind: Portraits of American Neo-Nazis and Klansmen.* New York: Penguin.

Faith, Karlene. 1993. "Gendered Imaginations: Female Crime and Prison Movies." *The Justice Professional* 8(1):53–70.

Feagin, Joe and Clairece Booher Feagin. 1996. *Racial and Ethnic Relations.* Upper Saddle River, NJ: Prentice Hall.

Feagin, Joe and Hernan Vera. 1995. *White Racism: The Basics.* New York: Routledge.

Feeley, Malcolm and Jonathan Simon. 1992. "The New Penology: Notes on the Emerging Strategy of Corrections and Its Implications." *Criminology* 30(3):449–474.

———. 1994. "Actuarial Justice: The Emerging New Criminal Law." In *The Futures of Criminology.* David Nelken (ed.). London: Sage.

Flavin, Jeanne. 2001. "Feminism for the Mainstream Criminologist: An Invitation." *Journal of Criminal Justice Education* 29 (4).

Fletcher, Connie. 1995. *Breaking and Entering.* New York: HarperCollins.

Foucault, Michel. 1980. *The History of Sexuality: Volume I: An Introduction.* New York: Vintage Books.

Frank, Nancy. 1988. "Unintended Murder and Corporate Risk-Taking: Defining the Concept of Justifiability." *Journal of Criminal Justice* 16:17–24.

Frankenberg, Ruth. 1993. *White Women, Race Matters: The Social Construction of Whiteness.* Minneapolis: University of Minnesota Press.

Franklin, H. B. 1989. *Prison Literature in America.* New York: Oxford.

Friedrichs, David. 1996. *Trusted Criminals.* Belmont: Wadsworth.

Fullwood, Sam. 1999. "Lawmakers Say They've Been Driven to Fight Racial Profiling; Many Black and Latino Representatives Count Themselves Among Motorists Stopped for No Other Reason than Appearance." *Los Angeles Times.* May 13:5.

Fussell, Paul. 1983. *Class: A Guide Through the American Status System.* New York: Summit Books.

Gamble, Sarah. (ed.). 1999. *The Routledge Critical Dictionary of Feminism and Postfeminism.* New York: Routledge.

Gandy, Oscar. 1993. *The Panoptic Sort: A Political Economy of Personal Information.* Boulder, CO: Westview.

Garland, David. 1999. "The Commonplace and the Catastrophic: Interpretations of Crime in Late Modernity." *Theoretical Criminology* 3(3):353–364.

———. 1990. *Punishment and Society: A Study in Social Theory.* Chicago: University of Chicago Press.

Gastwirth, Joseph and Tapan Nayak. 1997. "Statistical Aspects of Cases Concerning Racial Discrimination in Drug Sentencing." *Journal of Criminal Law and Criminology* 87(2):583.

Gellman, Barton. 1989. "Youth Program Unfair to Women, D.C. Suit Says." *Washington Post* May 12:C5:5.

Gilbert, Dennis. 1998. *The American Class Structure,* 5th ed. Belmont, CA: Wadsworth.

Gilliard, Darrell K. and Allen J. Beck. 1998. *Prisoners in 1997.* Washington, DC: U.S. Department of Justice.

Glazer, Myron and Penina Glazer. 1989. *The Whistle-Blowers.* New York: Basic Books.

Goodstein, Lynne. 1992. "Feminist Perspectives and the Criminal Justice Curriculum." *Journal of Criminal Justice Education* 3(2):165–181.

Gordon, Diana. 1990. *The Justice Juggernaut: Fighting Crime, Controlling Citizens.* New Brunswick, NJ: Rutgers University Press.

Gorman, Tessa. 1997. "Back on the Chain Gang: Why the 8th Amendment and the History of Slavery Proscribe the Resurgence of Chain Gangs." *California Law Review* 85 (2):441–478.

Grabosky, P., J. Braithwaite, and P. Wilson. 1987. "The Myth of Community Tolerance Toward White-Collar Crime" *Australia & New Zealand Journal of Criminology,* 20:33–44.

Greenfeld, Lawrence A. 1997. *Sex Offenses and Offenders.* Washington, DC: U.S. Department of Justice.

Greenfeld, Lawrence A. and Tracy L. Snell. 1999. *Women Offenders.* Washington, DC: Bureau of Justice Statistics.

Greenfeld, Lawrence A., Michael R. Rand, Diane Craven, Patsy A. Klaus, Craig A. Perkins, Cheryl Ringel, Greg Warchol, and Cathy Maston. 1998. *Violence by Intimates: Analysis of Data on Crimes by Current or Former Spouses, Boyfriends, and Girlfriends.* Washington, DC: Bureau of Justice Statistics.

Greider, William. 1996. *Who Will Tell the People? The Betrayal of American Democracy.* NY: Simon and Schuster.

——. 1994. "Why the Mighty GE Can't Strike Out." *Rolling Stone* April 21: p 36.

Gustavsson, Nora S. and Ann E. MacEachron. 1997. "Criminalizing Women's Behavior." *Journal of Drug Issues* 27(3):673–687.

Hacker, Andrew. 1995. *Two Nations: Black and White, Separate, Hostile, Unequal.* New York: Ballantine.

Hagan, John. 1994. *Crime and Disrepute.* Thousand Oaks, CA: Pine Forge Press.

Hajat, Anjum, Jacqueline B. Lucas, and Raynard Kington. 2000. *Health Outcomes Among Hispanic Subgroups: Data from the National Health Interview Survey, 1992–95.* Atlanta: Centers for Disease Control and Prevention.

Hale, Donna C. 1998. "Keeping Women in Their Place: An Analysis of Policewomen in Videos, 1972 to 1996." Pp. 159–179 in *Popular Culture, Crime and Justice.* Frankie Bailey and Donna Hale (eds.). Belmont, CA: West/Wadsworth.

Haley, John. 1989. "Confession, Repentance and Absolution." In *Mediation and Criminal Justice.* Martin Wright and Burt Galaway (eds.). Newbury Park, CA: Sage.

Hannon, Lance and Lynn Resnick Dufour. 1998. "Still Just the Study of Men and Crime? A Content Analysis." *Sex Roles* 38(1/2):63–71.

Hare, R. M. 1990. "Public Policy in a Pluralist Society." In *Embryo Experimentation.* Peter Singer, Helga Kuhse, et al. (eds.). Cambridge: Cambridge University Press.

Harlow, Caroline Wolf. 1998. *Profile of Jail Inmates 1996*. Washington, DC: U.S. Department of Justice.

Harring, Sidney L. 1983. *Policing a Class Society: The Experience of American Cities, 1865–1915*. New Brunswick, NJ: Rutgers University Press.

Harrington, Michael. 1989. *Socialism: Past and Future*. Berkeley, CA: Arcade Publishing.

Harris, Angela P. 1997. "Race and Essentialism in Feminist Legal Theory." Pp. 11–18 in *Critical Race Feminism: A Reader*. Adrienne K. Wing (ed.). New York: New York University Press.

——. 1990. "Race and Essentialism in Feminist Legal Theory." Pp. 253–266 in *Critical Race Theory: The Cutting Edge*. Richard Delgado (ed.). Philadelphia: Temple University Press.

Harris, David. 1999. "Driving While Black: Racial Profiling on Our Nation's Highways." An American Civil Liberties Union Special Report. Available through the criminal justice section of www.aclu.org.

Hart, Lynda. 1994. *Fatal Women: Lesbian Sexuality and the Mark of Aggression*. Princeton, NJ: Princeton University Press.

Harvard Law Review. 1988. "Developments in the Law: Race and the Criminal Process." *Harvard Law Review* 101:1472.

Hatchett, Shirley J., Donna L. Cochran, and James S. Jackson. 1991. "Family Life." Pp. 46–83 in *Life in Black America*. James S. Jackson, (ed.). Newbury Park, CA: Sage Publications.

Hatsukami, Dorothy K. and Marian W. Fischman. 1996. "Crack Cocaine: Myth or Reality?" *Journal of the American Medical Association* 276:1512.

Hawkins, Darnell. 1995. *Ethnicity, Race and Crime*. Albany: State University of New York Press.

Headlee, Sue and Margery Elfin. 1996. *The Cost of Being Female*. Westport: Praeger.

Hearings. 1990. Hearings before the Subcommittee on Financial Institutions Supervision, Regulation and Insurance of the Committee on Banking, Finance, and Urban Affairs, U.S. House of Representatives, 101st Congress, 2nd Session. "When Are the Savings and Loan Crooks Going to Jail?" Washington, DC: U.S. Government Printing Office.

Heidensohn, Frances. 1995(1985). *Women and Crime, 2nd ed*. New York: New York University Press.

Henry, Stuart and William Hinkle. 2001. *Careers in Criminal Justice, 2nd ed*. Salem, WI: Sheffield.

Henry, Stuart and Dragan Milovanovic. 1999. *Constitutive Criminology at Work*. Albany: State University of New York Press.

——. 1996. *Constitutive Criminology: Beyond Postmodernism*. London: Sage.

Herbert, Bob. 1999. "Breathing While Black." *New York Times* November 4: A29.

Hightower, Jim. 1998a. *There's Nothing in the Middle of the Road but Yellow Stripes and Dead Armadillos.* New York: HarperPerennial.

——. 1998b. "All the Free Speech Money Can Buy." Detroit *Metrotimes,* August 19–25.

Hills, Stuart, ed. 1987. *Corporate Violence: Injury and Death for Profit.* Savage, MD: Rowman & Littlefield.

Holdaway, Simon and Sharon K. Parker. 1998. "Policing Women Police." *British Journal of Criminology* 38:40–60.

Holmes, Malcolm D. "Minority Threat and Police Brutality: Determinants of Civil Rights Criminal Complaints in the U.S. Municipalities." *Criminology* 38(2):343–368.

Horton, Kerry F. 1996. "Images of Penality: Prison Films and the Construction of Discourse Regarding Punishment and Obligation." M.A. thesis. Ypsilanti, MI: Eastern Michigan University.

Horton, Paul B. and Chester L. Hunt. 1976. *Sociology,* 4th ed. New York: McGraw-Hill.

Hoyert, Donna, Kenneth D. Kochanek, and Sherry L. Murphy. 1999. "Deaths: Final Data for 1997." *National Vital Statistics Reports.* Hyattsville, MD: National Center for Health Statistics.

Hull, Gloria T., Patricia Bell Scott, and Barbara Smith (eds.). 1982. *All the Women Are White; All the Blacks Are Men, But Some of Us Are Brave: Black Women's Studies.* New York: The Feminist Press.

Human Rights Watch. 2000. "United States: Stark Race Disparities in Drug Incarceration." June 8, press release.

——. 1996. *All Too Familiar Sexual Abuse of Women in U.S. State Prisons.* New York: Women's Rights Project.

Humm, Maggie. 1990. *The Dictionary of Feminist Theory.* Columbus: Ohio State University Press.

Humphries, Drew. 1999. *Crack Mothers: Pregnancy, Drugs, and the Media.* Columbus: Ohio University Press.

Hurst, Erik, Ming Ching Luoh, and Frank Stafford. 1998. "The Wealth Dynamics of American Families, 1984–94." *Brookings Papers on Economic Activity* 1:267–337.

Hurtado, Aida. 1989. "Relating to Privilege: Seduction and Rejection in the Subordination of White Women and Women of Color." *Signs* 14(4):833–855.

Irwin, John and James Austin. 1997. *It's About Time: America's Imprisonment Binge.* Belmont, CA: Wadsworth.

Isikoff, Michael. 1990. "Justice Dept. Shifts on Corporate Sentencing." *Washington Post,* April 28.

Jenkins, Philip. 1994. *Using Murder: The Social Construction of Serial Homicide.* New York: Aldine de Gruyter.

Johnson, James H. Jr., Walter C. Farrell, Jr., and Jennifer A. Stoloff. 1998. "The Declining Social and Economic Fortunes of African American Males: a Critical Assessment of Four Perspectives." *Review of Black Political Economy* 25(4):17–40.

Johnson, Robert. 2000. "American Prisons and the African-American Experience: A History of Social Control and Racial Oppression." *Corrections Compendium* 25(9):6–30.

——. *Death Work: A Study of the Modern Execution Process,* 2nd ed. Belmont, CA: Wadsworth.

Johnson, Robert and Paul Leighton. 1999. "American Genocide: The Destruction of the Black Underclass." In *Collective Violence: Harmful Behavior in Groups and Governments.* Craig Summers and Eric Markusen (eds.). Lanham: Rowman & Littlefield.

Kandal, Terry. 1988. *The Woman Question in Classical Sociological Theory.* Miami: Florida International University Press.

Kangas, Steve. 1996. "Myths About Affirmative Action." *Liberalism Resurgent* http://www.aliveness.com/kangaroo/LiberalFAQ.htm.

Kennedy, Mark C. 1970. "Beyond Incrimination: Some Neglected Facets of the Theory of Punishment." *Catalyst* 5 (Summer):1–30.

Kennedy, Randall. 1997. *Race, Crime, and the Law.* New York: Random House.

King, Jeanne. 1998. "Two NYPD Officers Charge Discrimination Against Gays." Reuters wire service. October 28.

Kleg, Milton. 1993. *Hate, Prejudice and Racism.* Albany: State University of New York Press.

Klein, Dorie. 1995 (1973). "The Etiology of Female Crime: A Review of the Literature." Pp. 30–53 in *The Criminal Justice System and Women,* 2nd ed. Barbara Raffel Price and Natalie J. Sokoloff, eds. New York: McGraw-Hill.

——. 1998. "An Agenda for Reading and Writing about Women, Crime, and Justice." *Social Pathology* 3 (2) Summer:81–91.

Korton, David. 1995. *When Corporations Rule the World.* Kumarian Press & Berrett-Koehler Publishers.

Kozol, Johnathan. 1991. *Savage Inequalities: Children in America's Schools.* New York: HarperCollins.

Kramarow E., H. Lentzner, R. Rooks, J. Weeks, and S. Saydah. 1999. "Health and Aging Chartbook." *Health, United States, 1999.* Hyattsville, MD: National Center for Health Statistics.

Kuper, Leo. 1985. *The Prevention of Genocide.* New Haven, CT: Yale University Press.

Lacayo, Richard. 1992. "You Don't Always Get Perry Mason" *Time* June 1:38.

Lamy, Philip. 1996. *Millennium Rage.* New York: Plenum Press.

Lanier, Mark and Stuart Henry. 1998. *Essential Criminology.* Boulder, CO: Westview.

Lasswell, Thomas E. 1965. *Class and Stratum.* Boston: Houghton Mifflin.

Lazarus, Edward. 1991. *Black Hills, White Justice: The Sioux Nation Versus the United States, 1775 to the Present.* New York: HarperCollins.

Lee, Charles. 1992. "Toxic Waste and Race in the United States." In *Race and the Incidence of Environmental Hazards: A Time for Discourse.* Bunyan Bryant and Paul Mohai (eds.). Boulder: Westview Press.

Leighton, Paul. 1999. *Mopping the Floor While the Tub Overflows.* Monograph written for the Citizen's Alliance on Prisons and Public Safety. Available through http://www.paulsjusticepage.com.

Leighton, Paul and Jeffrey Reiman. 2001. *Criminal Justice Ethics.* Prentice-Hall.

Leinen, Stephen. 1993. *Gay Cops.* New Brunswick, NJ: Rutgers University Press.

Leonard, Christina. 1998. "Stalking Still Hidden but Growing." *Arizona Republic.* January 2: B1.

Leonard, Eileen B. 1982. *Women, Crime, and Society: A Critique of Criminology Theory.* New York: Longman.

——. 1995. "Theoretical Criminology and Gender." Pp. 54–70 in *The Criminal Justice System and Women,* 2d ed. Barbara Raffel Price and Natalie J. Sokoloff (eds.). New York: McGraw-Hill.

Levin, David J., Patrick A. Langan, and Jodi M. Brown. 2000. *State Court Sentencing of Convicted Felons.* Washington, DC: U.S. Department of Justice.

Levine, James. 1997. "The Impact of Racial Demography on Jury Verdicts in Routine Adjudication." *Criminal Law Bulletin* 33:523.

Levy, Barrie. (ed.). 1998. *Dating Violence: Young Women in Danger.* Seattle: Seal Press.

Lichter, Robert and Daniel R. Amundson. 1997. "Distorted Reality: Hispanic Characters in TV Entertainment." Pp. 57–72 in *Latin Looks.* Clara E. Rodriguez (ed.). Boulder, CO: Westview.

Lien, Pei-Te. 1998. "Does the Gender Gap in Political Attitudes and Behavior Vary Across Racial Groups?" *Political Research Quarterly* 51(4):869–894.

Light, Larry. 1998. "Executive Pay." *Business Week,* April 20: 64.

Little Rock. 1989. "The American Indian in the White Man's Prisons: A Story of Genocide" *Journal of Prisoners on Prisons* 1(1):41-56.

Lombardo, Lucien X. 1989. *Guards Imprisoned: Correctional Officers at Work,* 2nd ed. Cincinnati: Anderson Publishing.

Long, Robert. 1993. *Banking Scandals: The S & Ls and BCCI.* New York: H. W. Wilson.

Lusane, Clarence. 1991. *Pipe Dream Blues: Racism and the War on Drugs.* Boston: South End Press.

Lynch, Frank, Nancy Lynch, and Michael J. Lynch. 1992. *Corporate Crime, Corporate Violence.* Albany: Harrow and Heston.

Lynch, Michael J. 1996. "Class, Race, Gender and Criminology: Structured Choices and the Life Course." Pp. 3–28 in *Race, Gender, and Class in Criminology: The Intersection.* Martin D. Schwartz and Dragan Milovanovic (eds.). New York: Garland.

Lynch, Michael and W. Byron Groves. 1989. *A Primer in Radical Criminology,* 2nd ed. Albany: Harrow and Heston.

Lynch, Michael and E. Britt Patterson, (eds.). 1991. *Race and Criminal Justice.* Albany: Harrow and Heston.

Lynch, Michael and Paul Stretesky. 1998. "Uniting Class, Race and Criticism Through the Study of Environmental Justice." *The Critical Criminologist* 9(1):1.

MacKinnon, Catharine A. 1991 (1984). "Difference and Dominance: On Sex Discrimination". Pp. 81–94 in *Feminist Legal Theory.* Katharine T. Bartlett and Rosanne Kennedy (eds.). Boulder, CO: Westview Press.

Madriz, Esther. 1997. *Nothing Bad Happens to Good Girls: Fear of Crime in Women's Lives.* Berkeley: University of California Press.

Maguire, Kathleen and Ann L. Pastore, (eds.). 1999. *Sourcebook of Criminal Justice Statistics.* Tables 3.4 and 3.33. http://www.albany.edu/sourcebook.

Mandel, J. R. 1992. *Not Slave, Not Free: The African American Economic Experience Since the Civil War.* Durham, NC: Duke University Press.

——. 1978. *The Roots of Black Poverty: The Southern Plantation Economy After the Civil War.* Durham, NC: Duke University Press.

Mann, Coramae Richey and Marjorie S. Zatz. (eds.). 1998. *Images of Color, Images of Crime: Readings.* Los Angeles: Roxbury Publishing.

Mantios, Gregory. 1996. "Rewards and Opportunities: The Politics and Economics of Class in the U.S." in *The Meaning of Difference.* Karen Rosenbaum and Toni-Michelle Travis, (eds.). New York: McGraw-Hill.

Marable, Manning. 1983. *How Capitalism Underdeveloped Black America: Problems in Race, Political Economy and Society.* Boston: South End Press.

Marshall, Elliot. 1998. "DNA Studies Challenge the Meaning of Race." *Science* 282:654.

Martin, Susan E. 1992. "The Interactive Effects of Race and Sex on Women Police Officers." *The Justice Professional* 6(1):155–172.

———. 1990. *On the Move: The Status of Women in Policing.* Washington, DC: Police Foundation.

Martin, Susan E. and Nancy C. Jurik. 1996. *Doing Justice, Doing Gender.* Thousand Oaks, CA: Sage Publications.

Massey, Douglas and Nancy Denton. 1993. *American Apartheid: Segregation and the Making of the Underclass.* Cambridge, MA.: Harvard University Press.

Massey, James, Susan L. Miller, and Anna Wilhelmi. 1998. "Civil Forfeiture of Property: The Victimization of Women as Innocent Owners and Third Parties." Pp. 15–31 in *Crime Control and Women.* Susan L. Miller (ed.). Thousand Oaks, CA: Sage.

Mauer, Marc. 1997. *Intended and Unintended Consequences: State Racial Disparities in Imprisonment.* Washington, DC: The Sentencing Project.

McCormick, Anna. 1999. "Restorative Justice in a Northern Canadian Community: The Potential of Sentencing Circles to Address Issues Associated with Youth Crime Through Community Building." Paper presented at the Annual Meetings of the American Society of Criminology, Toronto.

McIntosh, Peggy. 1997(1988). "White Privilege and Male Privilege: A Personal Account of Coming to See Correspondences Through Work in Women's Studies." Pp. 291–299 in *Critical White Studies.* Richard Delgado and Jean Stefancic (eds.). Philadelphia: Temple University Press.

———. 1984. "Interactive Phases of Curricular Revision." Pp. 25–34 in *Toward a Balanced Curriculum.* Bonnie Spanier, Alexander Bloom, and Darlene Boroviak, (eds.). Cambridge, MA: Schenkman.

Meeks, Gregory W. 1999. "Q: Does the Supreme Court Need Affirmative Action for Its Own Staff?" *Insight on the News* 15(3):24–27.

Mencimer, Stephanie. 1997. "Getting the Treatment." *Washington City Paper* July 25.

Messerschmidt, James W. 1997. *Crime as Structured Action: Gender, Race, Class, and Crime in the Making.* Thousand Oaks, CA: Sage.

Messner, Steven F. and Richard Rosenfeld. 1994. *Crime and the American Dream.* Belmont, CA: Wadsworth.

Meyers, Marian. 1997. *News Coverage of Violence Against Women: Engendering Blame.* Newbury Park, CA: Sage.

Michalowski, Raymond. 1985. *Order, Law and Crime.* New York: Random House.

Michalowski, Raymond and Susan Carlson. 1999. "Unemployment, Imprisonment, and Social Structures of Accumulation: Historical Contingency in the Rusche-Kirchheimer Hypothesis." *Criminology 37(2).*

Miller, Jerome G. 1997. *Search and Destroy: African-American Males in the Criminal Justice System.* Cambridge: Cambridge University Press.

Miller, Jody. 1998. "Up it Up: Gender and the Accomplishment of Street Robbery." *Criminology* 36:(1):37–65.

Miller, Susan L. 1999. *Gender and Community Policing: Walking the Talk.* Boston: Northeastern University Press.

———. 1998. "Introduction." Pp. xv–xxiv in *Crime Control and Women.* Susan L. Miller (ed.). Thousand Oaks, CA: Sage.

Miller, Ted, Mark Cohen and Brian Wiersema. 1996. *Victim Costs and Consequences: A New Look.* Washington, DC: National Institute of Justice. (NCJ 155282).

Millett, Kate. 1970. *Sexual Politics.* New York: Doubleday.

Mills, C. Wright. 1956. *The Power Elite.* New York: Oxford University Press.

Moore, Michael. 1996. *Downsize This! Random Threats From an Unarmed American.* New York: Crown.

Morash, Merry and Lila Rucker. 1998. "A Critical Look at the Idea of Boot Camp as a Correctional Reform." Pp. 32–51 in *Crime Control and Women.* Susan L. Miller (ed.). Thousand Oaks, CA: Sage.

Morris, Anne, Marybeth Shinn, and Kimberly DuMont. 1999. "Contextual Factors Affecting the Organizational Commitment of Diverse Police Officers: A Levels of Analysis Perspective." *American Journal of Community Psychology* 27(1):75–105.

Moulds, Elizabeth F. 1980. "Chivalry and Paternalism: Disparities of Treatment in the Criminal Justice System," pp. 277–299. In *Women, Crime, and Justice.* Susan Datesman and Frank Scarpetti (eds.). New York: Oxford University Press.

Mullings, Leith. 1994. "Images, Ideology, and Women of Color." Pp. 265–289 in *Women of Color in U.S. Society.* Maxine Baca Zinn and Bonnie Thornton Dill (eds.). Philadelphia: Temple University Press.

Murphy, Sheigla B. and Marsha Rosenbaum. 1997. "Two Women Who Used Cocaine Too Much: Class, Race, Gender, Crack, and Coke." Pp. 98–112 in *Crack in America: Demon Drugs and Social Justice.* Craig Reinarman and Harry G. Levine (eds.). Berkeley: University of California Press.

Myrdal, Gunnar. 1944. *An American Dilemma: The Negro Problem and Modern Democracy.* New York: Pantheon.

Nagel, Ilene H. and Barry L. Johnson. 1994. "The Role of Gender in a Structured Sentencing System." *The Journal of Criminal Law and Criminology* 85(1):181–221.

National Catholic Reporter. 1999. "Bad INS Law Creates Cruel, Unusual Mess." *National Catholic Reporter* 35(March 12):28.

National Center for Woman in Policing. 1998. *Equality Denied: The Status of Women in Policing, 1997.* Washington, DC: National Center for Women in Policing.

National Narcotics Intelligence Consumers Committee. 1995. *The NNICC Report 1994: The Supply of Illegal Drugs to the United States.* Washington DC: DEA. DEA-95051.

Naughton, Jim. 1997. "A Confidential Report Details Salaries of Athletics Officials." *Chronicle of Higher Education* 43(29):A49-A50.

New Webster's Dictionary of the English Language. 1984. New York: Delair Publishing Company.

New York State Office of the Attorney General. 1999. Results of Investigation Into NYPD "Stop and Frisk" Practice. http://www.oag.state.ny.us/press/1999/dec/dec01a_99.htm.

Nisbet, Robert A. 1959. "The Decline and Fall of Social Class." *Pacific Sociological Review.* 2(Spring): 11–17.

Office of Juvenile Justice and Delinquency Prevention. 1998. *Disproportionate Minority Confinement.* Washington, DC: U.S. Department of Justice. NCJ 173420.

Ogawa, Brian and Aurelia Sands Belle. 1999. "Respecting Diversity: Responding to Underserved Victims of Crime." In *1999 National Victim Assistance Academy.* Grace Coleman, Mario Gaboury, Morna Murray, and Anne Seymour (eds.). Washington, DC: Office for Justice Programs. http://www.ojp.usdoj.gov/ovc/assist/nvaa99

Omi, Michael and Howard Winant. 1994. *Racial Formation in the United States,* 2nd ed. New York: Routledge.

Ontiveros, Maria L. 1997(1995). "Rosa Lopez, Christopher Darden, and Me: Issues of Gender, Ethnicity, and Class in Evaluating Witness Credibility." Pp. 269–277 in *Critical Race Feminism: A Reader.* Adrien Katherine Wing (ed.). New York: New York University Press.

———. 1997(1993). "Three Perspectives on Workplace Harassment of Women of Color." Pp. 188–191 in *Critical Race Feminism.* Adrien Katherine Wing (ed.). New York: New York University Press.

Oshinsky, David. 1996. *Worse Than Slavery: Parchman Farm and the Ordeal of Jim Crow Justice.* New York: Free Press.

Padilla, Laura M. 1997. "Intersectionality and Positionality: Situating Women of Color in the Affirmative Action Dialogue." *Fordham Law Review* 66:843–929.

Parenti, Christian. 1999. *Lockdown America: Police and Prisons in the Age of Crisis.* New York: Verso.

Pasztor, Andy. 1995. *When the Pentagon Was for Sale.* New York: Scribner.

Patterson, William (ed.). 1970. *We Charge Genocide: The Crime of Government Against the Negro People.* New York: International Publishers (reprint of 1951 edition published by Civil Rights Congress).

———. 1971. *The Man Who Charged Genocide: An Autobiography.* New York: International Publishers.

Pepinsky, Harold E. and Richard Quinney. (eds.). 1991. *Criminology as Peacemaking.* Bloomington: Indiana University Press.

Phillips, Susan and Barbara Bloom. 1998. "In Whose Best Interest? The Impact of Changing Public Policy on Relatives Caring for Children With Incarcerated Parents." *Child Welfare* 77(5):531–541.

Pierce, Jennifer. 1995. *Gender Trials.* Berkeley: University of California Press.

Pinkney, Alfonso. 1984. *The Myth of Racial Progress.* Cambridge: Cambridge University Press.

Pizzo, Stephen, Mark Fricker, and Paul Muolo. 1991. *Inside Job: The Looting of America's Savings & Loans.* New York: HarperPerennial.

Pizzo, Stephen and Paul Muolo. 1993. "Take the Money and Run: A Rogues Gallery of Some Lucky S & L Thieves." *New York Times Magazine,* May 9.

Platt, Anthony. 1974. "Prospects for a Radical Criminology." *Crime and Social Justice.* No. 1 (Fall): 1–14.

———. 1969. *The Child Savers: The Invention of Delinquency.* Chicago: The University of Chicago Press.

Platt, Anthony and Paul Takagi (eds.). 1980. *Punishment and Penal Discipline.* San Francisco: Crime and Social Justice Associates.

Pollak, Otto. 1950. *The Criminality of Women.* Philadelphia: University of Pennsylvania Press.

Pollard, Kelvin M. and William P. O'Hare. 1999. "America's Racial and Ethnic Minorities." Special issue. *Population Bulletin* 54(3). http://www.prb.org/pubs/bulletin/bu54-3/part6.htm.

Posner, Richard A. 1992. *Sex and Reason.* Cambridge, MA: Harvard University Press.

Potter, Gary W. and Victor E. Kappeler. (eds.). 1998. *Constructing Crime: Perspectives on Making News and Social Problems.* Prospect Height, IL: Waveland Press.

Préjean, Helen. 1995. "Dead Man Walking" (transcript of speech). Available on the Internet, Radical Catholic Page, http://www.bway.net/~halsall/radcath/prejean1.html.

Pyke, Karen D. 1996. "Class-Based Masculinities: The Interdependence of Gender, Class, and Interpersonal Power" *Gender & Society* 10(5):527–549.

Quinney, Richard. 1977. *Class, State and Crime.* New York: Longmans.

Radalet, Michael. 1989. "Executions of Whites for Crimes Against Blacks." *Sociological Quarterly* 30(4): 529–544.

Raeder, Myrna S. 1993. "Gender and Sentencing: Single Moms, Battered Women, and Other Sex-based Anomalies in the Gender-Free World of the Federal Sentencing Guidelines." *Pepperdine Law Review* 20:905–990.

Rafter, Nicole Hahn. 1997. *Creating Born Criminals.* Urbana: University of Illinois Press.

——. 1994. "Eugenics, Class, and the Professionalization of Social Control." Pp. 215–226 in *Inequality, Crime, and Social Control.* George Bridges and Martha Myers. (eds.). Boulder, CO: Westview Press.

——. 1990. *Partial Justice: Women, Prisons and Social Control.* New Brunswick, NJ: Transaction Books.

Rasche, Christine E. 1995(1988). "Minority Women and Domestic Violence: The Unique Dilemmas of Battered Women of Color," pp. 246–261. In *The Criminal Justice System and Women.* Barbara Raffel Price and Natalie J. Sokoloff. (eds.). New York: McGraw-Hill.

Redstockings, Inc. 1978. *Feminist Revolution.* New York: Random House.

Reed, Diane F. and Edward L. Reed. 1997. "Children of Incarcerated Parents." *Social Justice* 24:152–169.

Reiman, Jeffrey. 1998a. *The Rich Get Richer and the Poor Get Prison,* 5th ed. Boston: Allyn & Bacon.

——. 1998b. "Against Police Discretion: Reply to John Kleinig." *Journal of Social Philosophy* 29(1):132–42.

——. 1990. *Justice and Modern Moral Philosophy.* New Haven, CT: Yale University Press.

Renzetti, Claire M. 1998. "Connecting the Dots: Women, Public Policy, and Social Control." Pp. 181–189 in *Crime Control and Women.* Susan L. Miller (ed.). Thousand Oaks, CA: Sage.

Rice, Marcia. 1990. "Challenging Orthodoxies in Feminist Theory: A Black Feminist Critique." Pp. 57–69 in *Feminist Perspectives in Criminology.* Loraine Gelsthorpe and Allison Morris (eds.). Milton Keynes: Open University Press.

Richie, Beth E. 1996. *Compelled to Crime: The Gender Entrapment of Battered Black Women.* New York: Routledge.

Ridgeway, James. 1995. *Blood in the Face.* New York: Thunder's Mouth Press.

Rierden, Andi. 1997. *The Farm: Life Inside a Women's Prison.* Amherst: University of Massachusetts Press.

Rifkin, Jeremy. 1995. *The End of Work.* New York: G.P. Putnam's Sons.

Ripley, Amanda. 2000. "Unnecessary Force?" *Time* 145(4):34–37.

Rivera, Jenny. 1997(1994). "Domestic Violence Against Latinas by Latino Males: An Analysis of Race, National Origin, and Gender Differentials." Pp. 259–266 in *Critical Race Feminism: A Reader.* Adrien Katherine Wing (ed.). New York: New York University Press.

Roberts, Dorothy E. 1993. "Crime, Race, and Reproduction." *Tulane Law Review* 67(6):1945–1977.

Robinson, Matt. 1998. "Tobacco: The Greatest Crime in World History?" *The Critical Criminologist* 8(3).

Rodriguez, Clara E. 1997. "The Silver Screen: Stories and Stereotypes." Pp. 73–79 in *Latin Looks: Images of Latinas and Latinos in the U.S. Media.* Boulder, CO: Westview Press.

Rosenbaum, Marsha and Katherine Irwin. 1998. "Pregnancy, Drugs, and Harm Reduction." Pp. 309–318 in *Drug Addiction Research and the Health of Women.* Cora Lee Wetherington and Adele B. Roman (eds.). Rockville, MD: National Institute on Drug Abuse.

Rubenstein, R. L. 1987. "Afterword: Genocide and Civilization." In *Genocide and the Modern Age: Etiology and Case Studies of Mass Death.* Isidor Walliman, and Michael Dobkowski (eds.). New York: Greenwood Press.

Rusche, Georg and Otto Kirchheimer. 1968 (1939). *Punishment and Social Structure.* New York: Russell and Russell.

Russell, Katheryn K. 1998. *The Color of Crime: Racial Hoaxes, White Fear, Black Protectionism, Police Harrassment, and other Macroaggressions.* New York: New York University Press.

Samborn, Hope Viner. 1999. "Profiled and Pulled Over." *ABA Journal* 85:18.

Sample, Albert. 1984 *Racehoss: Big Emma's Boy.* New York: Ballantine.

Schemo, Diana Jean. 2000. "Despite Options on Census, Many to Check 'Black' Only." *New York Times* February 12:A1.

Schor, Juliet. 1998. *The Overspent American.* New York: Basic Books.

Schwartz, Martin D. and Dragan Milovanovic. (eds.). 1996. *Race, Gender, and Class in Criminology: The Intersection.* New York: Garland.

Schwendinger, Herman and Julia Schwendinger. 1970. "Defenders of Order or Guardians of Human Rights?" *Issues in Criminology* 5:123–157.

Scully, Diana. 1990. *Understanding Sexual Violence: A Study of Convicted Rapists.* London: HarperCollins Academic.

Segal, Debra. 1993. "Tales from the Cutting Room Floor." *Harper's* November 50–57.

Sellin, Thorsten. 1928. "The Negro Criminal: A Statistical Note." *Annals of the American Academy of Political and Social Science* 140:52–64.

———. 1976. *Slavery and the Penal System.* New York: Elsevier.

Shaw, Clifford R. and Henry D. McKay. 1942. *Juvenile Delinquency and Urban Areas: A Study of Rates of Delinquents in Relation to Differential Characteristics of Local Communities in American Cities.* Chicago: University of Chicago Press.

Shelden, Randell. 1999. "The Prison Industrial Complex and the New American Apartheid." *The Critical Criminologist* (10)1:1, 3–5.

Shine, Cathy and Marc Mauer. 1993. "Does the Punishment Fit the Crime? Drug Users and Drunk Drivers, Questions of Race and Class." Washington, DC: The Sentencing Project.

Simon, David. 1999. *Elite Deviance,* 6th ed. Boston: Allyn & Bacon.

Smart, Carol. 1995. *Law, Crime and Sexuality: Essays in Feminism.* London: Sage Publications.

Snell, Tracy L. and Danielle C. Morton. 1994. *Women in Prison.* Washington, DC: Bureau of Justice Statistics.

Solomon, Alisa. 1999. "A Dream Detained." *Village Voice* 44 (March 30):46–50.

Sorenson, Susan B., Julie G. Peterson Manz, and Richard A. Berk. 1998. "News Media Coverage and the Epidemiology of Homicide." *American Journal of Public Health* 88(10):1510–1514.

Spohn, Cassia. 1990. "Decision Making in Sexual Assault Cases: Do Black and Female Judges Make a Difference?" *Women and Criminal Justice* 2(1):83–105.

Starr, Douglas. 1998. *Blood: An Epic History of Medicine and Commerce.* New York: Quill (HarperCollins).

Staub, Ervin. 1989. *The Roots of Evil: The Origins of Genocide and Other Group Violence.* New York: Cambridge University Press.

Steffensmeier, Darrell. 1995. "Trends in Female Crime: It's Still a Man's World." Pp. 89–104 in *The Criminal Justice System and Women,* 2nd ed. Barbara Raffel Price and Natalie J. Sokoloff (eds.). New York: McGraw-Hill.

Sullivan, Mercer. 1989. *Getting Paid.* Ithaca, NY: Cornell University Press.

Surette, Rat. 1992. *Media, Crime and Criminal Justice: Images and Realities.* Pacific Grove, CA: Brooks/Cole.

Swift, Pat. 1997. "At the Intersection of Racial Politics and Domestic Abuse." *Buffalo News* December 27:B7.

Swinton, David. 1993. "The Economic Status of African Americans During the Reagan-Bush Era: Withered Opportunities, Limited Outcomes, and Uncertain Outlook," in *The State of Black America, 1993*. New York: National Urban League.

Thompson, Tracy. 1990a. "Subject of Lafayette Square Crack Sale Guilty in Other Cases." *Washington Post* January 1:C5.

——. 1990b. "D.C. Student Is Given 10 Years in Drug Case." *Washington Post* November 1:B11.

——. 1989. "Drug Purchase for Bush Speech Like 'Keystone Cops.'" *Washington Post* 15 December 15:C1.

Thompson, Tracy and Michael Isikoff. 1990. "Getting Too Tough on Drugs." *Washington Post* November 4:C1.

——. 1989. "Lafayette Square Drug Suspect Indicted," *Washington Post* September 27:D6.

Tjaden, Patricia and Nancy Thoennes. 1998. *Stalking in America: Findings from the National Violence Against Women Survey*. Washington, DC: U.S. Department of Justice.

Tolnay, S. E. and E. M. Beck. 1995. *A Festival of Violence: An Analysis of Southern Lynchings, 1882–1930*. Urbana: University of Illinois Press.

Tong, Rosemarie. 1989. *Feminist Thought: A Comprehensive Introduction*. Boulder, CO: Westview Press.

Tonry, Michael. 1995. *Malign Neglect: Race, Crime and Punishment in America*. New York: Oxford University Press.

Toth, Jennifer. 1995. *The Mole People: Life in the Tunnels Beneath New York City*. Chicago: Chicago Review Press.

Totten, Mark D. 2000. *Guys, Gangs, and Girlfriend Abuse*. Petersborough, ON: Broadview Press.

UCR. 1997. *Crime in the United States*. Federal Bureau of Investigation. Washington, DC: U.S. Department of Justice.

U.S. Department of Justice. 1999. *Sourcebook of Criminal Justice Statistics*. Washington, DC, GPO.

——. 1998. *Sourcebook of Criminal Justice Statistics*. Washington, DC, GPO.

——. 1996. *Sourcebook of Criminal Justice Statistics*. Washington, DC, GPO.

U.S. Sentencing Commission. 1999. *Sourcebook of Federal Sentencing Statistics*. Washington, DC: U.S. Sentencing Commission.

——. 1992. *Sentencing Commission Guidelines Manual*. Washington, DC: U.S. Sentencing Commission.

Van Ness, Daniel and Karen Heetderks Strong. 1997. *Restoring Justice*. Cincinnati: Anderson Publishing.

Veblen, Thorstein. 1969 (1919). *The Vested Interests and the Common Man.* New York: Capricorn Books.

Visano, Livy A. 1998. *Crime and Culture: Refining the Traditions.* Toronto: Canadian Scholars' Press.

Vold, George and Thomas Bernard. 1986. *Theoretical Criminology,* 3rd ed. New York: Oxford University Press.

Walker, Samuel. 1980. *Popular Justice: A History of American Criminal Justice.* New York: Oxford University Press.

Walker, Samuel, Cassia Spohn, and Miriam DeLone. 1995. *The Color of Justice.* Belmont, CA: Wadsworth Publishing.

Weeks, Robin and Cathy Spatz Widom. 1998. *Early Childhood Victimization Among Incarcerated Adult Male Felons.* Washington, DC: U.S. Department of Justice.

Welch, Michael. 2000. *Punishment in America.* Thousand Oaks, CA: Sage.

———. 1999. *Punishment in America: Social Control and the Ironies of Imprisonment.* Thousand Oaks, CA: Sage.

———. 1996a. *Corrections: A Critical Approach.* New York: McGraw-Hill.

———. 1996b. "The Immigration Crisis: Detention as an Emerging Mechanism of Social Control." *Social Justice* 23(3):169–184.

West, Candace and Don H. Zimmerman. 1987. "Doing Gender." *Gender & Society* 1:125–151.

West, Cornell. 1990. "Michael Harrington, Socialist." *The Nation* (January): 8–15.

Weyler, Rex. 1992. *Blood of the Land: The Government and Corporate War Against First Nations.* Philadelphia: New Society Publishers.

White, Jack. 1990. "Genocide Mumbo Jumbo." *Time* January 22:20.

White, Nicole. 1999. "NYPD White." *The Village Voice* 44(10):23.

White, Rob. 1998. "Social Justice, Community Building and Restorative Strategies." Paper presented at the International Conference on Restorative Justice for Juveniles, Fort Lauderdale.

Wightman, Linda F. 1997. "The Threat to Diversity in Legal Education: An Empirical Analysis of the Consequences of Abandoning Race as a Factor in Law School Admission Decisions." *New York University Law Review* 72:50–51.

Wildman, Stephanie M. 1997(1996). "Reflections on Whiteness: The Case of Latinos(as)." Pp. 323–326 in *Critical White Studies.* Richard Delgado and Jean Stefancic (eds.). Philadelphia: Temple University Press.

Wildman, Stephanie M. with Adrienne D. Davis. 1997. "Making Systems of Privilege Visible." Pp. 314–319 in *Critical White Studies: Looking Behind the*

Mirror. Richard Delgado and Jean Stefancic (eds.). Philadelphia: Temple University Press.

Willhelm, Sidney. 1970. *Who Needs the Negro?* Cambridge: Schenkman Publishing.

Williams, Chancellor. 1987. *The Destruction of Black Civilization.* Chicago: Third World Press.

Williams, Wendy W. 1991(1982). "The Equality Crisis: Some Reflections on Culture, Courts, and Feminism." Pp. 15–34 in *Feminist Legal Theory.* Katharine T. Bartlett and Rosanne Kennedy (eds.). Boulder, CO: Westview Press.

Wilson, W. J. 1996. *When Work Disappears: The World of the New Urban Poor.* New York: Knopf.

——. 1987. *The Truly Disadvantaged: The Inner City, the Underclass, and Public Policy.* Chicago: Chicago University Press.

Winerip, Michael. 2000. "Why Harlem Drug Cops Don't Discuss Race." *New York Times* July 9:A1.

Wing, Adrien Katherine, (ed.). 1997. *Critical Race Feminism: A Reader.* New York: New York University Press.

Winslow, George. 1999. *Capital Crimes.* New York: Monthly Review Press.

Wolff, Edward. 1995. *Top Heavy: A Study of the Increasing Inequality of Wealth in America.* New York: The Twentieth Century Fund Press.

Wolfgang, Marvin and Bernard Cohen. 1970. *Crime and Race: Conceptions and Misconceptions.* New York: Institute of Human Relations Press.

Wonders, Nancy. 1999. "Postmodern Feminist Criminology and Social Justice." In *Social Justice/Criminal Justice.* Bruce A. Arrigo (ed.). Belmont, CA: West/Wadsworth.

Wray, Matt and Annalee Newitz. (eds.). 1996. *White Trash Studies: Race and Class In America.* New York: Routledge.

Young, Vernetta D. 1986. "Gender Expectations and Their Impact on Black Female Offenders and Their Victims." *Justice Quarterly* 3:305–327.

Zehr, Howard and Harry Mika. 1998. "Fundamental Concepts of Restorative Justice." *Contemporary Justice Review* 1(1):47–55. ✦

Name Index

A

Above the Law, 231
Agozino, B., 201
A. H. Robins Company, 61
America's Most Wanted, 18, 231
Andersen, M., 15
Annunzio, F., 51
Austin, J., 72

B

Barak, G., 50, 69–70, 249
Barlow, M., 127, 230–231
Beauvoir, S., 133
Beccaria, C., 43–44
Beck, E., 98
Beirne, P., 42, 44
Belknap, J., 179
Bell, D., 128, 203
Benedict, H., 181–182
Bennett, W., 70, 101
Bernard, T., 43
Berry, G., 232
Binion, T., 19
Black, D., 48, 51–52
Blumstein, A., 110
Bonger, W., 96–97
Bonilla-Silva, E., 81
Box, S., 49
Braithwaite, J., 45, 49
Brandeis, L., 7–8
Braun, C., 197
Britton, D., 153, 177

B (continued)

Brown, R., 110
Brown v. Board of Education, 12, 75
Brouwer, S., 32
Bufkin, J., 207
Bullard, R., 88
Bureau of Justice Statistics, 119, 219
Bush, G., 125

C

Carmichael, S., 81
Catholic Church, 64
Chambliss, W., 44
Chesney-Lind, M., 15, 154
Childress v. City of Richmond, 226, 228
Christie, N., 95
Churchill, W., 90
Clear, T., 44, 108
Clinton, B., 198
Cohen, B., 97
Coleman, J., 52
Collins, A., 172
Collins, P., 15, 216, 224
Collins, W., 172
Columbus, C., 10, 90–91
Court TV, 19–20, 188
Cops, 69, 231
Crenshaw, K., 215
Currie, E., 45, 256

Subject Index